THE PLAYS OF SA[

Katherine Weiss is an Associate Professor of English at East Tennessee State University. She and Seán Kennedy are the editors of *Samuel Beckett: History, Memory, Archive* published in 2009 by Palgrave Macmillan. Additionally, she provided the notes and commentary to Methuen Drama's student edition of Tennessee Williams's *Sweet Bird of Youth* (2010) and has published several articles on Samuel Beckett and Sam Shepard, among other modern and contemporary playwrights.

In the same series from Methuen Drama:

THE THEATRE AND FILMS OF MARTIN MCDONAGH
by Patrick Lonergan

THE PLAYS OF SAMUEL BECKETT

Katherine Weiss

Series Editors: Patrick Lonergan and Erin Hurley

Methuen Drama

Methuen Drama

10 9 8 7 6 5 4 3 2 1

First published in Great Britain in 2013 by Methuen Drama

Methuen Drama, an imprint of Bloomsbury Publishing Plc

Methuen Drama
Bloomsbury Publishing Plc
50 Bedford Square
London WC1B 3DP
www.methuendrama.com

Paperback ISBN: 9781408145579
Hardback ISBN: 9781408157305

Available in the USA from Bloomsbury Academic & Professional,
175 Fifth Avenue /3rd Floor, New York, NY 10010.

A CIP catalogue record for this book is available from the British Library

CONTENTS

ACKNOWLEDGEMENTS

I am grateful to the Department of Literature and Language at East Tennessee State University and, especially, to Dr Judith Slagle, the department's chairperson, for the support provided to research this book. I would like to thank Ashley Fox for her help with transcribing the interviews and other laborious tasks I asked of her. Additionally, I extend my gratitude to my students at ETSU for their classroom discussions that helped to make this book possible.

I gratefully acknowledge the funding I received by the Research Development Committee (RDC) at ETSU. The support of the RDC made it possible for me to travel to Stuttgart, Germany, to dig through the Südwestrundfunk (SWR) archives and to travel to Baltimore, Maryland, to interview Wendy Salkind, Sam McCready, Bill Largess and Peggy Yates. Special thanks to Xerxes Mehta who helped me set up the interviews with the Baltimore actors, who advised me on the interview questions and who provided captions to the photographs in this book.

Thanks to the SWR archives and the Beckett International Foundation at the University of Reading, UK.

My gratitude goes to Drs Matthew Roudané, Elizabeth Weiss and Tom Laughlin for their willingness to listen to and comment on my ideas for the book.

This book is dedicated to Dr Jutta Brederhoff, whose friendship and mentorship mean more to me than words can express.

INTRODUCTION

Samuel Beckett began his career as a poet and novelist in the late twenties. However, it is his theatrical work, in particular his first performed stage play, *Waiting for Godot*, that brought him world recognition. Originally conceived of in French as *En attendant Godot*, Beckett's play was not seen by its first audience until 1953, four years after its completion. The difficulty in finding a stage for this remarkable play was undoubtedly the result of both post-war economics and the challenges the play asks of its performers, directors and stage technicians. *Waiting for Godot*, more than any other play before its première, challenges the conventions of theatre, and does so without a clear political aim. Beckett had no manifesto, no aim to get his intellectual audience to discuss the current political issues as do the plays of the German dramatist, Bertolt Brecht.

Despite often being labelled apolitical by scholars and students, Beckett was deeply involved in fighting the political injustices of his time. He was staunchly against censorship as is evident in his 1934 essay, 'Censorship in the Saorstat'. Moreover, he was opposed to injustices carried out against any group of people. While travelling through Germany in the thirties, Beckett was all too aware of the Third Reich's political tyranny. By studying the diaries Beckett kept during his travels through Germany, Mark Nixon and James McNaughton have shown that Beckett often ridiculed German authorities.[1] Later, he joined the French Resistance, 'translating, collating, editing and typing out scraps of information brought in by agents about German troop movements, information which was then microfilmed and smuggled out of France'.[2] In recognition of his important work with the Resistance, the French government awarded Beckett the Croix de Guerre[3] and the Médaille de la Reconnaissance.[4] His involvement in politics continued throughout his life, as is evident in his 1982 play *Catastrophe*, dedicated to the Czech writer Václav Havel, who was under house arrest for his advocacy of free artistic expression.

Beckett's play was staged for the International Association for the Defence of Artists. Regardless of this, Beckett wanted his plays to affect the audiences' nerves and emotions – not their intellects, as Brecht's plays sought to do. His refusal to provide interpretations for theatre professionals, his audiences and his critics testifies to Beckett's desire to keep his politics and his artistic aesthetics separate. Although traces of Beckett's political involvement can be found in his stage plays, as several scholars have pointed out in recent years,[5] the development of his aesthetics is not dictated by his political awareness.

Having a gift for languages, Beckett studied Modern Languages at Trinity College Dublin from 1923 to 1927. Despite this, Beckett began writing his prose and poetry in English. However, after the poor reception and devastating sales of *More Pricks Than Kicks* (1934) and *Echo's Bones* (1935), Beckett forsook his native tongue. Writing to his friend, Axel Kaun, Beckett revealed his growing discontent with the English language: 'More and more my own language appears to me like a veil that must be torn apart in order to get at the things (or Nothingness) behind it'. He continued, claiming that 'As we cannot eliminate language all at once, we should at least leave nothing undone that might contribute to its falling into disrepute. To bore one hole after another in it, until what lurks behind it – be it something or nothing – begins to seep through; I cannot imagine a higher goal for a writer today'.[6] Beckett's letter of 1937 does not explicitly announce his decision to turn to French; he had not yet made the decision to do so. However, it does reveal his frustration with English and perhaps languages more generally.

What we also learn from this letter is Beckett's move towards an aesthetic for which he would become known. While Beckett never gets rid of language altogether (even though he comes close to this in his late teleplays, *Nacht und Träume* and *Quad*, which I will discuss in detail in Chapter 3), his increasing minimalism and his radical language experiments are grounded in this letter. Indeed, it took writing in French for Beckett to be able to peel the veil off language to experiment with it more fully. In 1946, Beckett completed his first French work, the novel *Mercier et Camier*. Thereafter, he wrote several of his literary works in French, including most of his novels.

When asked to help Patrick Bowles translate his post-war novels *Malone Dies* and *The Unnamable* into English, Beckett did so. This collaboration led him to translate all of his French texts into English, and works he first conceived of in English he translated into French. Beckett was also proficient in Italian, German and Spanish. He directed several of his stage plays and all of his teleplays in Germany. Reading widely in these languages, Beckett's aesthetic has a global, at least in the Western sense, quality. While often Beckett is conceived of as either a French or an Irish writer, his work for theatre proves to be both and more. Many of his literary references reflect his interest in the literature, art and music of Europe. We find Shakespeare in *Happy Days*, Dante in *Play*, Schubert in *Nacht und Träume*, to mention a few. The names of characters throughout his dramatic writing, moreover, are suggestive of this global perspective. Estragon and Godot suggest a French space; Vladimir a Russian space; Pozzo an Italian space; Maggie in *All That Fall* an Irish space; Winnie in *Happy Days* an English space; and so on. Furthermore, his plays include jokes at the expense of the English and Irish, among others. Beckett's global perspective has contributed to an unusual style of writing, blending cultural debris into spaces that consequently appear to become indefinable.

While at university, Beckett went to the theatre regularly, and the plays he saw shaped his aesthetics. Beckett's biographer, James Knowlson, notes that as a young man Beckett saw W.B. Yeats's versions of Sophocles' *Oedipus the King* and *Oedipus at Colonus*.[7] Although there is no evidence that Beckett saw Yeats's *Purgatory* (1939), the dramatic visual similarities between Yeats's play and *Waiting for Godot* are undeniable.[8] And, although traces of the set of *Waiting for Godot* have been linked to the German Romantic paintings of Caspar David Friedrich,[9] the set of *Purgatory* (a country road, a stone and a ruined tree) and the two tramps is reminiscent of *Waiting for Godot*. Beckett was, after all, a close friend of Yeats's brother, the painter Jack B. Yeats, furthering the ties between both playwrights.[10]

Along with being influenced by Yeats's dramatic writings, Beckett saw John Millington Synge's plays, most notably *Playboy of the Western World*, *The Well of the Saints* and *The Tinker's Wedding* when they were revived for Dublin's Abbey Theatre. Knowlson recalls that Beckett felt the theatre of Synge 'had influenced his own theatre most of all'. He goes on to explain that Beckett was impressed by 'Synge's unusual blend of humour and pathos, his stark but resilient tragicomic vision, his imaginative power and clear-sighted pessimism. The rich texture and vitality of Synge's theatrical language and the striking, bold, simplicity of his verbal and visual imagery'.[11] In *Playboy of the Western World*, Christy's gallant tale of murdering his father, admired by the townspeople, reminds one of Pozzo's (*Waiting for Godot*) and Hamm's (*Endgame*) attempts to capture the attention of their listeners. As will be discussed in Chapter 1, these two tyrants struggle to assert themselves as storytellers. And in Beckett's *All That Fall*, the Rooneys and the townspeople are much like the blind couple and the humorously cruel townsfolk in Synge's *The Well of the Saints*.

The work of Sean O'Casey, too, left its mark on Beckett. As a young man still dabbling with the idea of being a scholar, Beckett wrote a short book review of O'Casey's *Windfalls*, a collection of poetry, short stories and one-act plays. While Beckett finds fault with the aesthetics of O'Casey's poetry and short stories, he praises his short dramatic texts: 'Mr O'Casey is a master of knockabout in this very serious and honourable sense – that he discerns the principle of disintegration in even the most complacent solidities, and activates it to their explosion'.[12] Beckett's analysis of O'Casey as an artist of 'disintegration' echoes his own aesthetic in later years. The disintegration of the body appears in his late theatre (for example, *Not I* and *Footfalls*); the body and voice in his plays struggle against disintegration. Beckett goes on to praise O'Casey's *Juno and the Paycock*, calling it

> his best work so far . . . because it communicates most fully this dramatic dehiscence, mind and world come asunder in irreparable dissociation – 'chassis' (the credit of having readapted Aguecheek and Belch in Joxer and the Captain being incidental to the larger credit of having dramatised the slump in the human solid).[13]

Beckett's insight into the antics of Joxer and the Captain is realised years later in his own stage work, particularly in *Waiting for Godot*'s Didi and Gogo as well as *Endgame*'s Hamm and Clov.

Upon graduating from Trinity College Dublin, Beckett took up an appointment at the École Normale Supérieure.[14] While in Paris, Beckett had the good fortune to meet James Joyce. Beckett admired the Irish writer, and as such spent much of his free time with the Joyces. And, like many of Joyce's friends and admirers, Beckett wrote essays to help promote Joyce's *Finnegans Wake*, then known as 'Work in Progress'. Their friendship left a lasting impression on Beckett as it was through his acquaintance with the older Irish writer that he seriously began to define his own work. In a 1956 interview with Israel Shenker, Beckett compared his aesthetics against those of Joyce's. Joyce, according to Beckett, was 'tending towards omniscience and omnipotence as an artist. I am working with impotence, ignorance'.[15] Impotence and ignorance, for Beckett, is an aesthetic of failure and lessness.

Beckett returned to Dublin in 1930 to take up a post at Trinity College. During the winter of 1931, Beckett, along with other members of the Modern Languages staff and their students, took part in his first real theatrical venture. They prepared a variety of plays 'one in Spanish; one an almost contemporary French play; and one a burlesque of Pierre Corneille's seventeenth-century four-act tragedy, *Le Cid*, called *Le Kid*'.[16] It is tempting to conflate his participation in the plays; Beckett's friend, Georges Pelorson, who also took part in the event, recalls that Beckett's involvement in the project was minor. He rarely showed up for rehearsals and wrote little to none of the adaptation of *Le Kid*. Pelorson, however, does credit Beckett with the renaming of *Le Cid*. It was another five years before Beckett tried to write a play of his own. His career in academics was short; he resigned from Trinity College Dublin in 1932 and left Ireland, first moving to London, then travelling throughout Germany before settling in France.

While Beckett claimed in 1947 that he began writing plays as a 'relief and for the sake of a challenge'[17] from the prose he was writing at the time, his intense involvement in theatre, radio and television suggests that Beckett's dramatic writings became a passionate obligation to express the inexpressible on stage.[18] Beckett's claim as to why he began to write for the stage is somewhat problematic. Before he embarked on *Waiting for Godot,* Beckett tried without avail to write two plays, *Human Wishes* and *Eleutheria,* neither of which was performed during his lifetime. In 1936 Beckett began to think about writing a play 'around the relationship between Dr Johnson and Mrs Hester Thrale, thirty-one years younger. He wanted it to cover the period after Mr Thrale's death in 1781 and before Hester decided to marry the Italian music teacher Gabriel Mario Piozzi in July 1784'.[19] Filling up several composition books with notes, Beckett struggled to find a way to bring together two very different themes that emerged in the preparation for the script. How would he manage to integrate 'the love of Johnson for Mrs Thrale' and 'the image of Johnson in decline, physically ill and morbidly preoccupied with his own physical deterioration, dying, and death'.[20] In the end, he abandoned *Human Wishes* after having completed a mere fragment of the script which was only published in 1984 in *Disjecta.* Interestingly, that which gave him so much trouble in *Human Wishes* became the staple of plays such as *Krapp's Last Tape* written nearly two decades later.

Beckett's second attempt at writing for the stage was more successful. *Eleutheria* was written in French and completed in less than two months.[21] After its completion in 1947, Beckett determined to keep this play from being made public whether on stage or in print. Knowlson speculates that his decision was based on the 'autobiographical tensions and reminiscences [which] seemed insufficiently distanced or inadequately integrated into the play'.[22] Despite its autobiographical nature, *Eleutheria,* as David Pattie points out, reveals 'Beckett's rather self-conscious attempt to draw attention to the theatricality of the play';[23] he even includes 'An audience member' in his cast of characters[24] (reminiscent of the canned applause in *Catastrophe*). Likewise, Knowlson explains that the play 'reveals Beckett's attitudes toward the theatre of the past, as well as point[s] forward to his own later, highly innovative drama. It parodies many features of traditional plays and experiments, not always happily, with more innovative techniques'.[25] Despite

Knowlson's and Pattie's praise, the play is too excessive for Beckett's own minimalist aesthetics, which he was still working through. With a cast of seventeen, the play, Beckett came to realise, would not find a stage given the nature of theatre spaces and budgets in post-war Europe.[26] Regardless, *Eleutheria* gave Beckett the momentum to write *En attendant Godot*. He went on to write nineteen stage plays, the last of which, *What Where*, was written in 1983.

By 1956, only two of Beckett's plays, *Waiting for Godot* and *Endgame*, had been staged. While not always met by appreciative audiences,[27] these two plays had an impact within literary and cultured circles. The BBC's new Third Programme, dedicated to cultural shows and radio plays, was interested in the dramatist's daring works. At the invitation of the BBC, Beckett wrote his first radio play, *All That Fall*, during the summer of 1956. *All That Fall* is Beckett's most overtly Irish and autobiographical dramatic work. As Ronan McDonald reveals, the play's 'Boghill is clearly based on Foxrock, the affluent commuter village outside Dublin where Beckett was brought up'.[28] Additionally, Knowlson shares excerpts from two letters Beckett wrote to friends which clearly point to the autobiographical quality of the play. To the poet Nancy Cunard, Beckett wrote 'Never thought about Radio play technique . . ., but in the dead of t'other night got a nice gruesome idea full of cartwheels and dragging feet and puffing and panting which may or may not lead to something'.[29] Echoing his own thoughts, Beckett wrote to the Irish writer Aidan Higgins:

> Have been asked to write a radio play for the 3rd [the BBC's Third Programme] and am tempted, feet dragging and breath short and cartwheels and imprecations from the Brighton Rd to Foxrock station and back, insentient old mares in foal being welted by the cottagers and the Devil tottered in the ditch – boyhood memories.[30]

In his subsequent writings, as H. Porter Abbott and S.E. Gontarski argue, Beckett undid these types of autobiographical references. The manuscripts reveal a conscious effort to distance personal experience from the work.[31] *All That Fall* is more than simply a record of Beckett's 'boyhood memories', however. In it, we discover Beckett's thoughts on radio techniques, which he explored and pushed to more extreme limits with each radio play he wrote. As Chapter 2 will delve into, Beckett explored what could be done with sound in the medium of radio. Challenging where sounds originated from, transforming music into a character and testing the dangers of silence in this particular medium fascinated Beckett. He went on to write seven radio plays between 1956 and 1963.

Another remarkable adventure for Beckett, as Chapter 3 will show, was the world of television. On his fifty-ninth birthday, Beckett began composing his first teleplay, *Eh Joe*. Shortly thereafter, *Eh Joe* was broadcast for both British and German viewers. Beckett had strong ties to the BBC and often communicated with Martin Esslin, Donald McWhinnie and other members of the broadcasting system's crew, as Jonathan Bignell and James Knowlson have noted.[32] However, it is in the German television studio that Beckett directed his teleplays. Reinhart Müller-Freienfels, director of the Süddeutscher Rundfunk (SDR), recalled that Beckett's first teleplay demonstrated an extraordinary awareness of camera technique. From thereon out, Beckett composed and directed seven teleplays for the SDR at the invitation of Müller-Freienfels. Beckett's teleplays were distinct from other television projects, both in Germany and Britain. Despite the uniqueness even of his first teleplay, as Müller-Freienfels pointed out in a lecture he gave on 6 February 1988 to commemorate Beckett's work at the SDR, Beckett had given much thought to the medium. *Eh Joe*, Müller-Freienfels remarked, could only have been written for television; the work is not theatrical or cinematic.[33]

Beckett's plays for stage, radio and television are often categorised as a part of the Theatre of the Absurd, a type of theatre that arose out of the ashes of World War Two. However, Beckett's plays do not look anything like the work of the other absurdists, namely Eugène Ionesco, Jean Genet and even Harold Pinter. 'Theatre of the Absurd', according to Martin Esslin, who coined the term, 'has renounced arguing *about* the absurdity of the human condition; it merely *presents* it in being – that is, in terms of concrete stage images'.[34]

He goes on to explain that it 'tends toward a radical devaluation of language, toward a poetry that is to emerge from the concrete and objectified images of the stage itself'.[35] What is more, in his chapter on Beckett, Esslin concludes that Beckett's plays, which have no plot and no story,

> are clearly attempts to capture the totality of an emotion in its most concentrated form. For if the self is ever elusive, split into perceiver and perceived, the teller of the tale and the listener to the tale – and also ever changing through time, from moment to moment – then the only authentic experience that can be communicated is the experience of the single moment in the fullness of its emotional intensity, its existential totality.[36]

For many years, Esslin's analysis of Beckett as an absurdist was taken at face value. However, Pattie and McDonald, among other Beckett scholars, have reassessed Esslin's assertion. Pattie argues, 'Absurdist playwrights saw man cut adrift in a world that does not make sense; that obeyed uncontrollable mechanical principles; a world in which personality was fluid, and the individual was always at the mercy of an obscurely threatening outside world'. However, Pattie goes on to point out that Beckett's work is 'more [of a] poem than philosophical demonstration'.[37] McDonald goes further, pointing out that 'Beckett himself, for telling reasons, explicitly renounced any association with the Theatre of the Absurd or more particularly with the premise upon which the critical grouping was based. For him this term was too "judgmental", too self-assuredly pessimistic'.[38]

Taking Beckett's lead, this book will not bring together his vast collection of plays under the umbrella of absurdism or existentialism. Rather, the unifying element that will be discussed is Beckett's uses of and references to technology. As such, this book is divided up into chapters that focus on each medium Beckett wrote plays for. Chapter 1 will focus on how Beckett uses technology in the stage plays. In plays such as *Waiting for Godot*, *Krapp's Last Tape* and *Happy Days*, technology is apparent in the props. Pocket-watches, tape recorders and musical-boxes, for example, help to develop themes concerning theatre conventions, time, memory, the failing body, the production of waste and gender. In contrast, Beckett's late works, such as *Come and Go* and *Footfalls*, do not employ technological props to such an extent. However, the structure of his late dramatic works continues to reflect his interest in technology; he is using technology formally in these works, showing how the characters' repetition and cyclical movements are part of a vast machinery. Moreover, Beckett's formal use of technology, as seen in his innovative use of the spotlight in *Play*, both reflects and challenges the conventions of the stage. Rather than shedding light on the action, in *Play* the technology of the spotlight tortures the characters as they are shrouded by what it is they need to say to end their torment.

From a discussion of the stage plays, this book moves into an exploration of Beckett's radio plays. These plays become vehicles to challenge conventional ideas of storytelling and progress. In *All That Fall* and *The Old Tune*, Beckett uses the sounds of transport technology to question the role of the storyteller and scientific progress through images of faltering machines, biological paralysis and death. The medium of radio is transformed into a vehicle that carries the voice outward, yet like the other machines the radio reflects the struggle against failure as the stories it births are primarily concerned with the struggle to go on. Despite the excruciating presence of this struggle in works like *Cascando*, there is humour in his radio plays. The humour in these works stems from the characters' anti-technological ravings. All six radio plays feature storytellers as being fragmented and isolated, and it is through Beckett's use of sound that he confronts his listeners with this absence and their futile compulsion to fill in the gaps.

Chapter 3 examines Beckett's plays for television. All of Beckett's teleplays contain images of voyeurism and surveillance. With the technique of the close-up, Beckett captures the audience's search for sense as an act of inscribing meaning onto the images it sees. In other words, through the narrative voice and the use of repetition, the teleplays place the viewer in the position of a voyeur struggling to inscribe meaning onto the white death-masks and fill in the black holes projected on screen; we struggle to gain control over the texts we see as the characters struggle to gain control over their narratives. For Beckett, then, the audience is a peeping Tom whose fetish is both viewing the unsuspecting victim and, while peering at him, writing a narrative to gain authorship over the image. It is interesting that in Beckett's teleplays the faces peered at are always male. As such Beckett challenges the conventional gaze of the camera. The male gaze has traditionally been associated with the camera eye. The camera, hence, becomes a tool for patriarchal control as it captures and objectifies the woman on film. Beckett, however, associates the camera's gaze with female ghosts confronting the male protagonists, exposing their inability to assert their power over women and their stories, consequently tormenting them with their own weaknesses.

Beckett does not separate the technical production of texts from their media. Instead he utilises the media and its technology to conceptualise the mechanical production of artistic creation, only to break it down. He uses technology in his dramatic works to structure the plays as worlds and situations, albeit often indefinable, that are winding down, fragmenting and falling apart. Often the technology itself is faltering or breaking down, mirroring the bodies on stage, the characters whose ageing bodies are limited. Later, Beckett does away with the body of maladies and stages mere body fragments. These stage presences are decomposing as they are presented to the audience. However, Beckett's dramatic images never finish decomposing, have never completely fallen to bits; his plays do not end and his characters endure the downward spiral of their situation.

Beckett's aesthetics of decomposition brought on by technology is in part a direct result of his movements during World War Two, a conflict which demonstrated to the world the devastating impact machines have on civilisation. Cities and the countryside were literally flattened into wastelands as Beckett recalls in his radio piece, 'The Capital of the Ruins', a non-fictional work in which he meditates on the presence of the Irish Red Cross in Saint-Lô, Normandy. In this radio commentary, Beckett commemorates the citizens of Saint-Lô, celebrating their resilience; they are heroic in their refusal to give up. Their will to survive is constant; it does not diminish when faced with the horror of rubble, malnutrition, sickness or injuries caused by masonry falling on them or children stepping on mines. He goes on to describe how 'its population of German prisoners of war, and casual labourers attracted by the relative food-plenty, but soon discouraged by housing conditions, continue, two years after the liberation, to clear away the debris, literally by hand'.[39] For Beckett this image of clearing away the rubble by hand in order to rebuild the town is 'a vision and sense of a time-honoured conception of humanity in ruins'.[40] In this radio piece, Beckett offers the Irish public a glimpse of a population that refuses to allow the ruins of their town to destroy their humanity. Interestingly, it is this image of humanity that haunts Beckett as much as the catastrophic events that led to the destruction of Saint-Lô. No matter how destitute their situation, they continue to work towards restoration.

However grim Beckett's thematic approach to modern technology may seem, his extensive and innovative use of technology surely points to a more complicated understanding of its role in modern life and the production of texts. Throughout, he explores images of mechanisation in relation to the individual storyteller and spectator, and creates self-reflexive texts to critique the media he uses, not to condemn modern technology but to utilise it to break down authorial structures. Destructiveness, to Beckett, is a possible way out of authorial institutions. In breaking down authority, Beckett awakens his audience from what the German philosopher Walter Benjamin calls their 'absent-mindedness',[41] but unlike Benjamin and Brecht, who were predominately concerned with a socialist awakening, Beckett keeps us from falling into the 'neatness of identification'.[42]

Beckett's dramatic writings are rich with interpretative possibilities. Chapters 1 to 3 offer my perspective of Beckett's plays centred on the question of technology. Chapter 4 provides four alternative perspectives by influential scholars and directors in Beckett studies. Graley Herren examines the teleplays in relation to the much debated topic of love. He takes on Alain Badiou, revealing that the philosopher has romanticised Beckett's depiction of love. Herren's own examination of the teleplays provides a grimmer analysis of love than Badiou's. Dustin Anderson re-examines the much discussed play, *Krapp's Last Tape*, providing new insight to the way Beckett's play and Bergson's theories on memory have anticipated contemporary cognitive science. In addition to these theoretical perspectives on Beckett, Chapter 4 includes essays by the veteran theatre director, Xerxes Mehta, whose productions of Beckett's late plays have toured Europe, and the edgy new director, Nicholas Johnson, who runs the Samuel Beckett Summer School. Both discuss how they approach Beckett's stage work. Mehta focuses on the ways in which his ghostly plays work on the eyes, ears and freedom of the players and viewers while Johnson looks at the various spectra of fidelity.

At the Beckett in Berlin Symposium in 2000, I had the opportunity to see the Maryland Stage Company's productions of Beckett's late plays. These productions, directed by Mehta and performed by Wendy Salkind, Sam McCready, Bill Largess and Peggy Yates, were praised by Beckett scholars and theatre goers alike. They demonstrated that productions of Beckett which strived for fidelity were not museum pieces, but rather vibrant works that haunt audiences. The company's production did, indeed, work on our nerves rather than our intellects. Chapter 5 includes four interviews, conducted in 2011, in which Salkind, McCready, Largess and Yates spoke about the theatrical and technical aspects of *Play, Not I, That Time* and *Ohio Impromptu*.

It was Beckett's exceptional career as a writer, and the popularity and importance of his first play that won him the Nobel Prize for Literature in 1969. Rather than being overjoyed by the news of the prize, Beckett and his wife, Suzanne Deschevaux-Dumesnil, were perturbed, deeming the award a 'catastrophe'. 'He saw only too clearly', Knowlson relates, 'how much his long-term future would be disrupted by the celebrity, in addition to his present peace being shattered'.[43] Despite his many obligations in the theatre as well as his loyalty and generosity to his friends, Beckett was a shy and private individual. He spent much of his time at his home in the country where he could write in peace. Paris had become a place in which he sorted out his social obligations whereas Ussy-sur-Marne was his refuge. In 1989, three months after Suzanne's death, Beckett passed away in a nursing home in Paris and was buried alongside his wife. A modest gravestone, indicative of his personality, bears their names.

CHAPTER 1
THE STAGE PLAYS

Samuel Beckett dabbled in all kinds of writing – from literary reviews to poetry, fiction and drama. He knew after his failed attempts at academia that he wanted to be a writer, but did not yet know what type of writing was his forte. Despite his struggle to find a form to fit his own vision, Beckett, even in the early thirties, made a name for himself, at least among other artists and writers. He won a poetry prize for 'Whoroscope' in 1930, which the poet and publisher Nancy Cunard and novelist Richard Aldington sponsored; he wrote short prose for journals such as *transition* throughout the thirties; and he published his collection of short stories, *More Pricks Than Kicks*, in 1934. However, his writing, while clever and experimental, was still too heavily influenced by his mentor, James Joyce. Joyce's style was seeping into Beckett's work, perhaps accounting for the numerous scholars who still compare the works of the two Irishmen.

It is possible that in writing plays Beckett found a way to break free from the styles of writers like Joyce, whom he admired. Although Beckett's first attempt at playwriting, *Human Wishes*, was aborted, he returned to writing for the stage a decade later. When Beckett completed *Eleutheria* he decided, with the help of Roger Blin (the director who was the first to produce *Waiting for Godot*), that the play was impossible to produce in post-war Europe. Once having finished *Eleutheria*, Beckett began *Waiting for Godot* and did not stop writing for the stage until 1983, five years before his death. Remarkably, Beckett wrote nineteen plays for the stage, seven for radio and five for television. Even more remarkable is that he did not abandon writing prose or poetry. He became prolific in all forms of literature.

Beckett's plays are radically different from any play before or after his time. He shows his audience and the theatre professionals daring enough to produce his plays that the stage is not a place of action but rather a place where political tyranny and personal ghosts can be confronted. His tyrants are ridiculed, robbed by the audience of their power. The ghosts of the past are harder, Beckett discovers, to vanquish. Theatre, for him, is a place where ghosts of the past haunt, sometimes even tyrannise, a space each night. Beckett does this by experimenting with form and content. In his plays, from *Waiting to Godot* to *Play*, Beckett, often in a self-reflexive manner, features technological props such as watches, clocks, tape recorders, musical-boxes and the technology of production (namely stage lighting) to challenge authorial figures and personal haunts. After *Play* Beckett writes shorter and increasingly minimalist plays. He rids the stage of props, but continues to rely on dramatic lighting. With each play, Beckett becomes more static, more minimalist, and yet each play becomes richer in its concerns with the tyranny of social and political constructions and the tyranny of the ghosts of the past.

Waiting for Godot

After struggling to make a career as a prose fiction writer for almost two decades, Samuel Beckett turned to theatre. Writing plays, he claimed, provided him with relaxation and a new challenge.[1] Yet Beckett was not a stranger to the theatre. As noted in the introduction, Beckett, as a young man in Dublin, attended the Abbey Theatre and was an admirer of J.M. Synge and Sean O'Casey. His knowledge of theatre and dramatic structure is present from the outset. Yet Beckett did not seek to reproduce conventional theatre. In *Waiting for Godot*, as well as his subsequent plays, Beckett refuses to carry out the conventions of dramatic structure. Conventional dramatic structure is equipped with the following: an exposition to inform the audience of the back-story which has led to the current conflict which will dominate the plot. The characters in such a play struggle, often successfully, to resolve the conflict, or problem. As the action unravels, a climax in the action is reached. Thereafter the action wanes into a resolution, or solution to the conflict. In Beckett's two-act play, *Waiting for Godot*, Vladimir (or Didi as he is referred to) and Estragon (or Gogo) wait each day for Mr Godot to arrive. As they wait, they talk to while away the time, but in their conversation little to no exposition is provided. Their conversation is a mixture of idle chatter, language wordplay and philosophical reflections. Their talk, moreover, is interrupted by the arrival of Pozzo and Lucky, a master and a slave who help the tramps get through the day. Godot does not arrive; there is no climax nor is there a resolution. Act two of *Waiting for Godot*, ultimately, is a repetition of act one. The play's structure is a recurring cycle much like the winding down of a watch or clock. Watches and clocks, interestingly, appear in the props Beckett employs in many of his early plays. Gadgets such as watches and alarm clocks in Beckett function to challenge theatrical conventions as well as explore the dangers of authorial institutions, of which the theatre is one.

Beckett incorporates the pocket-watch in *Waiting for Godot* and the alarm clock in *Endgame* to interrogate theatre as a system bound up in authorial power. To examine Beckett's investigation of theatre, we need to take a step back to look at how Beckett carefully constructs this argument. While plays prior to *Waiting for Godot* embodied a central conflict, reached a climax and ended with a resolution, *Waiting for Godot* subverts the audience's expectations for a climax (Godot's arrival) and a resolution (Didi's and Gogo's salvation or damnation). Rather, the conflicts in this play are the language games Didi and Gogo take part in and the master–slave relationship of Pozzo and Lucky. While Godot does not come as the audience expects, and Didi and Gogo hope, Didi and Gogo are visited by Pozzo and his slave Lucky. Pozzo is the first of Beckett's many parodied tyrants. His voice is booming, he uses a whip on Lucky to order him about and he is the only character in this play who owns and uses a pocket-watch. Although the whip undeniably marks Pozzo as Lucky's master, it is 'Worn out'[2] as is Pozzo's authority. Likewise, Pozzo's pocket-watch both points to his desire for power and his continued attempts to establish himself as a figure of authority.

Five times Pozzo looks at his watch. When Pozzo initially consults his watch, it is to reveal that 'the road seems long when one journeys all alone for . . . (*He consults his watch*) . . . yes . . . (*He calculates*) . . . yes, six hours, that's right, six hours on end, and never a soul in sight'.[3]

Here Pozzo uses a common, straightforward expression. Beckett first establishes Pozzo as using his watch to tell how much time has passed – a normal observation. When Pozzo looks at his watch a second time, however, Pozzo reveals that Lucky taught him beautiful thoughts some sixty years prior.[4] Because no watch can tell the passing of years, the audience must rethink the authoritative statements provided by Pozzo. He, after all, invents some of his calculations and uses his habit of turning to his half-hunter to support his erroneous claims. By looking at the pocket-watch before asserting how many years have gone by, Pozzo reveals that he needs to support his claims through his machine as much as he needs an audience to recognise his authority; without them his voice is lost to all.

This need for the pocket-watch is linked to Pozzo's demand that all eyes are on him. The necessity to be seen in Beckett, furthermore, alludes to the seventeenth-century philosopher Bishop George Berkeley, who claimed that to be is to be perceived (*esse est percipi*). Berkeley, Jonathan Kalb explains, 'believed that the material world had no independent existence outside sapient minds, which in turn exist only because God perceives them'.[5] Through his allusion to Berkeley, Beckett reveals that our existence, and more specifically authority, are not inherent; rather, both are constructed through our modern technology and through a participating audience.

At one such moment, Pozzo asks: 'Is everybody ready? Is everybody looking at me? (*He looks at Lucky, jerks the rope. Lucky raises his head.*) Will you look at me, pig! (*Lucky looks at him.*)'[6] before answering Gogo's question as to why Lucky does not put down his bags. Pozzo's need to be seen and heard is heightened in his comic attempt to entertain Didi and Gogo. Pozzo, here, looks at his watch while describing the end of the evening. Struggling to tell his tale well, Pozzo attempts to infuse his tale with the authority of a well-respected storyteller or author, by consulting his pocket-watch and frequently referring to clock time in his short monologue: 'this hour of the day', 'An hour ago' and 'say ten o'clock in the morning'.[7] When consulting his watch and speaking of time, Pozzo breaks from his '*lyrical*'[8] narrative to state a prosaic fact. Although his description of the change of the sky, as a sudden 'pppfff! finished!' when the sun sets and 'pop! like that!'[9] snapping his fingers when the moon rises, may seem ridiculous and unreal at first, Beckett slips us a teaser. Pozzo does indeed capture the strange and sudden change of the sky. In a letter to the American director Alan Schneider, Beckett includes his notes initially sent to Peter Hall who directed the English première of *Waiting for Godot*. It reads:

> The correct lighting in both acts is:
> 1) Unvarying evening light up to boy's exit.
> 2) Then suddenly darkness.
> 3) Then suddenly moonrise and moonlight till curtain.[10]

While audience members who have never seen or read the play may find Pozzo's description unnatural, they discover at the end of the first act that he is, in fact, accurate.

While Pozzo's description of the rising of the moon is accurate, it is also challenged. As an apology for having 'weakened a little towards the end', he says his memory 'is defective'.[11] Along with having an imperfect memory, his watch disappears at the end of act one, and in act two he, like the blind Hamm who depends on Clov in *Endgame*, is blind and completely dependent on Lucky who has become dumb. Shortly before describing the twilight to the tramps, Didi, '*Motionless, looking at the sky*', says: 'Time has stopped'.[12] Pozzo responds: '(*Cuddling his watch to his ear.*) Don't you believe it, sir, don't you believe it. (*He taps with finger on watch.*) Whatever you like, but not that'.[13] Pozzo's gestures, the cuddling and tapping of the watch, suggest that his half-hunter has stopped. Tapping it, Pozzo tries to set it in motion. Pozzo refers to concrete time (the ticking of a watch). Didi, however, is not concerned with the watch but rather comments on the fact that he and Gogo are going nowhere and are destined to go nowhere.

Later, in act one, Pozzo's pocket-watch mysteriously disappears. As Pozzo is about to depart, he searches for it and rationalises that he 'must have left it at the manor, on the Steinway'.[14] Pozzo's inability to remember that a few moments earlier he was looking at his watch confirms that his memory is poor and consequently his authority is crumbling. As McMillan and Knowlson convincingly sum up:

'[H]e is no longer in control of objects of bourgeois authority and comfort'.[15] Indeed, figures of authority, the play reveals, are slaves to social conventions. Twice, Pozzo, arisen from his stool, wishes to sit again without breaking the conventions of bourgeois society. His first attempt reads as follows:

> I am impertinent. (*He knocks out his pipe against the whip, gets up.*) I must be getting on. Thank you for your society. (*He reflects.*) Unless I smoke a pipe before I go. What do you say? (*They say nothing.*) Oh I'm only a small smoker, a very small smoker, I'm not in the habit of smoking two pipes one on top of the other, it makes (*Hand to heart, sighing*) my heart go pit-a-pat. (*Silence.*) It's the nicotine, one absorbs it in spite of one's precautions. (*Sighs.*) You know how it is. (*Silence.*) But perhaps you don't smoke? Yes? No? It's of no importance. (*Silence.*) But how am I to sit down now, without affection, now that I have risen? Without appearing to – how shall I say – without appearing to falter.[16]

Pozzo's choice of words is curious. Initially, he gets up because he says he is 'impertinent', but what is he disrespectful of – social convention regulating how long one may visit another? Then, when he wishes to sit again, he wonders how he can do so without 'affection' and without 'appearing to falter'. Does Pozzo wish to avoid seeming fond of Didi and Gogo, or rather does he attempt to avoid seeming diseased or flawed by his wavering? In ordering Lucky to slightly move his stool, and in smoking a second pipe, he justifies his further presence. Ironically, it is by breaking habit that allows him to stay and this break from habit makes his heart 'pit-a-pat'. Despite his decision to smoke another pipe before departing, an acceptable excuse to sit without hesitation, Pozzo's ill use of words throws his authority into question. Richard Schechner argues that Pozzo and Lucky, unlike Didi and Gogo, 'are free agents, aimless, not tied to anything but each other. For this reason, Pozzo's watch is very important to him. Having nowhere to go, his only relation to the world is in knowing "the time"'.[17] Despite being able to roam the country roads, Pozzo and Lucky are not free agents either. Pozzo lacks the free will to sit without an acceptable excuse. He is a slave to social convention compacted by the prop of the pocket-watch.

After preparing to leave a second time, Pozzo, wishing to stay a little longer, cannot continue his visit unless Gogo bids him to stay. Here Beckett creates a wonderful parody of polite bourgeois society. Gogo's 'Here we go' and Pozzo's 'Done it again' announces the artificiality of this exchange.[18] They are performing social conventions. Pozzo only agrees to sit down, albeit knowing all along he will, after Gogo's illogical assertion that he will catch pneumonia if he does not take a seat. Immediately after sitting again, Pozzo 'consults his watch' and says that he 'must really be getting along, if I am to observe my schedule',[19] but again stays so that he can give his performance of the twilight and so that Didi and Gogo can watch Lucky dance and hear him think. His wavering is the result of his habit of turning to his pocket-watch. Later in act two, when Gogo and Didi play at being Pozzo and Lucky, Gogo calls Didi a 'Punctilious pig'.[20] Although Pozzo abuses Lucky by calling him 'pig', Gogo's insult refers back to Pozzo, the slave to time, formality and etiquette as the adjective he uses to modify 'pig' reveals. Social conventions are again parodied when Pozzo finally leaves the stage in act one, bidding farewell to Didi and Gogo. In the hilarious 'Adieu' sequence,[21] Beckett's characters ape polite society. But actors are not exempt from Beckett's scrutiny: he mocks them when his characters bow to each other as they would during a curtain call – a theatrical convention that Beckett axed in plays after *Waiting for Godot*.

Perhaps Pozzo's pocket-watch goes missing because he has internalised its connotations of mechanisation without taking on its authorial power. He no longer needs the pocket-watch or any other timepiece; thus, Beckett erases the pocket-watch from the playing field. Helping Pozzo search for his watch, Gogo mistakes the beating of Pozzo's heart for the ticking of the missing object. By paralleling the human heart with a mechanical gadget, Beckett, in an existential gesture, laughs at the notion that the heart's beating, like that of the pocket-watch, verifies man's existence. Offering an interesting reading of clocks, Jean Baudrillard claims that the clock, which was once at the centre of the bourgeois interior, was the 'mechanical heart that reassure[d] us about our own heart'.[22] When Gogo mistakes Pozzo's heart for his pocket-watch, Beckett reveals that the beating of the heart, understood in relation to Western culture's fascination with clocks and watches, reminds us of the daily drudgery of our mechanised lives, and in doing so confirms our bleak existence. '[H]abit is a great deadener', Didi utters.[23]

It is through habit that Beckett's protagonists regulate and control their stories and existence. However, this authority collapses. Because of its repetition of sameness, mechanisation as represented on Beckett's stage paralyses his characters' creative processes. In his use of mechanical objects, Beckett stands as an example of how machine technology can be employed to create humour centred around a discourse of habit, mechanisation and both concrete and abstract time.

In the 2000 Meltdown production of *Waiting for Godot* at the Barbican Theatre in London, Gogo is depicted as a thief who steals Pozzo's pocket-watch. The director Luc Bondy's realist explanation for the disappearance of Pozzo's half-hunter is damaging to the play's carefully constructed anti-realism. Bondy provides a disappointing interpretation to a play that continually challenges authority. By stealing the watch, Gogo endeavours to position himself as having authority, giving him power over the other characters. Pozzo, however, recognises that Gogo has taken his pocket-watch and recovers it, re-establishing his authority. With the text's mysterious disappearance of the pocket-watch, Beckett throws the issue of power, and by extension authority, into question. While all the figures on stage try to verify their existence, the play allows the spectators to ask who, if anyone, is in control. When the pocket-watch is lost, Pozzo declines into a blind, timeless being. The text reveals the futility and increasing desperation over the dilemma of gaining authorship over one's existence.

Even for Didi and Gogo, the issue of authority and authorship arises. In his frustrated attempts to discuss the reasons why, out of four Evangelists, only one is believed to have recorded the true events at the crucifixion, Didi asks Gogo if he remembers the Gospels. Gogo replies, 'I remember the maps of the Holy Land'.[24] In response,

Vladimir You should have been a poet.

Estragon I was. (*Gesturing towards his rags.*) Isn't that obvious? (*Silence.*)[25]

The silence at the end of their exchange allows the audience to laugh at the absurd notion that Gogo's rags signify him as a former poet. This joke plays on the romanticised image of the poet as a starving and struggling artist. If Gogo was a poet, he is one without the ability to be an author. In fact, he cannot even 'return the ball'.[26] His position of authority is further undermined when we learn that each night when he sleeps in his ditch he is attacked by some violent gangs. It is interesting to note that in the original French text the word meaning ditch, *fossé*, resembles the word *fosse* meaning grave. This wordplay also exists in the German translation, with *Graben* as ditch and *Grab* as grave, both words originating from the same stem.[27] In the French and German, Beckett hints that Gogo returns to his grave; he is a corpse unable to produce a corpus of work. Gogo resembles the protagonist in *Krapp's Last Tape* in that he is a failed author – a writer who can no longer produce texts. He merely repeats himself and suggests suicide throughout the play. It is Didi, not Gogo, who is given the lyrical, philosophical lines.

Didi is the one character in *Waiting for Godot* who attempts to question authorship and authority by wondering why one version of the two thieves and not another is the authoritative text. And yet he is unable to resolve the problem. He wonders how, if all four Evangelists were present, they could have recorded the same event differently. Didi does not contemplate the possibility that the Evangelists had faulty memories like Pozzo or that their versions are different because they wished to express different ideologies. Each may have attempted to make the gospel their own. Didi's meditation, moreover, suggests that the author is only given authority through an audience who listens. Only the one version is remembered because it offers the audience hope as well as a puzzle to solve. The audience wonders which one of the two – Didi or Gogo – will be saved.

Whereas religion lacks the answers that Beckett's characters seek, time provides them with a new vision. Ruby Cohn observes that in *Waiting for Godot* 'Lucky promises four times that "time will tell", but that is what it does not do. Time passes without telling'.[28] Although her analysis in *Just Play* is often insightful, here Cohn underestimates Beckett's use of the cliché 'time will tell'. Time does tell; it fills the air with cries, expressing that all decays and dies. Once Lucky thought and danced beautifully but his ability to do so has diminished, and in the second act even his ability to think aloud has disappeared. The repetition of 'time will tell' together with the increasing frenzy of Lucky's thinking in act one reveal the passing of time as a rapid movement towards decay and deterioration rather than a slow decline.

In act two, soon after entering the stage, the blind Pozzo and dumb Lucky fall to the ground and are unable to get back up. Helpless on the ground and unable to see the rising of the moon or his pocket-watch (even if he had found it), Pozzo is a pathetic figure of fallen tyranny. He is tormented by questions of 'when' and furiously says,

> Have you not done tormenting me with your *accursed time*! It's abominable! When! When! One day, is that not enough for you, one day like any other day, one day he went dumb, one day I went blind, one day we'll go deaf, one day we were born, one day we shall die, the same day, the same second, is that not enough for you? (*Calmer.*) They give birth astride of a grave, the light gleams an instant, then it's night once more.[29]

Pozzo is not only furious because as he claims the blind have no notion of time but also because, along with his failed sight, his memory has failed. He has no notion of the past. Unable to see or remember, Pozzo is left in a world with no days and nights; he is on an endless journey, doomed to repeat himself. After the departure of Pozzo and Lucky in act two, Didi repeats a slightly varied version of Pozzo's monologue. Pozzo's monologue suggests that birth and death occur within the same day or second because he cannot tell them apart whereas Didi, reflecting on his own desperate waiting for each day to end, emphasises the 'time to grow old' even though 'the grave-digger puts on the forceps'.[30]

Despite Pozzo's attempts to fix time with his pocket-watch in act one, from the outset Beckett shrouds the play in ambiguity. Didi and Gogo, having no gadgets to regulate the passing of time, exist in a world of uncertainty. After Gogo suggests that they leave within the first few minutes of the play, Didi reveals that they are bound to the spot because they are waiting for Godot. Upon questioning Didi as to whether they are waiting in the right spot and whether today is not Friday or Thursday instead of the Saturday of their appointment, Didi says angrily, 'Nothing is certain when you're about'[31] and begins to wonder which day Godot said he would come. Dougald McMillan and Martha Fehsenfeld point out that 'Godot's human existence was made less definite by the deletion of a portion of the manuscript which refers to a piece of paper in Godot's own hand giving the time and place of the appointment'.[32] In this unpublished manuscript, Godot, having written on paper, marks out his existence. The omission, however, not only obscures Godot's existence but also obscures the fixed time of the appointment and consequently challenges Didi's certainty of it and his authority over Gogo. After becoming frustrated and perhaps confused with Gogo's continuous questioning, Didi tells Gogo that Godot 'didn't say for sure he'd come'.[33] Later, the audience is placed in the position to doubt Didi. At the end of the first act, Godot's messenger tells Didi that 'Mr Godot told me to tell you he won't come this evening but surely tomorrow'.[34] And, in the second act, the play closes with Didi anticipating the boy's message.[35]

Two things are significant here. First, Didi's ability to anticipate the boy's message, in the statements that Godot will not come tonight but will tomorrow, suggests that each day the same message is brought. When Didi sees the boy he says, 'Off we go again'[36] reminiscent of Gogo's earlier remark 'Here we go' when he beseeches Pozzo to be seated. As a result, like Franz Kafka's 'Before the Law' in which the countryman awaits to be given permission to enter the gate, Didi and Gogo continue to wait without ever meeting Godot. The only mercy bestowed on them is that they can pass the time with each other. Secondly, the boy says that Godot *won't* rather than *can't* come. If the message had been that Godot was unable to meet with Didi and

Gogo, there would be a hint of regret and apology with the possibility of coming in the future. Because Godot's absence is voluntary, his failure to appear suggests indifference and even malice. Hence, the play ends with a harsh realisation – Godot, the highest authority in the play, allows for the endless waiting of Gogo and Didi. Their fate is much like Sisyphus' punishment.

Using a watch or an alarm clock and references to time, both *Waiting for Godot* and *Endgame* '[assault] the basic unities of the conventional theatre: time, place, and plot'.[37] By obscuring these elements, *Waiting for Godot* must have thrown its first audiences off balance, as it reminds them of the passing of time during their own waiting. Relying on theatrical conventions, early audiences must have waited for the conflict, climax and resolution. When nothing happened, they either left disappointed or acclaimed *Waiting for Godot* a success for breaking theatrical conventions.[38] After seeing the play in 1956, Vivian Mercier wrote:

> Its author has achieved a theoretical impossibility – a play in which nothing happens, that yet keeps audiences glued to their seats. What's more, since the second act is a subtly different *reprise* of the first, he has written a play in which nothing happens, *twice*.[39]

Today's audiences, even those of us who have seen and read *Waiting for Godot* and *Endgame* numerous times, are placed in the position of waiting – waiting for Pozzo and Lucky to enter, waiting for our favourite lines and waiting for the boy's message, waiting for Clov to exit and waiting for the senseless moves in the chess game to end.[40] Ultimately Beckett shows us, through Pozzo's pocket-watch and Clov's alarm clock, through references to time and to social conventions, that plays are primarily about waiting. In awakening his audience to their habit of waiting, he destabilises authorial conventions.

Endgame

Beckett's second staged dramatic work, *Endgame*, is a play in one act in which four characters live their miserable existence in what seems to be a basement room. Hamm, the most boisterous of the four, is a blind and wheelchair-bound invalid who bosses Clov, his companion and servant, about. Despite being the only character who can move about on stage, fetching various items from the kitchen, Clov, too, is an invalid as he can no longer sit. As such, he laboriously moves around the stage, looks out the windows with the use of a ladder and threatens to leave Hamm throughout the play. The two supporting characters are Hamm's parents, Nagg and Nell, both of whom are so old and decayed they reside in ashbins, unable to move about except to raise themselves partially up. The audience sees them in one exchange, clinging onto the rim of the ashbins as they attempt to kiss and speak to one another. Interestingly, *Endgame* is Beckett's least minimalist play. Props are much more plentiful in this play than any of Beckett's other produced plays. Among the props are a dog's biscuit, a stuffed dog, insecticide, a ladder, a telescope and an alarm clock. Like the pocket-watch in *Waiting for Godot,* the alarm clock is utilised to upset the dramatic structure and the power dynamics between the figures in *Endgame.* While Clov does not bring out the alarm clock until late in the play, when it is brought out on stage it resonates with the themes dealt with throughout, reminding us of Hamm's attempts to tell stories to while away the time as well as of how such objects define existence.

Hamm's first words, which later he repeats in his last soliloquy, are 'Me – (*he yawns*) – to play'.[41] It is through Hamm's self-declaration that Beckett creates a struggle between the characters Hamm and Clov. In other words, by asserting that this play is about and initiated by 'me', Hamm struggles to be the creator of the play that Clov unveils when he removes the sheets covering the ashbins and Hamm before the audience. The audience sees Hamm acting the tyrant throughout even to the point of insisting that all listen to him while he tells a story that he has been constructing, presumably, for some time. Curiously, Hamm refers to his own story as an 'audition',[42] suggesting that he seeks more than merely passive listeners; he wishes them to judge his storytelling. He is not only an author but also, as his name suggests, he is a ham actor; his text as well as his performance of it are overdone.[43]

Beckett famously forwent expressive acting in his later plays. Although in these earlier plays, Beckett still creates characters who emote, in works such as *Not I*, *Play* and *Come and Go*, Beckett seeks acting that is ideally colourless – without a hint of emotion in the voice or gesture. In *Endgame*, Beckett already plays with this concept through the ridiculous over-emotional Hamm who grates on everyone's nerves. Through this, Beckett reveals that the struggle his characters are up against is that of being heard. Being looked at is not enough; an audience must see and hear critically even when judgement is harsh. His father, Nagg, the audience learns, never listened to his son even when he cried in his crib. When Hamm cried as a baby, Nagg placed him out of earshot. And now he will only listen to his son if he is given a sugar plum. Yet, when Nagg learns that he will not get his sugar plum despite being promised one, he claims that he was not listening in any case.

Hamm's story is spoken twice – first to his father and then in a compressed version to Clov – and reveals both his obsession with fathers and his concern with asserting his authority through references to time, as did Pozzo. The plot of the story is simple, although not narrated in a simple way, about a father who on Christmas Eve seeks food to nourish his ill son. The stranger, whom Hamm designates as the narrator, hesitates giving the father food because the 'brat'[44] may already be dead. Instead, taking on the role of protector, he offers the man shelter and a job as a gardener. In the process, the narrator cancels out the father's protective role by encouraging him to abandon his son. But, ironically, as a gardener, the father is responsible for growth. The date, Christmas Eve, moreover, signifies the birth of Christ, but Hamm's narrative is a subversion of this theme. It is not about the birth of Christ but rather Christ's possible death.

In his first telling of the story, Hamm alludes to several instruments of measurement. He says that the temperature is 'zero by the thermometer', the brightness of the sun is measured as 'fifty by the heliometer', the force of the wind is measured as 'a hundred by the anemometer' and the humidity is 'zero by the hygrometer'.[45] The references to these meters reflect Hamm's attempt to create an accurate and precise story, much like Pozzo's references to time. Moreover, to get his story right he provides all round numbers – zero, fifty and one hundred. Regardless of his endeavour to be precise, Hamm's measurements are absurd. While his references to these astrological instruments reveal Hamm's desire for and inability to obtain power and authority, these measurements do little more than reveal Hamm's measuring out of the story so that he will not finish it too soon.

Like the blind Pozzo, Hamm has no notion of time but regardless asks Clov 'What time is it?'[46] Clov replies ambiguously, 'The same as usual' and when pressed for more, he replies: 'Zero'.[47] Unable to see or move, Hamm is disempowered and, like the audience, cannot see what time it is. In addition, the ambiguous 'Zero', while numerically may signify that the time is midnight, also implies nothingness. Clov's answer suggests that time stands still, echoing Didi's own despairing remark when looking at the sky in *Waiting for Godot*. Indeed, within the auditorium time stops for the audience. Although we watch a picture moving through time and space, we are unaware of the exact ticking of the clock until Clov brings out the alarm clock. Moreover, each night when asked the time it is at the same moment within the play, and Clov's reply is that of the weary actor.

Beckett further pokes fun at theatrical conventions through Clov. From the onset, Clov struggles to tidy the stage. In his continual struggle, Clov positions himself as the play's author. The play opens with Clov removing the sheets that cover the furniture, ashbins and Hamm. By uncovering the set, Clov reveals and begins the play. What is to follow is his creation. However, Clov's desire to do his 'best to create a little order' is disrupted at the play's conclusion by Hamm's demand that he 'Drop it!'[48] Through the power struggle between Clov and Hamm, Beckett implies that to order the mess is impossible. The artist, Beckett has stressed, must not ignore the chaos by tidying up; instead, he should 'find a form that accommodates the mess'.[49] Indeed, in the very act of cleaning up, the author/artist figure, according to Beckett, fails to create. Beckett in 'Three Dialogues' wrote, 'the shrink from' the artist's task is 'art and craft, good housekeeping, living',[50] all of which Clov is guilty of. Clov struggles between his love for order (represented in his housekeeping), art and craft (represented in the toy dog he is making for Hamm) and his creative impulses. When creating order on stage, Clov undermines artistic creation. The stage and auditorium is silent and still, and each prop is in its place when a play has concluded. The artistic production is dead – 'under the last dust'[51] – and what remains is a bare stage with all its machine technology exposed.

Towards *Endgame*'s conclusion, the audience sees Clov placing the alarm clock on the wall where a picture with its 'face to [the] wall' hangs.[52] Replacing the artistic object with a mechanical one,[53] Clov seems to be asking the question: 'What constitutes art?' He fills in the unseen image of the canvas; the artwork becomes an alarm clock. Yet, in doing so, Clov also rejects the work of art for a gadget. In both readings, *Endgame* reflects modernist concerns about the increasing reliance on mechanical technology, which both constitutes some works of art and threatens to destroy others. What is more, when Hamm questions Clov as to what he is doing, Clov, who is in the process of hanging up the alarm clock in the place where the picture hung, responds 'Winding up'.[54] This phrase not only refers to the winding up of a clock, but also suggests that Clov is attempting to wind up the play, meaning both to end the play and to begin it once again. While the alarm clock potentially destroys the artwork because of its mechanical reproduction of time and implications of habit, it also works to 'wake the dead'.[55] In Beckett's own production in 1967 for the Schiller-Theater Werkstatt in Berlin, and subsequent productions, the placement of the alarm clock was changed. Instead of moving it from the wall to Nagg's ashbin, Clov '*Puts clock first on Nagg's bin then after thought on Nell's*'.[56] In 'winding up' the scene is resurrected and recreated as it will potentially reawaken Nell from death. As such, the alarm clock becomes an instrument which allows Clov to potentially gain independence from Hamm, albeit simultaneously imprisoning him on the stage.

The phrase 'winding up' also resonates with the inevitable process of *winding down*. Michael Worton convincingly argues that Clov's placement of the alarm clock and his statement that 'Something is taking its course'[57] reflect the play's structure as a 'diminishing spiral'.[58] The play, he goes on to argue, implies that 'our lives are a series of passive repetitions and that we are merely cogs in a machine that is slowly running down'.[59] Along with the metaphor of the winding-down clock, the numerous references to death and the description of the outside as 'Corpsed'[60] reveal the play and the constructed world outside the stage as dead and in a process of decomposing. From the outset, the audience learns that the play is 'Finished, it's finished, nearly finished, it must be nearly finished'.[61]

In using an alarm clock, Beckett further challenges notions of theatrical time and space. The play cannot officially end until the alarm goes off, but in going off, it will potentially awaken Nell from the dead and paradoxically begin the play all over again. In effect, the performance ends without ending. Moreover, despite its associations with authority, this gadget is dependent on human intervention, and therefore when winding up the alarm clock Clov remains on stage as the play ends. Before Hamm *'covers his face with handkerchief'* and *'remains motionless'*, he says, 'Since that's the way we're playing it . . . (*he unfolds handkerchief*) . . . let's play it that way . . . (*he unfolds*) . . . and speak no more about it . . . (*he finishes unfolding*) . . . speak no more'.[62] As Cohn points out, in Beckett's own production he forewent the curtain call.[63] The frozen tableau at the end of the play is a new game; it teases the audience with the possibility of beginning again – a potential act two in Godot style – once Clov turns back towards the stage or until the alarm reawakens the action.[64] Without a curtain call *Endgame*, even after the audience departs, theoretically does not conclude, and even though Hamm suggests an end when his monologue moves from 'speak no more about *it*' to 'speak no more', the play does not close. Hamm does not remain silent and his final words, 'You . . . remain',[65] open several possible readings, none of which is resolved. The 'you' is ambiguous as it may refer to Hamm, his handkerchief, Clov (who like Hamm physically remains on stage) and/or the audience who have not yet left the auditorium. Although Hamm claims that 'the end is in the beginning',[66] what Beckett reveals is that the beginning is in the end.

Krapp's Last Tape

In Samuel Beckett's one-act play *Krapp's Last Tape*, the ageing protagonist is consumed by two machines – his pocket-watch and his tape recorder – both of which make up his obsession with clock and calendar time. While the pocket-watch is a significant prop in this play, as it was in *Waiting for Godot*, Beckett's best-known mechanical object is undoubtedly Krapp's tape recorder. Several scholars argue that Krapp's tapes are not merely reflections of events long gone; he makes and remakes his personal history using this machine technology.[67] In addition to serving as a tool that allows Krapp to reimagine his memories, the tape recorder challenges dramatic action by reducing movement on stage. Rather than seeing the end of a love affair, the audience watches an old man sit rigidly while listening to the memory of the end of his love affair. He becomes an audience member to his own past.

Regardless of Beckett's vague note, '*A late evening in the future*',[68] *Krapp's Last Tape* takes place during a specific clock time of which we are not told, and on a specific calendar date: Krapp's sixty-ninth birthday. On this evening, as on past birthdays, Krapp listens to tapes from his past and records a new tape. This play is steeped in the cultural and theatrical notions of clock and chronological time which Beckett, in turn, challenges. In what is perhaps his most conventional and nostalgic play, Beckett, through the use of the pocket-watch and tape recorder, depicts the paralysis that occurs when past memories are obsessively recalled.

The play opens with Krapp '*a moment motionless*', before he '*heaves a great sigh, [and] looks at his watch*'.[69] Immediately after Krapp looks at his pocket-watch, he begins his birthday ritual of eating bananas, drinking wine and whisky, fumbling through reel tapes and listening to old tape recordings of past birthdays. This initial act of looking at his pocket-watch begins the play and establishes its structure and themes. When Krapp looks at his pocket-watch in the middle and towards the end of the play, he unknowingly reveals that he is controlled by time and paralysed by the past. Listening to himself remembering a tape of some ten or twelve years prior, Krapp switches off after the memory of the woman in the green coat is completed and the voice on the tape is on the verge of commencing a new thought with 'When I look –'. At this moment, '*Krapp switches off, broods, looks at his watch, gets up, goes backstage into darkness*'[70] to pour himself a drink. The action of Krapp looking at his pocket-watch completes the unspoken words on the tape. In other words, the phrase could read 'when I look at my watch'. However, when Krapp resumes the tape, the audience discovers that the remaining part of the phrase is '– back on the year that is gone'.[71] Ultimately, both Krapp's gesture of looking at his pocket-watch and his listening to the tape illustrate Krapp's obsession with time.

Krapp's sensitivity to the passing of time is a habit. Every year he sets out on a retrospective of the past year and, during his birthday ritual, he watches the passing of time on his pocket-watch. His fixation with time is juxtaposed against another habit. After looking at his pocket-watch each time, Krapp goes backstage to drink. Krapp's gesture of checking the time and thereafter taking a drink signifies that he is paralysed by his habit. Krapp's habit of looking at his watch, Cohn argues, is an attempt at self-imposed discipline.[72] Likewise, N. Katherine Hayles suggests that when Krapp looks at his pocket-watch, he is 'timing his drinks in an effort to keep them to a reasonable level'.[73] However, Krapp's attempt to moderate his alcohol consumption is unsuccessful. His appetite for booze grows from one to three glasses of wine and from wine to whisky. After his last trip backstage, moreover, he is seen coming back '*a little unsteadily*'.[74] Krapp's drinking both offers him a temporary escape from his current existence and, in becoming drunk, reveals that he, like Pozzo and Hamm, is losing control over his past.

In an attempt to gain control Krapp sets out to tape a memoir of his past year 'separating', as he puts it, 'the grains from the husks'[75] – that is, Krapp sifts through and prioritises the events of the year gone by. Using the tape recorder as a journal and a photo album, Krapp tries to order his life and construct a history out of the past. The audience sees Krapp carry in '*an old ledger*'[76] which holds the written chronicles of his life. Using the notes in his ledger, Krapp searches for 'Box . . . three . . . spool . . . five'[77] to provide himself with a sense of worth. Perhaps he seeks to affirm his decisions. It is often assumed that Krapp returns to this particular tape to remember, relive and regret his past decision to forsake love in order to become a writer, but his reading of the ledger suggests that he does not remember all the memories recorded on the tape. When reading the contents of the tape, he is '*Puzzled*'.[78]

While the tape recorder initially works to offer an exact repetition of the past, the machine, in its repetitions and its differences, does something more. It is through this machine that Beckett interrogates the ways in which we narrate our past. '[E]verything we see and hear Krapp doing', Paul Lawley explains, 'is authorial: on the tape he (re)imagines his past, and on the stage he edits it into his present'.[79] The memory of the woman in the punt whose love he forsook, as Lawley suggests, is not an exact repetition of the event. The audience sees Krapp in the process of editing while both setting out on a new tape and listening to his past in retrospect. When he winds forward, he cuts; when he winds back, he repeats; and when he switches off, he provides pauses and interruptions in his text. Manipulating his material, he is simultaneously editor and author.[80]

Although the audience can only be sure of how he attempts to capture the past on his sixty-ninth birthday, Krapp's process reveals how he may have recorded his other tapes. On his present birthday, Krapp '*loads [a] virgin reel on [the] machine, takes [an] envelope from his pocket, consults back of it, lays it on table, switches on, clears his throat and begins to record*'.[81] In clearing his throat, Krapp, like Pozzo, Hamm and the storytellers in Beckett's radio plays, prepares to tell a story. At this moment, his speech is distinct from that of the fumbling, cracked voice we hear reacting to the tapes. And, when Krapp pauses and broods, instead of allowing the tape recorder to capture his silence, he switches off the machine. This switching off is a denial of the realism within Krapp's text. Beckett reveals that Krapp is not capturing his past as it happened, but rather he constructs a certain image of himself through the telling of his past.

After brooding, Krapp begins again with 'Everything there, everything, all the —'[82] but realises that he has not switched the machine on and must begin again. This time he alters the phrase:

'Everything there, everything on this old muckball, all the light and dark and famine and feasting of . . . (*hesitates*) . . . the ages!'[83] After his frustration at having to begin again, Krapp adds the harsh description of the earth to the original interrupted sentence. How much of what Krapp records is written on the envelope the audience does not know. However, as seen in this example, the envelope does not dictate his every word; Krapp deviates from his original thought. Once is enough for him, but the ritual of taping compels him to say it again. In its repetition, he says it with a difference.

Krapp's act of recalling the past year allows the audience, at least partially, to conceive of his history. The recordings and ledger in *Krapp's Last Tape* provide the audience with recorded memories of former Krapps, which allow them to construct Krapp's history and identity. Certain aspects of Krapp remain the same – his attention to eyes, his appetite for bananas, alcohol and women, and his struggle between binaries,[84] while others are different. His voice, '*clearly Krapp's at a much earlier time*', at thirty-nine is strong and pompous,[85] while at sixty-nine is '*Cracked*'.[86] And, in his thirty-nine-year-old retrospect, he laughs at himself ten or twelve years earlier, exclaiming: 'Hard to believe I was ever that young whelp. The voice! Jesus!'[87] By noting the difference in his voice, Krapp at thirty-nine reveals that his voice has changed, and as the audience hears, continues to change with the passing of time.

Twenty-seven years earlier Beckett wrote in *Proust*: 'There is no escape from yesterday because yesterday has deformed us, or been deformed by us'.[88] In *Proust*, Beckett speculates as to whether we are altered by the past, or whether it is we who alter the past. In *Krapp's Last Tape*, he discovers that both are possible. The recording of time is an attempt to capture and thus take control of the past. But like the black ball that the young Krapp tosses to the white dog, these memories cannot be kept. Time alters and erases them as it alters Krapp's voice and erases his vocabulary. He cannot remember the meaning of the words 'equinox'[89] and 'viduity',[90] words that were familiar to the thirty-nine-year-old Krapp. Hence, while the tape recorder functions to capture memories, it also replaces Krapp's memory, thereby highlighting its limits.

Krapp, furthermore, edits out certain memories and emphasises others in an effort to construct who he *was* as well as who he *is*. The activity of listening to and editing the past allows him to rewrite the past and present. Krapp's past recordings structure and distort his present undertaking and the viewers' perception of Krapp. The vision on the pier, which was once deemed his chief memory to record, is wound forward and other tapes are even swept impatiently and '*violently to the ground*'.[91] These discarded memories are trodden on as he goes to his cubbyhole to drink.

Using the metaphor of a clothing line, Katharine Worth explains that the tapes function as a way for Krapp to have his memories in a retrievable format, and Worth recognises that the memories that are remembered are not those that Krapp originally thought would be of much value.[92] As time passes, some memories are forgotten while others take on new significance for Krapp. The thirty-nine-year-old Krapp says that what he has 'chiefly to record' is his 'vision at last'.[93] Krapp at sixty-nine winds forward his vision because it is no longer meaningful to him. Nevertheless, when the sixty-nine-year-old Krapp tapes his new and last retrospect, he chiefly records his failure as a writer, his failed aspirations to cut out bananas, booze and women, and his burning desire to be gone.

While the tape recorder allows Krapp to remember, and keep remembering, his lost past, it also displaces Krapp's emotional and physical needs. The act of reviewing the past draws Krapp further into the past, into himself and into the machine. Many actors playing Krapp have drawn attention to the relationship Krapp has with his machine. Pierre Chabert, who performed in *La dernière bande* in 1975, recalls Beckett's direction that Krapp should 'Become as much as possible one with the machine'.[94] Krapp's attitude and gestures towards the memories reproduced on the tape function to transform the tape recorder into something other, something human. Chabert goes on to observe, 'Krapp is a solitary old man. He has emotional relationships with objects, as he does with words. Beckett asks the actor to "humanise" objects'.[95] Through Krapp's gestures and attentiveness to the memory of the woman whose love he forsook, a theme that will recur in Beckett's teleplay *Eh Joe*, the machine transforms into a version of the woman which Krapp can physically hold onto. Knowlson and Cohn have pointed out that Beckett instructed Martin Held, in his 1969 Schiller-Theater Werkstatt production, to caress the tape recorder as though he were sensually and erotically caressing the woman's body once again.[96] Donald Davis, who played Krapp at the 1960 Provincetown Playhouse production, too, commented on Krapp's embrace with the tape recorder during the punt episode, and suggested that Krapp 'anthropomorphized the machine'.[97] In the BBC2 television production of *Krapp's Last Tape*, Krapp, played by Patrick Magee (the actor the play was originally written for), slowly lowered his head while listening to the memory of the woman on the lake until his head was completely down at 'Let me in'; Krapp's face once again rests on her breast represented in the spools of the recorder.

The final image of the tape recorder's red mechanical eye glowing on the darkened stage suggests that the machine consumes Krapp. As darkness swallows Krapp, the machine remains visible. Through his emotional dependency on the tape recorder the viewers recognise that Krapp's entire world revolves around this machine. Krapp has become increasingly mechanised, and as such has become increasingly isolated. In the light of debates on technology within modernism, the audience can read the play as a metaphor for man's mechanisation through his long-term involvement with machines.[98] For example, Krapp at sixty-nine moves like the very machine that has replaced his memories and his women. Indeed, Donald Davis reveals that he and the director Alan Schneider did not want to disrupt Beckett's sense of balance 'between sound and silence, between speed and slowness'.[99] Davis's attention to the speed and slowness (and for that matter, mobility and immobility) reflects the movement of the tape recorder. In contrast to his laborious movements and motionlessness, Krapp moves with '*all the speed he can muster*'[100] when he moves off and on stage, and his violent sweeping of the boxes to the ground is carried out with a sudden burst of anger. 'When he becomes impatient and agitated activity comes in a quick burst and then, just as abruptly, switches back to motionlessness, as if he too were a machine with a binary on–off switch', Hayles observes.[101] Likewise, the eating of the bananas is structured on quick and slow movements. Magee's Krapp peels the banana with considerable urgency and, before speedily devouring it, pauses for a moment with the banana in his mouth. John Hurt's Krapp at the New Ambassador Theatre in London in 2000, and in the 2000 *Beckett on Film* project, emphasised such movement to a greater degree than previous Krapps. The banana, in particular, hangs from Hurt's mouth, calling to mind the phallus, until it almost breaks off; at which point he resumes eating hastily.

Beckett, like other modernist writers, also explored the tension between the sterility of machine technology and the messiness of the human body. With this in mind, we can see that Krapp's inability to produce faecal matter further aligns him with his tape recorder. The audience learns that for many years Krapp has been constipated. At thirty-nine, he regrets to say that he has consumed three bananas, 'Fatal things for a man with my condition',[102] and at sixty-nine, he says he has nothing to say: 'What's a year now? The sour cud and the iron stool'.[103] Beckett told Patrick Magee, that 'sour cud' and 'iron stool' stood for rumination and constipation.[104]

The image of human waste, be it regurgitation or faecal matter, is often juxtaposed to technology in literary works of the twentieth century, theorist Tim Armstrong reveals in *Modernism, Technology and the Body*. Armstrong explains that, in the late nineteenth and early twentieth century, there was a general movement to maximise production and minimise waste. This reached an extreme with Horace Fletcher, C.W. Post and J.H. Kellogg. Believing that human waste kept the human body from running efficiently, these inventors of American cereal strove to minimise the storage of human waste.[105] Anson Rabinbach, moreover, explains that this movement began with an American engineer, F.W. Taylor, whose 'goal was the maximisation of output – productivity – irrespective of the physiological cost to the worker. As an engineer he believed that the body was a "machine", which either operated efficiently or it did not'.[106] As Armstrong persuasively argues, the man–machine metaphor fails, as modernist writers show, 'where the body declares its irreducible presence, and linear time is replaced by the cyclic time of the body' through its production of waste.[107]

Krapp, in essence, is a modernist writer who bids farewell to love at thirty-nine in order to devote his life to writing. In doing this he, in effect, gives up the waste of emotional love to maximise his production as a writer. Despite Krapp's failure to give up his sexual life, he does not partake in the excessiveness of love. At sixty-nine, Krapp says:

> Fanny came in a couple of times. Bony old ghost of a whore. Couldn't do much, but I suppose better than a kick in the crutch. The last time wasn't so bad. How do you manage it, she said, at your age? I told her I'd been saving up for her all my life. (*Pause*).[108]

Playing on the name Fanny as well as the image of a constipated man, Beckett puns on the word consummation.[109] Fanny represents a union that although *consummated* is *constipated*, that is, their union lacks emotional waste whereas the woman in the punt represents Krapp's constipated emotional needs. Because the memory remains on tape only to be recalled with the help of a sterile machine, Krapp is unable to flush away his emotional longing. Krapp cannot produce written texts because he hoards his memories of love and loss onto a machine which ultimately leads to an unproductive artistic life.[110]

James Knowlson rightly posits that 'From being a positive, purposeful form of stocktaking, recording and listening to the tape recorder have now become a mechanised habit, a birthday treat and ritual action in the old man's barren life'.[111] Despite his dreams of becoming a writer and attempting to recollect his memories, his women and himself, Krapp remains a failed author. He says bitterly, 'Seventeen copies sold, of which eleven at trade price to free circulating libraries beyond the seas. Getting known'.[112] On the one hand, his failure lies in his flushing away what may have been his 'chance of happiness'[113] while, on the other hand, his failure lies in his mechanisation, a form of constipation, of his past. Krapp uses his machines to stash away his emotions. Controlled by his machines, he cannot become an author or even a lover.

Happy Days

Happy Days, even more so than *Krapp's Last Tape*, features a character's dependence on machines. Both plays include props that allow for them to tap into the past – a past that also haunts them. For Winnie, Beckett's first leading lady, a musical-box plays a tune that both she and her husband Willie connect to. In addition to the musical-box, Beckett's 1961 play includes the ringing of a bell, which resembles an amplified alarm clock, and a revolver which Winnie takes from her bag. All three are based on revolving cylinders, and it is through these mechanical props and sounds as much as through the burial of Winnie, that Beckett investigates how the past recurs to haunt Winnie. Instead of evolving towards a better state of mind, Winnie desperately clings to the past and to her routines while her days wind down and she sinks into the earth.

Martha Fehsenfeld, a scholar and friend of Beckett's, attended rehearsals of the 1979 production of the play at the Royal Court Theatre in London. In her rehearsal diary, Fehsenfeld wrote that for Beckett, who was directing the production, the musical-box was 'a prop of [Winnie's] inward life'.[114] Many scholars have overlooked the importance of this remark; most do not even mention it. Instead, Beckett's comment that Winnie is 'Like a bird with oil on its feathers'[115] has become the predominant image to define the role of Winnie. However, the cultural history of mechanical life reveals a connection between Winnie's musical-box and her bird-like mannerisms.

The earliest mechanical gadgets were often in the shape of a bird. One of the more famous inventors of automatic life in the early eighteenth century, Jacques de Vaucanson, created a mechanical duck that quacked, digested food and excreted the food as waste.[116] The inner workings of this and other early automatons were similar to musical-boxes; they, too, had to be wound up and ran on cylinders much like manual clocks and watches. As such, it is no surprise that these inventions were often named 'clockwork figures'.[117] Indeed, Billie Whitelaw, who was cast as Winnie in the Royal Court Theatre production, characterised Winnie as such a 'clockwork figure'. She understood that Winnie, like a figurine in a musical-box replaying its sad and monotonous song, replays her bygone days, as is evident in her performance. This image is key to understanding the way in which Winnie rewinds and replays her past, struggling to transform the pain into a happy memory.

As is evident in this play, Beckett was keenly interested in the ways in which individuals struggle between the desire to disown their past with the need to speak of it. The inability to resolve this tension results in a recalling or replaying of the past, which the cylinder technology helps to illustrate. Memories of bygone days have left a trace on Beckett's protagonist. In Winnie's need to fill in the silence with constant talk of the past, trying to remember her classics perhaps in an attempt to forget memories of an unhappy childhood, she displays signs of trauma. Trauma, according to Cathy Caruth, is that which 'returns to haunt the victim'. It is 'not only the reality of [a] violent event but also the reality of the way that its violence has not yet been fully understood'. The unwelcome repetition of the event is 'not just an unconscious act of the infliction of the injury', but rather 'a voice that cries out from the wound, a voice that witnessed the truth'[118] that the survivor cannot reconcile.

The manifestation of trauma, as it is depicted in the arts, takes on three characteristics: repetition, exactness/stability, and fragmentation. Adam Phillips argues that 'Repetition is the sign of trauma; our reiterations, our mannerisms, link us to our losses, to our buried conflicts', and he continues to point out that repetition often 'obscures its own history, the conflicts it was born out of, the problems which made it feel like a solution'.[119] The second indicator of trauma, according to Phillips, is 'the need for things to have an exact position'.[120] Antonia Rodríguez-Gago takes note of this need for exactness in Beckett's stage work. She writes, 'In Beckett's early plays, past memories are kept in various containers, dustbins in *Endgame*, tapes in *Krapp's Last Tape*, a mound in *Happy Days*, jars in *Play*, or [they] are embodied through sound and repeated in the stories the characters tell'.[121] Quite literarily, Beckett imprisons his storytellers, perhaps to show how their memories, their pasts, imprison them. Lastly, the third indicator of trauma, fragmentation, is indicative of a 'too-closeness', or the lack of critical distance from trauma. Survivors have no distance from the traumatic event, Adam Phillips argues; their experience is one of intimacy and as such is manifested in distortion and fragmentation.[122]

Through its repetition, fragmentation and stage image of a woman caught in a mound, Beckett's theatrical *tour de force* can be read as the struggle to have a voice – to speak of and reinvent one's past, turning unhappy days into happy ones. With this said, *Happy Days* can be read in terms of Beckett's experience of working with the reconstruction of Saint-Lô, Normandy – a town that was devastatingly bombed during World War Two.[123] Herbert Blau and Martin Esslin, long ago, have alerted readers to the traces of World War Two and the atomic bomb, giving us new ways to read many of Beckett's seemingly deracinated sets. To build upon their reading, Phyllis Gaffney asserts that the image of Winnie in *Happy Days* 'echoes the real experience of a Saint-Lô citizen who was found by rescue-workers standing upright, unable to move, stuck in the ruins of his house' and 'Winnie's care to look her best recalls the women of the town, who would emerge into the sunlight from their dusty cellars, beautifully turned out in starched white blouses'.[124]

Having been a witness to the aftermath of the bombing of Saint-Lô, Beckett wrote to his friend, Thomas MacGreevy, 'St.[-]Lô is just a heap of rubble, la Capitale des Ruines as they call it in France. Of 2,600 buildings 2,000 completely wiped out, 400 badly damaged and 200 "only" slightly'.[125] Moreover, Beckett recorded his impressions for a radio broadcast that was never aired. In 'The Capital of the Ruins', he writes of the city's destruction and its lack of medicine to treat the sick and injured. He also takes great care to point out the efforts to reconstruct the city literarily by hand and the 'imaginative people' of Saint-Lô who continued to 'smile at the human conditions'.[126]

Echoes of this are present in *Happy Days*. The destitute landscape in *Happy Days* is described as an '*Expanse of scorched grass*'[127] and Winnie's medicine, toothpaste and lipstick are 'running out',[128] yet she repeatedly smiles and even concludes the play with 'Oh this is a happy day, this will have been another happy day!'[129] Her relentless 'happiness' attests to her endurance. Interestingly, it is the endurance of the people of Saint-Lô that stays with Beckett – that is, the endurance to survive and the struggle to preserve one's past despite the urge to forget. What we witness in *Happy Days* is a remembering of the past – a remembering, however, that attempts to rewrite the past in its attempt to re-see unhappier times as happy days.

That which endangers Winnie's happiness is time, is the past. From the outset of the play, Beckett manifests time as a threat in the form of the piercing bell. In the first versions of this play, the agonising sound that keeps Winnie from sleeping takes the concrete form of an alarm clock situated near her black bag on the mound.[130] Despite Beckett's attempt to defamiliarise the sound from the object, the piercing bell continues to serve the function of an alarm clock, waking Winnie, regulating her days and marking the passing of time. When awoken by the bell, Winnie mumbles her prayers and then tells herself to 'Begin, Winnie. (*Pause.*) Begin your day, Winnie'.[131] Apart from being stuck in a mound of earth in the blazing sun, her day is not much different from the audience's. She goes through the routine of brushing her teeth, taking her medicine, fixing her make-up and putting on her hat. These daily routines are carried out without much thought. The stage directions reveal that Winnie wipes her glasses '*mechanically*'.[132] Winnie, in other words, goes about her day, repeating her daily habits – but does so mechanically, as unconscious acts perhaps to keep a more unpleasant thought away.

Once awoken, Winnie insists on following through with the 'old style'. She keeps up her appearance mostly by keeping up habits, as the women of Saint-Lô did, and she attempts to remember forgotten quotations. Frequently, she asks, 'What are those wonderful lines?'[133] In trying to remember the forgotten lines, Winnie takes part in attempting to reconstruct the past – a narrative that privileges the classics. S.E. Gontarski, Derek Goldman and Ruby Cohn have rightly posited that the cultural debris littering the play represents the very mound of earth imprisoning Winnie.[134] She is stuck in the old ways and the old sayings, and these habits are like the ballast that chains Beckett's dog to his vomit.[135] While habit and memory are impossible to break away from, Beckett suggests that holding on to the 'old style' too vehemently is also detrimental as it leads to paralysis. Winnie, like an archive, embodies cultural debris, but by doing so constructs a narrative that is always lacking, always fragmented, and as such she is imprisoned.

Winnie continues to remember and retell her story as is demonstrated in Beckett's attention to the musical-box. While Winnie only once retrieves the musical-box, when she does so, she '*winds it up, turns it on, listens*', happily '*sway[ing] to the rhythm*' of the 1905 operetta waltz duet 'I love you so' from *The Merry Widow*.[136] The musical-box tune also stirs up happy memories for Willie as he continues the tune once the musical-box winds down. This tune, which reappears at the play's conclusion when Winnie sings once her husband attempts to climb up the mound to join her (for what purpose, we do not know), harks back to happier times for the married couple, but what those times entail we also do not know. Now, in their destitute wasteland these memories are re-enacted by consciously winding up the mechanism which holds a degraded version of the operetta. Musical-boxes almost never provide the tune in its entirety. Invariably, after winding up such a box, one hears only a fragment of the song, fixed into the mechanism's memory. As such, the musical-box functions very much like Winnie's mind, and by extension the human mind. Fiona Shaw, who recently played Winnie in Deborah Warner's production of *Happy Days*, noted in a 2008 interview on New York public radio that when Winnie recollects her memories she is 'nearly remembering' the event before it 'collapses in her mind'.[137] Beckett, as Shaw comes close to expressing, suggests that the construction of the past is an attempt to rebuild, and invariably fabricate, where memory has collapsed.

The revolver, too, connects to Winnie and Willie's past. For Winnie, the revolver, or Brownie, stirs up mixed emotional responses. When she first pulls out the revolver after dipping into her bag, she '*kisses it rapidly*'[138] and returns it to the bag. However, later in act one, when she takes out the revolver, she is '*Disgusted*'[139] but leaves the miserable object on the mound. It is at this point, too, that we learn about Willie's suicidal thoughts. Here we see how the revolver works very much like the musical-box, yet the sound that escapes this gadget is very different. Winnie rewinds Willie's past agony when she reminds him of his suicidal tendencies: 'Remember Brownie, Willie? (*Pause.*)

Remember how you used to keep on at me to take it away from you? Take it away, Winnie, take it away, before I put myself out of my misery'.[140] Even though the revolver reminds Willie and Winnie of the painful past, Winnie nevertheless claims that 'Oh I suppose it's a comfort to know you're there, but I'm tired of you'.[141] The audience is left to ponder why a revolver is a comfort.

The newspaper Willie reads, *Reynolds News*, also informs the audience of the couple's past and the world in which they live. In earlier versions of *Happy Days*, the items in Willie's newspaper were explicitly about war. In them, he read, 'Rocket strikes Pomona, seven hundred thousand missing', 'Rocket strikes Man, one female lavatory attendant spared' and 'Aberrant rocket strikes Erin, eighty-three priests survive'.[142] Each of the news items comments on the destruction caused by war technology, even those that are obviously jokes. What Beckett has left his audience with, however, is much less explicit. The title of the newspaper is perhaps a reference to *Reynolds Weekly News*, a popular newspaper which ran from 1850 to 1950. Eleven years after the press folded, Beckett features it in his play. It must have been important to Beckett that what Willie reads is an old newspaper. The newspaper sheets are yellow; thus, what Willie reads is, indeed, part of the past – a past that this old married couple connects to. We learn of 'His Grace and Most Reverend Father in God Dr Carolus Hunter dead in tub'.[143] The obituary that Willie reads brings up happy memories for Winnie – memories of a flirtatious and promiscuous past. Beckett further emphasises this desire for a long-lost youth which involved play and frolic with the wanted ads. Winnie perhaps longs for a 'smart youth' or a 'bright boy',[144] but she is stuck with the marriage partner she chose – Willie.

Print media used to recollect the past appears again when Willie looks at a pornographic postcard. After noticing that Willie is closely examining a postcard, Winnie, burning with curiosity, manages to convince Willie to hand it over to her. Despite never being told what sexual act is depicted in the postcard, from Winnie the audience learns that 'this is just genuine pure filth! (*Examines card.*) Make any nice-minded person want to vomit!'[145] Although Winnie's words express her disgust, her action of examining the card and looking closer suggests that, like Willie, some part of her is turned on by the obscenity in the card. Indeed, her earlier reminiscences of her first ball, her second ball, and her first kiss in a tool-shed helps to establish Winnie as a woman with real sexual desires and a sexual past that does not always involve her husband.[146] Winnie's reaction, furthermore, is tied to her memory of Mildred – a story which may relate to sexual trauma.

Not until the second, and last, act does Winnie recollect her most painful memory: 'There is my story of course, when all else fails'.[147] By referring to the narrative as 'my story', Winnie sets up an ambiguous relationship to the tale. She, on the one hand, tells us that it is a mere story, a fiction. On the other hand, the personal pronoun 'my' testifies that Winnie is closer to the tale than she wishes to admit. Her emotional response helps establish this. Winnie inadvertently reveals that this is 'her story', her history. The pain of the past haunts her, but as is characteristic of trauma victims, she has distorted the event into an obscure tale of a mouse running up Mildred's thigh. Paul Lawley compellingly argues that Winnie's story, along with numerous sexual references in the play, stands for 'a sexual violation'.[148] To begin with, this child, who snuck out of her room at night, undresses her new waxen doll, 'Scolding her . . . the while'.[149] Undressing a doll is, of course, a natural curiosity for children. However, the scolding of the doll while it is being undressed is not. When Winnie breaks off this story with 'Suddenly a mouse –',[150] the audience immediately is left hanging with a burning curiosity to know what happened. The audience wants to peer into this closed door to discover what keeps Winnie from continuing. Instead, Winnie calls out to Willie for help and when he does not respond, she 'call[s] to the eye of the mind . . . Mr Shower – or Cooker',[151] a memory that in act one 'floats up – into [Winnie's] thoughts'.[152] She does not want to remember how this 'coarse fellow' and his partner gape at her, wondering why she is 'stuck up to her diddies in the bleeding ground'[153] and if she has 'anything on underneath'[154] – a question that echoes Mildred's wondering what Dolly has on underneath her clothing.

While remembering the Mr Shower/Cooker incident, as in the tale of Mildred, Winnie interrupts the memory and then returns to it. In the first instance, she files her nails, punctuating the memory of Mr Shower/Cooker with comments about her nails as if to keep a certain distance from the past; it will not, she seems to be saying, disrupt her daily habits. At the end of this recollection, she even states that she is 'Thankful for it in any case'.[155] In the second act, buried up to her neck and without the possibility of filing her nails or entertaining herself with any other habit to distance herself from the pain of the past, she attempts to shut it out by closing her eyes. The bell, however, forces her to face her past. Urgently, she again calls for Willie's help. In his silence, the '*Narrative*' of Mildred resurfaces with

> Suddenly a mouse . . . (*Pause.*) Suddenly a mouse ran up her little thigh and Mildred, dropping Dolly in her fright, began to scream – (*Winnie gives a piercing scream*) – and screamed and screamed – (*Winnie screams twice*) – screamed and screamed and screamed and screamed till all came running, in their night attire, papa, mamma, Bibby and . . . old Annie, to see what was the matter . . . (*Pause*) . . . what on earth could possibly be the matter. (*Pause.*) Too late. (*Pause.*) Too late.[156]

This return suggests that Winnie suffers from a traumatic incident similar to Mildred's. Even in her attempts to distance herself from her trauma by fixing the memory in a controlled past, her history screams out through its fragmentation and repetition. In her attempt to forget the painful incident, the memory of the incident resurfaces and the wound becomes increasingly painful. The repetition of the word 'screamed', as well as Winnie's screaming, is a reliving of the event, but a reliving without clarity.

Beckett was all too aware of the paralysis that can occur from trauma. In his 1973 play *Not I*, Beckett depicts the turmoil of a woman who has been speechless all her days until the moment of the play. She is a creature who needs to speak of her past despite being unable to acknowledge that those painful wounds are hers. Her mouth, the only visible part of her, appears to the audience like a gaping wound. Likewise, despite May in *Footfalls* (1975) never being 'done . . . revolving it all?',[157] she keeps her memories at a distance, using the third person singular, like Mouth, and using a pseudonym, like Winnie, when recollecting the past. By incorporating the image of the musical-box, the revolver and the sound of the alarm clock in *Happy Days*, Beckett depicts Winnie as struggling between remembering and forgetting her past, a struggle which ultimately results in the return of wounds of unhappier days.

Play

The characters in *Play* find themselves repeating the clichéd love story, ripe with infidelity, of their bygone days. The story the characters tell is simple: a husband, who Beckett refers to as M, cheated on his wife, W1, with a woman very similar to her, W2. Their indiscretions are not recalled in a nostalgic yearning to remember as they are in *Krapp's Last Tape*, nor as a way to get through their days as they are in *Happy Days*. These characters are forced to speak of the past by the spotlight that swivels from one to another. More than ever before, Beckett explores the technology of the stage to examine memory as closely linked with torture (a theme Beckett returned to in *What Where*, as will be explored in Chapter 3). Technology becomes the means through which to recall the past but not a means to understand it.

The involuntary repetition of their past memories and the stage image, with its grey urns against the enveloping darkness, invite a comparison to purgatory as many scholars have noted. However, the stage is a place where even repenting does not release the figures from their agony. W1, the wife in the love triangle, asks, 'Is it that I do not tell the truth, is that it, that some day somehow I may tell the truth at last and then no more light at last, for the truth?'[158] Beckett suggests that even if she told the truth, the spotlight would not release her. Shortly after, she states: 'Penitence, yes, at a pinch, atonement, one was resigned, but no, that does not seem to be the point either'.[159] She struggles to find something which will release her from this ongoing torture. What she and, through her, the audience discover is that repenting, an action that usually results in forgiveness, in *Play* merely adds to a heap of empty rhetoric. What the audience leaves with are not answers, but a sense of frustration and agony.

What makes this frustration and agony for the characters, actors (as Salkind, Yates and Largess reveal in Chapter 5) and audience worse is that the story that this man, his wife and his lover tell is repeated at an incredibly fast pace. The play's second movement, a repetition of the first half of the play but faster still, gives the impression of an endless performance. The figures are not only trapped by their urns, they are also trapped by their need to be heard. Yet because their memories have become increasingly mechanised their individual voices have become increasingly lost. Although memories of their very nature recur, sometimes voluntarily and sometimes involuntarily, Beckett reveals that memories become more easily reproduced with modern technology. Krapp could go back to his memories, remembering and regretting endlessly as the tapes are played. Winnie in *Happy Days* finds that memories are recalled when listening to her musical-box. Technology allows one to capture and remember moments by gazing at a reproduction of the image. Mechanically reproduced and recalled memories, however, do not offer a more accurate, or individualised image of the past as seen in *Play*, particularly when all three characters speak at once.

Beckett explores this mechanism to recall memory, noting that the theatrical gaze is an inquisitor. It is tempting to link the spotlight directly to the eyes of the audience, yet in his note on lighting Beckett explains that the spotlight is distinctly separate from that of the audience in the stalls: 'The source of light is single and must not be situated outside the ideal space (stage) occupied by its victims'.[160] Beckett carefully constructs the technician operating the spotlight as 'a fourth player'[161] in order to direct the gaze of the audience and thereby reproducing the authorial role of technology in the production of a play. The light does not originate from the auditorium, and thus the critique of the audience's gaze is not one that should cause the viewing audience to mindlessly replicate the function of the uncritical viewer. Rather it functions like a camera, bridging the distance between the audience and stage. Beckett, interestingly, would use this very technique in his first play for television written only three years after

Play was completed. By using the technology of a spotlight, Beckett explores its function as a prosthetic eye which directs, reproduces and enhances the gaze of the audience. The single mobile spotlight, Beckett notes, is 'a unique inquisitor' 'swivelling at maximum speed from one face to another as required',[162] serving to both interrogate and provoke the characters into an agonising performance for the audience's eyes. The audience pries into their faces with the aid of the spotlight and searches for recognisable facial expressions, as they will later pry into the death-masks of Beckett's teleplays.

The spotlight becomes the prosthetic eyes and ears of the audience through its illumination of a purgatorial world not immediately visible, audible or comprehensible to human sensory organs. Anthony Minghella, in his adaptation of *Play* into the medium of film, has visualised the spotlight as a movie camera, cutting and zooming in and out of each figure. In making the sound of the camera audible, and in beginning and concluding each sequence with what appears to be unrecorded film strips, Minghella asks his audience to recognise the camera as a prosthetic lens aiding and editing for our biological eye. Like a television or movie camera, the spotlight works to capture the images onstage and places the audience in the framed image, but the final product is not an exact replica.

Rudolf Arnheim, defending the artistic nature of film in 1933, claims that film is always a reconstruction of the image filmed and outlines all the ways in which the medium breaks from mere reproduction.[163] Beckett's story of a love triangle, a theatre and screen cliché, breaks the conventions that the banal storyline dictates through the defamiliarised setting and the 'fourth player' flickering the spotlight from each character. By utilising the spotlight, Beckett stages the light as an authority, directing the eyes of the audience towards where to look. Without the prosthetic eye of the spotlight, the human eyes in the stalls would fruitlessly peer through the dark.

Theorist Andreas Huyssen identifies the technological gaze as masculine. In his discussion of Fritz Lang's 1927 film classic *Metropolis*, he argues that the 'male gaze is ultimately that of the camera', objectifying the female body.[164] With this in mind, the spotlight parallels the eye of the male authority on- and offstage, and this light functions to illuminate both the director dictating the way in which the play is seen and M's 'playing with' both his wife and lover. W2 says that when she questioned M as to whether there was anything between him and his wife he said: 'Anything between us [. . .] what do you take me for, a something machine?'[165] M, here, is paralleled to the manipulative, unseeing and unthinking machine of the light. His role in the narrative was that of the male authoritative gaze that objectified both his wife and lover in a game and a performance which he cannot seem to make sense of or end even after he left both women. He says, 'I simply could no longer –'.[166]

While M was unable to make sense of and control his former situation, he is privileged with the recognition of their situation as a performance. M says, 'I know now, all that was just . . . play. And all this? When will all this –'. He continues this line of inquiry after the light returns to him: 'All this, when will all this have been . . . just play?'[167] M draws the distinction between his past life as play and his current agony. He refers to the past as a performance, yet ironically he does not recognise his current situation as a performance which he must replay for another machine – the light. The self-reflexive title of this play reveals that it is a play about the agony of performing. Stage performance, the work demonstrates, is agonising because of its repetitive actions and the actor's need and agony of being seen and heard.

In comparing stage to film, philosopher Walter Benjamin argues that unlike theatrical conventions the camera isolates the actor from the audience: 'The audience's identification with the actor is really an identification with the camera. Consequently the audience takes the position of the camera; its approach is that of testing'.[168] Beckett undermines Benjamin's argument by staging a play which employs the spotlight in a way that exposes theatre as mirroring film. The audience is placed in the position of identifying with the light instead of the actors. The privileged inquisitive gaze of the audience mirrors the spotlight and as a result is also guilty of torturing the actors. Beckett's use of the spotlight further unsettles Benjamin's formula that the actor of the stage acts for an audience while the actor of film acts for the camera. Beckett's actors are trapped into acting for the spotlight rather than for a live audience. When the spotlight shines on W1 she, like Mouth in *Not I* who attempts to shut out the eyes watching her, says, 'Get off me! Get off me!'[169] She addresses the prosthetic eye of the audience; it is the spotlight, not the faces of the masses, that torment her as is evident in the interviews in Chapter 5.

With the torturous staring of the spotlight, Beckett creates the sensation of looking into an unseeing eye. The spotlight focuses on individual characters, but despite the function of the prosthesis to enhance vision, the spotlight blinds the actors and audience. The characters, acting for and seemingly gazing into the spotlight, question whether they are seen. W2, like Winnie in *Happy Days*, says: 'Are you listening to me? Is anyone listening to me? Is anyone looking at me? Is anyone bothering about me at all?'[170] She begins by addressing her question to 'you', the specific perceiver – the spotlight. However, by addressing the other questions to 'anyone', W2 questions the audience, yearning to know whether she is seen. Likewise, M says:

> And now, that you are . . . mere eye. Just looking. At my face. On and off.
> –
> Mere eye. No mind. Opening and shutting on me. Am I as much –
> (*Spot off M. Blackout. Three seconds. Spot on M.*)
> Am I as much as . . . being seen?[171]

Here, M focuses the gaze on the audience. It is possible that the spectators do not clearly perceive M because all three characters resemble one another and appear to be part of their urns. Their voices, moreover, are ideally toneless, and their words are performed at breakneck speed. *Play* places the audience in the position of the inquisitive eye that does not fully understand the inmates on stage, and as a result cannot release them from their purgatorial roles as performers. The performance, performed ideally without expression except where indicated, parodies the mechanised performance of the actor stuck in the same play for years. It has become their habit, and as Beckett argued over thirty years earlier, habits are paralysing.[172]

Plays, Beckett reveals, are fragmented bits pieced together for an audience. During rehearsals a play is split up into beats and later pieced together for the stage performance. In this theatrical work, Beckett dramatises the fragmentation that exists in stage productions by staging three figures that attempt to tell their story, as do most of Beckett's characters. Their storytelling, however, is fragmented through the spotlight. Often the characters are cut off in mid-sentence, and M is even cut off in mid-word:

> **M** Why not keep on glaring at me without ceasing. I might start to rave and – (*Hiccup*) – bring it up for you. Par–
> (*Spot from M to W2.*)
>
> **W2** No.
> (*Spot from W2 to M.*)
>
> **M** –don.[173]

Through the fragmentation of the story being told, Beckett undermines the stage image. The audience is placed in the position of editing the fragments together to try to make sense of them. Yet sense is not easily made of this very difficult play even though the story is quite simple. Director George Devine saw clearly that the difficulty of the play lies in the use of the spotlight. In his notes relating to the London première of *Play*, he jotted down: 'Audience privileged/actors tortured'.[174] The audience may appear to be privileged because the spotlight appears to extend their vision; however, this prosthesis also hinders sight.

The privileged, prosthetic eye of the audience cannot edit together the fragments to provide understanding nor can this eye illuminate the purgatorial experience it sheds light on. W2 says that 'No doubt I make the same mistake as when it was the sun that shone, of looking for sense where possibly there is none'.[175] As part of a vision-centred and vision-generated culture (which Beckett exploited to an even greater extent with his teleplays) the audience looks where the light shines, searching to be enlightened. However, Beckett's use of the spotlight comments on the audience's mistake in attempting to look for meaning where there may be none. The spotlight is an artificial light that, through its illumination of the images onstage, places the audience in the dark. In other words, it is a staring, technological eye that initially seems to enhance the audience's sight, allowing them into this purgatorial world, but instead of illuminating the play it reveals the audience's and the characters' lack of insight.

Come and Go

By the time Beckett completes *Come and Go* in 1965 he has eliminated stage props altogether, with one exception.[176] What remains are the traces of the mechanical props featured in his earlier plays. The cyclical movement of Ru, Vi and Flo in *Come and Go* is a mere remnant of the cyclical props like the musical-box and tape recorder of Beckett's past plays. The tightness of the lighting design in *Come and Go* also remains, echoing *Play* and creating a mysterious, ghostlike world in which the three figures disappear and reappear as they come and go into the lighted area.

Through the cyclical movements of the characters and the lighting technology, Beckett depicts characters haunted by memories that they cannot or will not speak of. In their struggle to remember and to speak, many of Beckett's characters become involved in the process of repeating stories by storing up memories, or archiving them beyond the point of being helpful as Krapp does when he records memories of past years on tape reels. Yet, despite Krapp's desire to remember, he continually forgets. As such, for Krapp and many of Beckett's subsequent characters, the past becomes a ghost haunting him as it escapes the recorder – Krapp's past haunts the present, and this spectre of the past, consequently, defines the future. While in *Come and Go* there is no tape recorder to make the connection between the memories that are stored and recalled, Ru, Vi and Flo haunt the stage as they are haunted by the past which they attempt to recall.

The philosopher Jacques Derrida may be helpful here. He explains in his book *Archive Fever*, that a struggle in humans exists between keeping secrets and going public, hiding away and making known, a struggle which arises in *Come and Go*. Secrets are kept from the audience and from the characters. Ru, Vi and Flo whisper to one another but these secrets are never shared among all three of them nor among the audience; rather they remain unknown, as the content of *Come and Go* does not give the audience much to go on.

Unlike *Play*, in which the past would be discernible if the characters spoke more slowly, in *Come and Go* the three women either speak in whispers or in audible speech that is slower than normal, with the dialogue made up of fragments. Both styles of delivery leave the audience in the dark. As such this play deals with memories that are locked away. Because the memories are not named, they cannot be collected, catalogued and made public – their bodies struggle to keep the memories inside and out of public view. There is, according to Derrida, 'no archive desire without the radical finitude, without the possibility of a forgetfulness which does not limit itself to repression'.[177] It is the very knowledge of the failure to remember and the inevitable forgetting, or silencing (as with repression), of the past that potentially drives Beckett's characters to repeat the past and to record those repetitions, whether it be on tape (*Krapp's Last Tape*), or in the struggle to leave behind footprints (*Footfalls*) that inscribe existence. The desire to archive is the desire to leave a trace of the past – a trace that will speak to the future.

In *Come and Go*, Beckett's characters are haunted by memories which they struggle to make public while the pain of the past keeps them from voicing those memories fully. The whispered secrets of Ru, Vi and Flo, secrets which provoke the '(*Appalled.*) Oh!'[178] from each character, are never heard. Despite being made public to one another (sometimes actors whisper nonsensical words, sometimes they make up secrets), this act of archiving fails as the secrets are not moved into the public domain and thus do not satisfy the audience's desire to know.

Drawing on his knowledge of the manuscripts, Knowlson reveals that the secrets, at least in early drafts, concerned 'the imminent death of the friend who has just left them'.[179] Death would no doubt threaten the memory they share. While Flo's, Ru's and Vi's whispers remain unheard by an audience that has not seen the manuscript drafts, the memory they share is made public, at least in part. The memory, however, appears in fragments scattered throughout Beckett's short play of roughly eight minutes when performed. And, indeed, not until directing the play at East Tennessee State University in 2010 did I recognise that these shattered bits fit together, although not without cracks showing. These fragments read as follows:

> **Flo**   Just sit together as we used to, in the playground, at Miss Wade's.
>
> **Ru**   On the log.[180]
>
> . . .
>
> **Ru**   Holding hands . . . that way.
>
> **Flo**   Dreaming of . . . love.[181]

This memory of love is reminiscent of Krapp's memory of his decision to break off a romance with a woman he loved.[182] The ledger entry of Krapp's breakup is called 'Farewell to – (*he turns the page*) – love',[183] echoing the typographical structure of *Come and Go*'s 'Dreaming of . . . love'. Krapp's turning of the page creates a pause similar to that of the ellipses in *Come and Go*. Indeed, Beckett's plays are littered with characters sitting on stones (*That Time*), on logs (*Come and Go*), in fields (*Not I*), dreaming of love. On the one hand, Beckett creates nostalgic plays – plays that recall and are often melancholic about the past.

On the other hand, Beckett speaks to nostalgia through the estrangement of nostalgia. Nostalgia, in Beckett, goes beyond the mere reminiscing of the past; it is often aligned with wishing to fix the past. In other words, nostalgia is the desire to reconstruct and archive the past. The memory of sitting on a log in a playground together, dreaming of the love they one day may have, suggests that they never experienced romantic love. *Come and Go* revolves around the tension of the absence of love, or that of never being loved. As such, they cannot make public a confession of love. And, if making public is an archival desire as Derrida argues, then these women cannot 'archive' – they cannot compile and store memories and tokens of love.

Despite being so focused on a past that amounts to nothing, of love that is never consummated, *Come and Go* concludes with gapping openness. Ambiguity surfaces. When nearing the end of the play, Vi says, 'May we not speak of the old days? (*Silence.*) Of what came after? (*Silence.*) Shall we hold hands in the old way?'[184] In the first question Vi poses, she attempts to silence the memory of 'the old days'. However, the characters have already begun to speak of the past and the audience has begun to speculate on their nostalgia. Thus, Vi may indeed be using the question rhetorically: *we shall speak of the past* and *we shall hold hands as we once did*. Her second utterance is a silencing of the aftermath; she asks that they *do not speak of what came after the old days*. The question leaves the audience to ponder whether there was some shattering event, some catastrophe that cannot be spoken of and that perhaps kept love at bay. What these women do have in their spectre world is one another. When Vi asks if they shall hold hands, she reaches out for love, albeit not romantic love. Her wish is granted as Ru and Flo slowly join hands with her in a strange web connecting each to one another.

The concluding line, 'I can feel the rings',[185] which is spoken by Flo, is perhaps the most puzzling. It is tempting to visualise rings on their fingers and indeed, John Crowley's production for the 2000 *Beckett on Film* project did so in its close-up, showing Flo feeling Vi's and Ru's ringless fingers. The suggestion, however, that the rings refer to marriage rings is too sentimental to be Beckett.[186] This line, indeed, sparked much conversation when directing the play. The actresses in the East Tennessee State University production understood that this line is multifaceted. The rings are the 'oh's of Ru's, Flo's and Vi's few colourful responses, and the very movement they have been going through on stage. They are, after all, in a repetitive cycle, echoing the reels turning on Krapp's tape recorder. The image 'becomes an emblem of [the play's] own theatrical and semantic "aboutness"', according to Keir Elam.[187] It was decided, moreover, that the rings could reflect the rings of the log they sat on as girls. The rings thus reflect the past, history and the desire to record memories as with the tape reels seen in *Krapp's Last Tape*. But again, to stop there does the play a disservice. The rings further represents the way Ru, Vi and Flo hold hands, creating 'the pattern of an unbroken chain, an emblem that, traditionally, has been used to symbolise eternity', as Knowlson suggests,[188] and an emblematic spiral 'ceaselessly spinning [a] central consciousness, made available to us in words of unerring simplicity and humanity', as Xerxes Mehta argues.[189] Indeed, the archive functions as a cycle, spinning in a cyclical fashion and reconstructing the past to speak to the future.

In *Come and Go*, the cycle ensures that these women remain in our memories, sharing similar dreams and urges. Yet simultaneously they are paralysed in a cycle, an archive that fails because they fail to make audible the secrets that have fragmented the unity they perhaps once had; they are paralysed because they wish to silence their voices – their past.

Footfalls

Footfalls, completed a decade after *Come and Go*, also revolves around the tension between remembering and forgetting, telling and silencing, archiving and destroying an unknowable 'it'. Unlike *Come and Go*, however, this later play explores trauma to a greater extent. Trauma is closely linked to the failure to archive. It is, as Dominick LaCapra and Cathy Caruth theorise, an involuntary *acting out* of the past that has been unsuccessfully integrated into one's history. Those suffering from trauma, LaCapra explains, are 'performatively caught up in the compulsive repetition of traumatic scenes – scenes in which the past returns and the future is blocked or fatalistically caught up in a melancholic feedback loop'.[190] While repetition is a characteristic of trauma and the archive, in trauma the repressed experiences resurface, haunting the individual. Whereas Derrida tells us that '*a technique of repetition*'[191] is necessary for the archive, Caruth and LaCapra reveal that repetition without intentional technique is a sign of trauma. Technique involves the process of reproduction and reconstruction. In trauma, repetition is not productive; it does not reconstruct the past for the public's eye, but rather festers in the private, interior walls of the mind, haunting and slowly destroying the person who houses the traumatic past. Beckett's *Footfalls* is a complex exploration of the archive and May's failure to make her past move into the present to shape her future.

Repetition, while a sign of trauma, is also indicative to the machines seen in earlier plays by Beckett. He, however, no longer needs a prop to make clear that trauma is ultimately an automatic and unwanted recalling of the past, a mechanical repetition of sorts. Another significant trace found in this play that occurred in Beckett's earlier work is the sound of the chime, which appears before each episode of *Footfalls*. The chime, echoing the alarm clock in *Endgame* and the ringing of the bell in *Happy Days*, begins May's day. The audience hears the chime, the lights go up, and May is seen pacing and heard 'revolving it all' in her 'poor mind'.[192] The 'it' that May refers to remains hidden, perhaps repressed. She keeps revolving 'it all' in her mind, but struggles to voice what that 'it' which haunts her is.

May's pacing is a compulsive, mechanical repetition of the past haunting her. Knowlson reveals that in the early drafts of the play, two titles, *It All* and *Footfalls*, were used alternatively. Beckett abandoned the title *It All* because he 'insist[ed] that the image of the woman pacing relentlessly up and down is central to the play'.[193] Even when she stands still, May continues to revolve the memory in her mind as she 'Tries to tell how it was' when 'she fancies none can hear'.[194] That is, she attempts to inscribe her past in the present. However, she only speaks of the past when she believes she is alone, and only does so in fragments, leaving much unknown. Thus, while there is repetition, as seen in her pacing, May does not externalise her traumatic past, other than to the audience who she does not acknowledge.

Because May is unable to tell the audience what 'it' was that set her pacing, the audience is left in the dark. 'In *Footfalls*', Steven Connor argues insightfully, 'we are never sure what it is we are being asked to watch so intently, never left secure in our position as spectators, because of the movement in the different narratives between spectatorship and spectacle'.[195] For Connor, this and other plays by Beckett featuring female leads display 'representation as power'.[196] As such, Beckett's plays about women reveal that Beckett was deeply aware that women are often the object of the gaze, as is evident in *Happy Days* when Winnie recalls how Mr Shower/Cooker gapes at her, and in his teleplay . . . *but the clouds* . . . . The audience gazes at May and thus is guilty of leaving her powerless, according to Connor. Yet, the audience, too, is left powerless when they are unable to make sense of what they are witnessing. In essence, the audience cannot read May because she locks herself in, perhaps like O in *Film*, to flee the audience's hungry eyes and intellects – she believes she is far from the voyeuristic eye. Indeed, the voice of her mother tells us that May

has not been out since girlhood. (*Pause.*) Not out since girlhood. (*Pause.*) Where is she, it may be asked. (*Pause.*) Why, in the old home, the same where she – (*Pause.*) The same where she began. (*Pause.*) Where it began. (*Pause.*) It all began. (*Pause.*)[197]

May has remained a prisoner to her trauma, turning it over in her mind since she was a child. She has remained both physically and mentally locked in. Beckett's initial decision was to light the set with only a dim strip of light 'strongest at floor level, less on body, least on head'[198] which fades out between each episode. However, when directing the play at the Schiller-Theater Werkstatt in 1976, he included 'a vertical accent to the horizontal light on the strip which would remain lit after each part'[199] to avoid the confusion that the play was over each time the lights faded out. The decision to include this 'vertical accent' is intriguing as it is reminiscent of light coming in through a door which is open a crack, as Asmus observed, reinforcing that May is, indeed, inside. As the door is open, May is figuratively locked in; a prisoner of her past.

Interesting shifts, moreover, occur in the mother's monologue. When she tells her listeners that May is in the old home, she stops herself from using the word born. Instead, she replaces it with the awkward 'began'. Knowlson gives a glimpse of Beckett's understanding of what is happening to May. He recalls that Beckett was haunted by Carl Jung's revelation during his lecture in London in 1935 that an individual could be traumatised by not recognising that he/she had been born.[200] Yet, what this concept means to Beckett is difficult to say. The audience is left to wonder if birth is the trauma that May has experienced, or whether there is some other experience that leads May to reject being born, much like Mouth in *Not I*. For Mouth, birth is being cast '. . . out into this . . . before her time . . . godforsaken hole called . . . called . . . no matter . . . parents unknown . . .'.[201] Her lonely and loveless existence results in her literal disintegration; she is a mouth, voicing a story that she refuses is her own. Likewise, both the mother and May in *Footfalls* refuse to accept their life stories. As a result of the shifts in language and Knowlson's insight, the audience is invited to ponder in the pause provided, *where she began what? Life?* The mother continues by changing 'she' to 'it'. But again, the 'it' is an unknown; the pronoun has transformed, no longer signifying May. The audience is left with the question, *where what began* in the old home.

When the mother and then later May, as her mother, ask, 'Will you never have done? (*Pause.*) Will you never have done . . . revolving it all', May halts her pacing and responds with the question, 'It?'[202] The audience is left with a mystery, one of Beckett's many teasers as to what the 'it' is that May cannot archive.[203] The audience is left, however, also wondering whether May herself knows. Perhaps this memory is so horrific she cannot face 'it'. In May's attempt to archive the wound, she fails to make the 'it' knowable.

Elaine Scarry, in her seminal work *The Body in Pain*, theorises that extreme pain results in a destruction of language – pain leaves us with the inability to express with words, to rationalise what has happened. She writes that 'physical pain does not simply resist language, but actively destroys it'.[204] Beckett goes further than Scarry does, suggesting that mental pain, too, destroys language. Facing the trauma, that which has resulted in her being a recluse who cannot express the wound with words of logic, would perhaps release her from her pacing. May has not worked through her trauma, that is, she has not made it public; she has not exteriorised it. Perhaps she has lost the ability to do so.

When May attempts to 'tell how it was', she is only able to give 'The semblance'[205] of it. Here, May announces twice that she can only show herself the barest trace of how it was, this 'Faint, though by no means invisible'[206] memory. What she reveals is this.

> At nightfall. (*Pause.*) Slip out at nightfall and into the little church by the north door always locked at that hour, and walk, up and down, up and down, his poor arm. (*Pause.*) Some nights she would halt, as one frozen by some shudder of the mind, and stand stark still till she could move again. But many also were the nights when she paced without pause, up and down, up and down, before vanishing the way she came.[207]

May's reference to herself in this monologue as 'she' is reminiscent of *Not I*. 'Repetition and (self-)denial', Elam reveals in his study of Beckett's short plays, 'converge'.[208] Here, a female narrator and character attempts to tell her story while at the same time disavowing it along with her history. The past is both made public and, as Boulter argues, made flesh, in addition to being spectral or ghostly.[209] Unable to recollect and reconstruct this past as her own, May remains stuck in the past, much like Winnie and the figures in *Play* are. She is not able to reconstruct this past into a tool for the future or for the public.

The other curious shift in her monologue is the change from 'his poor arm' to 'that poor arm'.

> Soon then after she was gone, as though never there, began to walk, up and down, up and down, that poor arm. (*Pause.*) At nightfall. (*Pause.*) That is to say, at certain seasons of the year, during Vespers.[210]

As May revolves this memory in her mind, she erases the pronouns, the details that may one day release her from her purgatorial pacing. When I directed *Footfalls* at ETSU this third section was the most difficult to work with. Bethany Stokes, who played May and May's mother, wondered who the man was that May clings to when pacing up and down the aisle of the church and why she pushes him out of this faint memory. The pronoun is lower case indicating he is not divine. Reluctant to admit her thoughts on the play, Stokes divulged that the memory is reminiscent of marriage, or a wish for marriage. Although the pacing, the mother tells the audience, began when May was a girl, the audience wonders if this is yet another image of wishing to be loved.

Additionally, the image is one of being led, or guided, by some male figure, perhaps a father. There are several references to sons and fathers in Beckett's landscapes. In *Nohow On*, for example, the image that haunts the pages is of two individuals, an old man and presumably his son, plodding on, hand in hand. Seán Kennedy argues insightfully that 'Beckett's memories of the father are sustained by memories of the landscape, just as memories of the landscape are inseparable from memories of the father'.[211] While the memory of the father in Beckett is linked to land (the exterior), memories of the mother which appear in *Krapp's Last Tape* and *Rockaby*, among other plays, are always interior. *Footfalls* is puzzling because in it memories of the mother and perhaps the father (in the reference to the arm) are interior; they are connected to the home and church. The mysterious man, who May alludes to, was one who perhaps attempted to guide May out of the darkness. However, she 'vanishe[d] the way she came'. As such, this father figure who attempted to help, who offered May guidance, sadly fails, like the figure in *Not I* whose 'gestures of helpless compassion'[212] lessen after each of Mouth's denials that the traumatic telling of her story is, indeed, hers.

The second story May tells is of a dialogue between a mother and daughter, perhaps her mother and herself at an earlier time. In May's telling of the exchange between Mrs Winter and Amy, the audience learns that the mother is troubled by a peculiar feeling she had in church. When asking her daughter whether she 'observe[d] anything . . . strange at Evensong',[213] she receives an odd response. Amy claims not to have been sitting beside her mother when, according to the mother, she was present:

Mrs W: But I heard you respond. (*Pause.*) I heard you say Amen. (*Pause.*) How could you have responded if you were not there? (*Pause.*) How could you possibly have said Amen if, as you claim, you were not there?[214]

The immediate connection here is to May's never having been born and her need to 'hear the feet, however faint they fall'.[215] Sitting in church, where she is still and quiet, she cannot be assured that she exists. Here Beckett draws once again on the seventeenth-century philosopher Bishop Berkeley, who theorised that human beings know they exist because they are seen by God. This concept fascinated Beckett so much that he even began his general script of his 1973 film with Berkeley's *esse est percipi*. Beckett reveals, however, that even in church Amy/May is not assured that she is seen by a divine being. Because she is not convinced of her existence, May cannot make her life public; she cannot archive her experiences in photographs and journals the way most of us archive our lives.

Likewise, May exhibits the tension between expressing and pushing away her past when she begins to tell of the conversation that arose between Mrs Winter and Amy after the evening service.

> Old Mrs Winter, whom the reader will remember, old Mrs Winter one late autumn Sunday evening, on sitting down to supper with her daughter[216]
>
> . . .
>
> But finally, raising her head and fixing Amy – the daughter's given name, as the reader will remember – raising her head and fixing Amy full in the eye she said –[217]

Here, it is as though May both murmurs, *this did not happen to me*, and recognises that the experience is important to record. The repetition of 'the reader will remember' suggests that a text is being written and read much like the one read in *Ohio Impromptu*. In transforming her experiences into a narrative about another mother and daughter May does, indeed, attempt to archive the experience. Consequently, May transforms the audience into readers, but readers with faulty memories. The audience does not remember Amy and Mrs Winter, although they speculate that May's narrative is a record of her past. However, her inability to acknowledge the narrative as her own past – her refusal to say I – results in her failure to archive this memory. What is more, this failure to archive cancels out her future; May is paralysed, as Didi and Gogo are, by habit, by her internal cycle of revolving the past trauma.

The narratives May tells, like the creature we see pacing the stage, is 'Tattered', 'a tangle of tatters'.[218] The London début in 1976 (as well as the ETSU production in 2010) left audiences 'baffled by this elusive little play'.[219] In not being able to comprehend what 'it all' means, the audience pays more attention to the visual image of the play. The image of a skeletal woman, in a grey tattered gown and dishevelled grey hair, pacing in what is obviously an uncomfortable hunched position speaks volumes. Her existence and her past, Beckett suggests, is beyond reconstruction. Despite her many attempts at correcting her narratives to make them more exact or for that matter more obscure – a characteristic that appears throughout Beckett's plays as early as *Waiting for Godot* and *Endgame* – reveals that May is unable to tell her story correctly. She can never fix her past and, thus, she can never archive it. Her trauma has resulted in this 'tangle of tatters' never to be untangled, never to be sewn together. Despite her attempts to express how it was, May cannot work through her trauma. May is utterly unlike Winnie in *Happy Days*, who has a bag holding remnants of her past (an archive of sorts). Winnie is, as Beckett put it, an 'organized mess'.[220] May is a helpless mess.

Conclusion

Samuel Beckett's aesthetic as a playwright is distinctly different from that of other modern playwrights. Using technology thematically and formally, Beckett challenges the conventions of dramatic structure. In doing so, in plays such as *Waiting for Godot, Endgame* and *Play*, he assaults authorial intentions and political tyranny. In other stage plays, namely *Krapp's Last Tape, Happy Days, Come and Go* and *Footfalls*, Beckett uses mechanical repetition, even when the technological is no longer present, to explore the ways in which the past haunts his characters and, by extension, his audience. His characters struggle to be authors, to assert their power over their tales or to come to terms with a painful past, but ultimately the audience witnesses that all their attempts are hindered by mechanical repetitions and habit.

Moreover, in Beckett's stage plays, spanning five decades, we witness the evolution of Beckett's aesthetic more clearly than we do in his radio or television work. Ultimately Beckett moves from a stage that, although it has a minimal set, is littered with props such as watches, clocks, tape recorders, newspapers, revolvers and musical-boxes, to name a few, to a stage that is devoid of props and sets. Beckett's late works, such as *Footfalls*, *That Time* and *Not I*, are sparse. Stark lighting and a body, or merely part of one, is enveloped in darkness. Movement is reduced, but more often than not cyclical. Traces of his machines remain, but no physical objects. This sparseness is intensified in the radio plays where sounds provide merely a haunting of the objects usually seen on a stage.

CHAPTER 2
THE RADIO PLAYS

Samuel Beckett began writing for radio at the invitation of the BBC's Third Programme during the summer of 1956. Despite his initial struggles to create a play for radio, what came of the invitation would be *All That Fall*, an innovative work that runs just over sixty-nine minutes. Moreover, the BBC's invitation inspired Beckett to write an additional five radio plays and one adaptation of Robert Pinget's *La manivelle* in a six-year span.

For Beckett, radio offered unique possibilities for exploring the production of sound in dramatic texts, as is evident in a letter he wrote to the American director Alan Schneider. Shortly after finishing *All That Fall*, Beckett wrote to Schneider, who was directing *Endgame*, that the play was 'a matter of fundamental sounds (no joke intended), made as fully as possible, and I accept responsibility for nothing else'.[1]

In addition to his new awareness of sound that radio brought to *Endgame*, the genesis of *Krapp's Last Tape* is directly connected to the BBC's broadcast of *All That Fall*. On hearing a recording of the play, Beckett became intrigued by the raspy voice of Patrick Magee, the Irish actor who played Mr Slocum. Moreover, the recorder sent to him so that he could hear the play intrigued him. He was fascinated with this new recording device. Both Magee's voice and his interest in the mechanisms of the tape recorder resulted in his writing *Magee Monologue*, the first draft of what Beckett would develop into *Krapp's Last Tape*[2] (a detailed discussion of Beckett's exploration of technology in this play is provided in Chapter 1). Indeed, radio presented Beckett with the possibility of investigating the technology of sound as well as the figurative possibilities the medium brought with it. As such, these plays often depict the struggle to create. In this they are more self-reflexive than his plays for the stage. In addition to their self-reflexivity, Beckett's plays for radio increasingly move away from realist representations into a world of ghosts. For Beckett radio is a box which buries voices and a vehicle which carries them forward. Those voices carried into the audience's homes are haunting, ghostly voices, mere traces that never become whole.

All That Fall

First broadcast on the BBC in 1957, *All That Fall* opens with the sounds of an old, overweight woman, Maddy Rooney, making her way to the train station to pick up her blind husband, Dan. On her journey to the station, she meets her fellow townspeople. Christy, a dung salesman, stops to talk with Maddy. After their exchange, his hinny will not move 'a muscle'.[3] Mr Tyler, who sounds his bicycle-bell before Maddy announces his arrival, stops with Maddy for a bit. Before continuing on his way, he despairs that his 'back tyre has gone down again'. 'The back! The chain! The oil! The grease! The hub! The brakes! The gear! No!', he continues, 'It is too much!'[4] The proprietor of the racetrack stops to give Maddy a lift in his car. The sound of the starter, gears and horn threaten the silence of the play. In addition to hearing the parts of each machine, the sequence in which they appear constructs an understanding of transport history. The play moves from the cartwheel, bicycle, van, motor car and concludes with the train. This history represents a technology of progression; yet this progression, the audience discovers, is an incomplete cycle. Through the act of listening to these bits and pieces and Maddy's recollection of the past Beckett challenges notions of progress, as the sounds that dominate this radio play ultimately reveal the stalling and faltering of machines.

The sounds of these machines parallel the way in which Beckett composes an awareness of radio. Beckett's audience becomes aware that machines, including radios, are composed of unseen mechanisms. What the audience hears on the radio are not the only elements involved in the production of carrying a voice into our homes; there are also mechanisms, which the audience cannot see, that go into the production of radio broadcasts. Linda Ben-Zvi observes that

Beckett 'forces the audience to acknowledge the presence of these usually hidden shapers of texts'.[5] In effect, the audience discovers that the sounds they hear are artificially created by isolated tracks put together by a broadcasting technician.

Yet in *All That Fall* the bits and pieces of sound do not always amount to a complete visual understanding of what is happening. Maddy, despite being the audience's guide through this soundscape and communicating to them what she sees so that they can translate what they hear into an image, leaves much of the information incomplete; her memory fails her as Winnie's does in *Happy Days*. After Maddy's encounter with Christy she is about to reveal 'what' happened 'So long ago',[6] but breaks off, refusing to acknowledge the event and consequently denying the audience this information. Her ability to recall the past, like Winnie's, is compacted when she partially quotes some old lines. She only half remembers John Ford's *The Lover's Melancholy*: 'Sigh out a something something tale of things, Done long ago and ill done'.[7] The 'something something' has replaced 'lamentable' because presumably Maddy has forgotten the original. Like the machines that falter, her memory putters out. In only providing some of the quote, Beckett reveals that recollection for repetition, a mechanical act, is never complete. However, Maddy's recollection of Ford's original lines brings about a new composition. With these fragments Maddy composes something new; she has made Ford's lines her own. Her text reads as her manifesto: she sighs out a tale of things, done long ago and ill done. Her story is composed of material from the past and her tale is retold poorly because of the pain the past stirs up. When speaking to herself, she reveals that she is 'destroyed with sorrow and pining' and is childless.[8] Immediately after her lamentation, Maddy calls out 'Minnie! Little Minnie!',[9] revealing that at one time she had a daughter. Her sorrow, the audience speculates, is of loss.

Indeed, death and sterility saturate the radio play. With each encounter Maddy inquires as to the health of someone. Each time we learn about the infertility or sterility of the person in question, and with the news the drivers' machines falter. '[S]uch mechanical failure is thematically poignant as well', explains Louise Cleveland, 'since each vehicle is closely identified with the body of its owner and the failures partake of comic entropy'.[10] The news of Christy's wife and his daughter is not good. Although he does not reveal what ails them, he tells Maddy that they are 'No better' but 'No worse'.[11] The stable condition of Christy's wife and daughter parallels that of his hinny. Christy's hinny will not budge until the third welt it receives on its rump.

When Mr Tyler joins Maddy for a chat, he tells her his daughter is 'Fair, fair. They removed everything, you know, the whole . . . er . . . bag of tricks. Now I am grandchildless'.[12] Although he initially responds that she is 'fair', the extra information Mr Tyler departs with reveals his daughter's infertility. His failed attempt to continue his family lineage is represented by a higher technological authority – the van. The van, with its *thunderous rattles*,[13] announces itself as both a vehicle with more power and a technological god. Like Zeus, the god of thunder, it breeds destruction and reminds man of his powerlessness. After the 'narrow squeak' with Connolly's van, Mr Tyler curses God, man and 'the wet Saturday afternoon of my conception'[14] because his tyre has gone flat despite his having 'pumped it hard as iron before I set out'.[15] The pumping of the tyre is suggestive of Mr Tyler's attempts to create. When the tyre goes flat, it represents his impotence as well as a mechanical miscarriage. He cannot assert his authority over a machine just as he cannot rely on sexual reproduction to forward his family heritage. Cursing his own conception, Mr Tyler reveals a paradoxical relationship towards conception and authorship. While he wishes to assert his authority, he curses God for creating man and curses the day he himself was conceived.

After Mr Tyler departs, Maddy greets Mr Slocum as he pulls up beside her. She asks how his mother is doing. Mr Slocum responds that 'she is fairly comfortable. We manage to keep her out of pain',[16] and offers to give Maddy a lift, perhaps to relieve her of her own pain in walking. Nonetheless, the effort to get her into and out of the car results in its own struggle and pain. Sounds from Mr Slocum and Maddy's strenuous efforts are heard; he nips her frock when slamming the door and his inability to get the motor started causes her to feel 'awful'.[17] Mr Slocum says:

(*Dreamily*.) All morning she went like a dream and now she is dead. That is what you get for a good deed. (*Pause. Hopefully*.) Perhaps if I were to choke her. (*He does so, presses the starter. The engine roars. Roaring to make himself heard*.) She was getting too much air! (*He throttles down, grinds in his first gear, moves off, changes up in a grinding of gears*.)[18]

Although Mr Slocum claims he keeps his mother out of pain, he is characterised by violence. Mr Slocum mutters, grinds his gears, shoves Maddy into the car and blows the horn violently. In addition, once on his way he squashes a hen in his reckless acceleration towards the station. Maddy's reaction depicts Mr Slocum's car as a machine that has the ability to destroy fertility: 'What a death!', Maddy exclaims, 'One minute picking happy at the dung, on the road, in the sun, with now and then a dust bath, and then – bang! – all her troubles over. (*Pause*.) All the laying and the hatching'.[19]

Laying and hatching are obvious references to fertility. Dung, however, represents both fertility and waste. Even though Maddy laments the mother hen's death, it is also a relief. No longer must the hen trouble itself with the wasteful act of creation nor must it continue picking at waste products. Not only does the motor car kill the hen, but ironically the car also dies. Temporarily dead, the motor car can only be revived by choking *her*. Because of the close proximity of this sentence to Mr Slocum's annoyance with Maddy and Patrick Magee's intonation in performance, this sentence provides dark humour as it surpasses its literal meaning and suggests that Mr Slocum may indeed be dreaming of choking Maddy – nipping the old hen in the bud.

Whereas each vehicle parallels the hierarchical position of its driver, positions of authority in this radio play are continually ridiculed and undermined. Christy travels with a cartwheel pulled by a hinny and sells dung. He is associated with the sale and commodification of animal waste and thereby occupies a low position in the hierarchy of the play. Christy, the only character capable of fertilising and composing life, does not succeed because he has transformed the act of creation into a commodity and as such his authority is wasted.

Mr Tyler, as Maddy reveals, is a retired bill-broker. His bicycle and the designation of his former career as a middle-man to transact business or negotiate bargains places Mr Tyler in the middle of the play's hierarchy. It is important, too, that unlike Christy, who is always referred to by his Christian name, Mr Tyler is not. However, his retirement suggests that he is no longer useful even as a middle-man, and Connolly's van nearly flattens him. Like his bicycle tyre, Mr Tyler, whose name sounds strikingly like tyre, has lost his air of authority. No matter how many times he pumps himself up again, he remains a deflated man.

Mr Slocum, the Clerk of the Racecourse, holds the highest position of authority. He owns his own motor car which, although less powerful in mass and velocity than the train, is historically more advanced and more mobile. W.H. Lyons points out in his meticulous study of *All That Fall* that a motor car with balloon tyres in the mid-twenties (the time in which the radio play is set) in Ireland would still have been rare.[20] The rarity of this vehicle sets Mr Slocum up as a celebrity, positioning him above the rest. Asserting his authority, Mr Slocum orders the porter to help Maddy out of the car when they have reached the station and then drives away. Cleveland claims that 'The ultimate mechanical bride is, of course, the motor car' and adds, 'Mr Slocum's name is certainly an allusion to procreation as well as race tracks, as the gearbox pun emphasizes'.[21] While Mr Slocum functions as the highest form of authority, he is connected not with creation but with destruction. He destroys both machine and animal life. '[C]rucifying his gearbox',[22] he is aligned with the death of Christ, and in killing a mother hen he destroys an image of motherhood and fertility. In addition to destroying the hen, Mr Slocum is the failed admirer of Maddy, and his name, a pun on his virility, furthers the theme of infertility and impotence.

Maddy has become isolated by Mr Slocum's roaring machine that engulfs her in the dust it whirls sky-high. Indeed, she is crucified but, unlike Christ, whose legend lives on, she is ignored by all, even at times by the audience. Despite various individuals stopping for a brief chat with her as they journey towards the station, once at the station and among other company they are no longer interested in her. Beckett's exploration of isolation brought on by technology echoes Walter Benjamin's claims that each new technology has the potential to further isolate humans. Quoting Georg Simmel, Benjamin writes: 'Before buses, railroads, and streetcars became fully established during the nineteenth century, people were never put in a position of having to stare at one another for minutes or even hours on end without exchanging a word'.[23] *All That Fall* is a case in point. The cartwheel, bicycle and motor car can theoretically halt so that the drivers can communicate with others. However, the train, according to Maddy's husband, Dan Rooney, isolates each individual in his compartment. Dan explains that in the train he felt confined 'like a caged beast'.[24] Describing his existence as being stuck in a cage, living an isolated, disembodied life, Dan unwittingly describes the medium of radio – a box which figuratively conceals the body while concurrently projecting the voice outward.

The machines occupying Maddy's world increasingly isolate her. Throughout the radio play, Maddy refers to herself as not being alive despite fighting to be heard as a real presence. When Mr Tyler says that 'it is a blessed thing to be alive in such weather, and out of hospital',[25] Maddy responds: 'I am not half alive nor anything approaching it'.[26] Here, she negates the audience's imagination by denying her existence, despite her presence as sound. Consequently, Maddy and the world around her have been interpreted as figurative ghosts.[27] Towards the end of the play, she recalls a lecture she attended in which a psychologist explained that the trouble with a certain patient was that 'she had never really been born!'[28] As previously discussed in Chapter 1, Beckett attended one of Jung's lectures in 1935 and was fascinated by Jung's remark that an individual could exist without being born. Jung's observation reflects Beckett's use of radio. Voices coming out of the radio box exist because we hear them, but they have not been born. Their bodies remain in this mechanical womb.

At other times Maddy struggles to reassert her existence. When the porter begins to speak with Mr Slocum after being ordered to help Maddy out of the car, Maddy states: 'Don't mind me. Don't take any notice of me. I do not exist. The fact is well known'.[29] With this statement, Maddy admonishes the porter for not greeting her; she does so to reassert her presence. When listening to the dialogue between the porter and Mr Slocum, the audience, in effect, temporarily erases Maddy from the scene. Likewise, when no one speaks to Maddy at the station, she again attempts to assert her existence: 'Do not imagine, because I am silent, that I am not present, and alive, to all that is going on'.[30] '[D]espite Mrs Rooney's insistence on her presence', Thomas Van Laan points out, 'in actual fact, as long as she is silent she does not and cannot exist'.[31] The audience further hears Maddy struggling to remain in the radio play when she interrupts the dialogues between the other characters on the platform by confronting them and the audience at home with her presence: 'Do not flatter yourselves for one moment, because I hold aloof, that my sufferings have ceased. No'.[32] Maddy cannot control the other characters. Nevertheless, while the others continue to ignore her, Maddy interrupts with her description of her surroundings – a sight that is painful for her as she breaks off with 'I stand here and see it all with eyes . . . (*The voice breaks.*) . . . through eyes . . . oh if you had my eyes . . . you would understand . . . the things they have seen . . . and not looked away . . . this is nothing . . . nothing . . . what did I do with that handkerchief?'[33] What Maddy has seen and to whom she is referring to are left unknown.

After the train arrives and the old couple begin their journey home Dan speaks, relating the events on the train. Resting on the side of the road, he explains in a *'narrative tone'*[34] that while in his compartment he thought of retiring, but regardless of the money he would save, 'the horrors of home life' and the 'howling neighbour's brats'[35] discouraged him. The attention given to 'home life' in the form of a list of gerunds suggests that domesticity for Dan represents habit and order. Years prior to writing *All That Fall*, in a dialogue with the French artist Georges Duthuit, Beckett urged that artists must resist ordering that which seems chaotic.[36] Dan avoids habit and order. Nonetheless, he provides a list which, in effect, is an ordered definition of 'home life'. In this he is like Clov. The habit of ordering, Beckett reveals in this play for radio, is inevitable; thus, all artists fail. In his recognition of the failure to escape habit, Beckett suggests that the outcome of the text is not as important as the process, or journey.

Like so many of Beckett's narrators, Dan also is unable to be done with his narrative, perhaps because he is full of loathing for fertility and youth. Dan is aligned with destruction. The references to the neighbour's brats and Dan's confession to having 'nearly attacked the boy. (*Pause*.) Poor Jerry!'[37] many times point to the Beckettian disgust with reproduction. Even though Dan wishes to destroy life rather than create it, as a narrator Dan's acts of destruction allow him to create. His 'composition'[38] comes about through his experience on the train, and the train's great power represents the ultimate destruction of life. Despite not revealing what caused the interruption in a thirty-minute run, Dan's composition is partially completed by Jerry: 'It was a little child fell out of the carriage',[39] Jerry tells Maddy.

The massive machinery of the train results not only in the greatest isolation among its passengers, but also results in the greatest destruction, that of a human life. Many scholars have called this work an unresolved whodunit.[40] Indeed, Beckett's radio play refuses to provide a closed system. The ball-like object, Dan's confession that he sometimes desires to kill a child and his attempts to keep Jerry from answering Maddy, some have argued, imply that he is guilty of the child's death.[41] The end, however, remains ambiguous; and if Dan is responsible for the child's death he is not charged (here, at least) with the crime.

The radio play does not end in the silence of the unsolved mystery. Rather, it ends with an excess of sound.[42] The storm performs the same function as the sound effects of the train, which drown out human speech as it arrives in a '*Crescendo*'.[43] It washes away Dan's composition, flooding all voices and sounds. Producing an excess of sound, the storm floods all growth and leaves a once-fertile landscape with uprooted waste. But in drowning out all previous sounds, the radio play continues.

Embers

Beckett's second radio play, broadcast on the BBC in 1959, features an old man, Henry, who goes to the seaside, sits on a bench and calls on voices of the past to help him while away the day. In addition to calling on dead loved ones, Henry tells a story of an old man, Bolton, seeking help from a doctor, Holloway, to give him an injection. *Embers*, thus, is the typical stuff of Beckett. Yet in this play for radio, Beckett explores the new medium he is working in even further than he did with *All That Fall*.

The central innovation is the radio play's self-reflexivity. *Embers* begins with Henry simply saying 'On'.[44] When he does so, he positions himself as a radiophonic narrator, switching on the sound channels. The word 'on', in other words, denotes a *switching on* of sound and thereby commencing one's narrative. Furthermore, the stage directions reveal that after Henry says 'On' twice, the audience hears his *'Boots on shingle'*.[45] Henry must order himself to continue walking and take his place on the bench by the sea. Once sitting, Henry *switches on* his stories. Henry, Jonathan Kalb remarks, is a man 'wrestling with his imagination – a spectacle we witness in the form of sound-effect commands barked out as if to obedient radio technicians'.[46] Kalb characterises Henry as a director barking out orders to create the appropriate sound-text, yet he does not recognise Henry as a storyteller struggling to sustain his authority. Whereas Kalb draws a distinction between a director and storyteller, the boundaries between these roles will be blurred in this chapter. Henry, like so many of Beckett's protagonists, attempts to maintain directorial control over the stories he tells.

Henry's ability to switch sounds on, however, falters. When Henry barks out his orders, he repeats himself, revealing his inability to make his commands stick. In the repetition of each command, the exclamation mark following the repeated command and in Jack MacGowran's raised voice in the original BBC broadcast, Beckett exposes Henry's frustration. Towards the end of the radio play, Henry can neither summon his father nor his wife Ada to keep himself company. His only recourse is to continue his tale of Bolton and Holloway to reinvigorate his position as author. Increasingly, however, he becomes more like Bolton, who pleads to Holloway for something to take away his loneliness. Instead of providing company, his narrative reflects his isolation. Trying to escape through his

Holloway–Bolton story, Henry 'finds only confirmation of that very isolation'.[47] His only comforts are the ghosts of his wife, Ada, and daughter, Addie, who, by the end of the radio play, no longer appear. Even Addie's music and riding masters are dead authorities. Beckett labels them 'masters' instead of 'teachers', which establishes them more bluntly as authorities over Henry's daughter. However, in Henry's mind the ghost of Addie continually undermines their authority. She cannot play Chopin's Fifth Waltz without playing '*E instead of F*',[48] and there is always something wrong with her posture when out riding her horse. Paul Lawley reads Addie as another reflection of Henry's 'own creative predicament'.[49] Her inability to play the Waltz and properly ride a horse positions her as Henry's failed creation, and as such always reminds him of his own failure to create.

Beckett further challenges Henry's authority by juxtaposing clocks/time and dead bodies. Images of clock technology are directly connected with the formation of habits, the mechanisation of bodies and authorial structures. Henry contemplates whether one could

> Train it to mark time! Shoe it with steel and tie it up in the yard, have it stamp all day! (*Pause.*) A ten-ton mammoth back from the dead, shoe it with steel and have it tramp the world down! Listen to it![50]

The desire to mark time and create a timepiece is directly associated with Henry's attempt to uphold his authority. He concludes by ordering the audience to listen to the mammoth marking time. The audience, however, hears nothing because the mammoth is dead. Henry's effort to create a timepiece fails because he treats the horse as a concrete machine rather than decomposing biological material. In another reference to time, the audience learns that the absence of Henry's father's body 'held up probate an unconscionable time'.[51] Although it is not unusual that probate would be held up, this statement is also emblematic, revealing that without a body the signifier 'dead' is empty. Moreover, together with meaning 'excessive', the word 'unconscionable' refers to 'waste', an important image in

Krapp's Last Tape and *All That Fall*, as already discussed. Here both the clock and the father lose their original meaning; rather they are decomposed into waste products. Like dying embers, they no longer are emblems of warmth, security or authority.

When narrating the Holloway–Bolton story, Henry speaks the words 'white world' eight times and 'not a sound' twelve times in this short radio play of nearly forty-five minutes. The image of the 'white world', a place covered with snow, parallels the image of a white (or blank) page. Together with representing Henry's own failure to stamp out his story and leave behind the black marks of existence, the image of the blank page represents an erased page. Henry's use of the repetition of 'white world' mirrors his use of his gramophone, another mechanical gadget, first featured in *All That Fall*. The ghost of Henry's wife explains, 'There is no sense in that. (*Pause.*) There is no sense in trying to drown it'.[52] Ada reveals that the gramophone does not provide Henry with the sufficient amount and quality of sound to erase the sound of the sea. The failure of the gramophone to rise above the sound of the sea echoes Henry's failure to conjure up the ghosts of his father, and later his wife. He calls for them from the depth of his consciousness but receives no answers.

By utilising the gramophone and the words 'white world', Henry tries to both mark his existence on the page by conjuring up old ghosts and tries to wipe the page clean of his former self in order to recreate and reanimate himself into an author. The overwhelming need to tell stories, in Beckett, is tied to the need to justify one's existence, as Fletcher argues: '*Embers*, for the first time, introduces the theme which from then on proceeds to dominate Beckett's radio drama, that of the storyteller and his obsessive need to justify his existence and find an identity through and by the telling of stories'.[53]

The image of the 'white world', moreover, recalls Beckett's 1937 letter to his friend Axel Kaun, in which the young Beckett claims that he will set out 'To bore one hole after another in it [language], until what lurks behind it – be it something or nothing – begins to seep through'.[54] Twenty-two years later Beckett applies his mistrust of language to sound. While his image of boring holes into language constructs language as a physical although meaningless object, his investigation into sound reveals that as Henry strives to erase the soundscape punctuating the play. He fails because he has not sufficiently misused sound. His page remains intact. Only by marking the white page can one test the frailty of sound. A 'white world', after all, in radio refers to 'white noise', noise that exists but is inaudible to the human ear. The recurring reference to 'not a sound' does not literally mean that there is no sound. Rather, it comments on the inability to hear the noise of the 'white world'. Ironically, however, the repetition of 'not a sound' both makes the sound/noise audible and erases its significance. It becomes, like the ticking of a clock, a sound that is no longer heard because of its mechanical repetition.

The concept of an inaudible yet present sound/noise echoes throughout *Embers*. Ada and even Henry, to some extent, are ghosts; they exist despite not being perceivable to the human eye.[55] Hence, although Henry endeavours to affirm his existence through his narrative, the audience is placed in the position of both doubting Henry's and Ada's materiality and acknowledging their aural presence. The concept of unperceived existence (i.e. the absence of body seen and the presence of white noise) is crucial to the medium of radio. Through it, Beckett destabilises Bishop Berkeley's 'to be is to be perceived' and uses the idea of unperceived and unheard existence as a theme to explore the need to hear and see objects.

The radio play concludes with a banality – a plumbing problem. When Henry consults his 'Little book',[56] he discovers that despite repeatedly murmuring 'white world', his world is not a blank page: 'Tomorrow . . . tomorrow . . . plumber at nine, then nothing. (*Pause. Puzzled.*) Plumber at nine? (*Pause.*) Ah yes, the waste'.[57] Henry refers to human waste literally, but this waste, while affirming his existence, also reflects his decomposition. The appointment marks the white page as waste marks the otherwise sterile, white world. As the twentieth-century French philosopher Dominique Laporte theorises: 'No doubt beautiful language has more than a little to do with shit, and style itself grows more precious the more exquisitely motivated by waste'.[58] An elaborate style is excessive, wasteful. And, '[o]f all Beckett's plays', Zilliacus observes, '*Embers* is the most saturated with sound'.[59]

In saturating the play with sound, Beckett places the audience and Henry in a similar role – that of struggling to wash away the overflow of sound only to recognise the impossibility of sterilising the soundscape. Indeed, Beckett creates yet another narrator who deals with the problem of language and waste in various ways. While Krapp hoards his waste and as a result finds himself unable to create text, Henry shits on the page, but rather than leaving the page marked with his waste he attempts to remove it. His appointment with the plumber reveals his failed effort to flush it away and his failure to deny his existence.

The Old Tune

Beckett's third venture into radio, his adaptation of *La manivelle* written by his friend, the Swiss writer Robert Pinget, was broadcast on the BBC in 1960. As it is an adaptation, *The Old Tune* is often neglected by scholars because adaptations are generally not considered to be original works. *The Old Tune* may not be a 'Beckett original' in the strictest sense; nonetheless, Beckett has made this adaptation his own, setting the play in Ireland and peopling it with two ageing Irish men who meet after many years and reminisce nostalgically about the past. As Cream and Gorman talk about the old days and rail against modern ways, they are interrupted by the passing of cars. Through the sounds of Gorman's barrel-organ, the sounds of road traffic and references to modern machinery, this radio play bears the Beckettian mark in its exploration of technology, communication and the process of storytelling.

From the onset, the audience is aware of three predominant sounds, the noise of modern traffic, the sound of an old-fashioned barrel-organ and the sound of the human hand hitting the barrel-organ: '*Background of street noises. In the foreground a barrel-organ playing an old tune. 20 seconds. The mechanism jams. Thumps on the box to set it off again. No result*.'[60] These opening stage directions reflect both the decreasing popularity of radio plays and the breakdown of authorial mechanisms. Beckett's protagonists, the decrepit Gorman and Cream, have experienced the beginning of cinema and perhaps even television, as the radio play takes place around 1957 (revealed through the references the men make to the moon expeditions). The barrel-organ, although fairly popular in the 1920s, was quite rare after World War Two. Radio plays, too, lost their popularity with the arrival of television in the late 1950s. While radio still remains popular for music programs, few today listen to radio plays. Beckett seemed to have an ambivalent relationship to the medium of radio. Even though radio offered him an opportunity to experiment with sound, he recognised radio's limitations and short lifespan. This radio play in particular, expresses the death of the art of radio drama. Yet, what Beckett adds to the history of radio is a rich play lamenting the disappearance of old art forms.

Like Beckett's other radio plays, this one critiques the medium it was constructed for. Both the barrel-organ and the radio are boxes that have a knob or handle which must be turned to be switched on. As the audience recognises in *Rough for Radio I*, the action of switching on the radio is a miniature of cranking of the barrel-organ. However, in changing Pinget's title *La manivelle*, which translates to 'the crank', 'daily routine' and 'drudgery', to *The Old Tune*, Beckett shifts the focus from the mechanism that cranks out the music to the music marking the toil of daily life. Gorman and Cream's chance meeting is a break from their laborious lives, but their narratives, and Gorman's recourse to crank the barrel-organ, are rooted in habit. They crank out the past, and these recollections form their stumbling old tunes.

When the mechanism of the barrel-organ jams in the opening, Gorman thumps on the box, which yields no result, thus revealing his lack of control over his machinery. The word 'machinery' only appears once, and then in conjunction with the courts; however, this word resonates throughout the radio play. Learning that Cream's son is not the judge in a sex offence case but employed in the county courts, Gorman says: 'All that machinery you know I never got the swing of it and now it's all six of one to me'.[61]

His confession that he never got the swing of the court system is equally true of his barrel-organ. Gorman's barrel-organ fails partly because he does not comprehend its mechanisms. Instead, he has become mechanised and worn down by the laboriously repetitive movement of the crank. His act of cranking out the tune, however, is his act of composition. The music's return is significant. Prior to the tune resuming each time, Gorman says: 'When you think . . .'[62] and after the tune breaks off he recalls a new memory to add to his repertoire. The barrel-organ functions much like Krapp's tape recorder. When switched on, it helps Gorman recall and restart his narrative. Unlike the philosopher Walter Benjamin's storyteller whose art is that of 'repeating stories',[63] Gorman's cranking is a mechanical repetition. To create music, Gorman must crank his instrument, but this repetition of sameness results in paralysis. Initially, Gorman's hand is active as he pounds on the barrel-organ in an attempt to resurrect the tune, but when the machine falters twice more, he does not attempt to assert authority over it. He allows his once active hand to lie inert, becoming more modest in his role.

Like the barrel-organ, Gorman and Cream play 'an old tune' when they recollect the past. Their memories are rooted in a romanticised Ireland. Nostalgic of the past, Cream says, 'Ah in our time Gorman this was the outskirts, you remember, peace and quiet'[64] and Gorman adds,

> Do I remember, fields it was, fields, bluebells, over there, on the back, bluebells. When you think . . . (*Suddenly complete silence. 10 seconds. The tune resumes, falters, stops. Silence. The street noises resume.*) Ah the horses, the carriages, and the barouches, ah the barouches, all that's the dim distant past, Mr Cream.[65]

After his description of a romanticised rural landscape, Gorman resumes his tune as if to turn on his memories. However, his memories and the tune are interrupted by the noise of modern traffic, reminding the audience and the protagonists that their memories are in the distant past.

Gorman and Cream's obsession with the past is established in their physical objects and Beckett's characterisation of these old cronies. Gorman, the owner of the broken-down barrel-organ, has an '*Old man's cracked voice, frequent pauses for breath even in the middle of a word, speech indistinct for want of front teeth, whistling sibilants*.[66] Cream, too, is an old man with *'cracked voice, stumbling speech, pauses in the middle of sentences, whistling sibilants due to ill-fitting denture'*.[67] In the only production of this radio play, moreover, these cracked voices are distinctly Irish. Most who have heard Barbara Bray's production for the BBC with Patrick Magee and Jack MacGowran will agree that it is these cracked and whistling voices that compose music. The audience listens intently to the composition of their rotting Irish lyric. Along with the quality of Magee's and MacGowran's voices, Beckett's use of names such as Drummond Place and Sheen Road, his references to an idealised countryside and his use of many phrases such as 'Ah Mr Cream, always a great one for a crack'[68] identify these two men as Irish and the place as Ireland.

Lamenting the bygone days and railing against modernity, Cream says, 'My dear Gorman do you know what it is I'm going to tell you, all this speed do you know what it is has the whole place ruinated, no living with it any more, the whole place *ruinated*, even the weather. (*Roar of engine.*)'.[69] To 'ruinate' is to reduce to ruins, and to bring destruction upon. However, Cream's description of the cityscape is misleading. The street is not obliterated or decayed into a waste land like it is in *Endgame* or *Happy Days*. The audience hears passing cars and footsteps. Rather, Cream and Gorman's nostalgic Ireland of peaceful fields has been destroyed by technological progress. The constant noise of cars indicates that mobility has become more accessible, yet, as a result, silence has been sacrificed and individuals have become increasingly isolated. The Mr Slocums of the past no longer exist. In effect, new forms of technology have destroyed the landscape and the old way of life by building up a new one.

That which isolates Cream and Gorman and aborts their reminiscences is the noise of motor vehicles. In this short play of thirty-two minutes, the *'Roar of [an] engine'* is heard eighteen times, which in production often drowns out the dialogue. Gorman and Cream must frequently ask 'Eh?' after cars pass.[70] Clas Zilliacus correctly sums up the isolation in the play as follows: 'Instead of plot there is stasis, instead of development abortive retrospection. The past remains hypothetical. . . . [T]he play implies that everyone is solitary'.[71]

Depicting modern technology as interrupting the interaction between these two storytellers, Beckett, on one level, theorises that modern technology and mechanical reproduction isolate and fragment communities. Modern modes of transport, as discussed in relation to *All That Fall*, placed people in a position of 'having to stare at one another for minutes or even hours on end without exchanging a word'.[72] In this radio play, Beckett represents cars as creating an even greater distance, as now individuals do not sit in close proximity to one another. Modern humans isolate themselves from others by entering their cars. Not only have they physically placed themselves in cages, but they have also shut out each other's gaze.

Even when they leave their vehicles, they move about as if the walls of their cars continued to surround them. Beckett represents this ultimate isolation in the passers-by. When Cream and Gorman ask each passer-by for a light, they are ignored. Each time this occurs, the audience is presented with an image of modern isolation. Modern humans hear but choose not to stop and listen. They have become 'wrapped up'[73] in themselves and as such are deaf and blind to each other. As a result of the modern individual's isolation, Benjamin explains that the modern storyteller no longer produces a narrative to communicate with others. He 'is no longer able to express himself by giving examples of his most important concerns'.[74] Cream and Gorman lack authority to compose narratives that would counsel each other because they lack the courage to expose their concerns and wounds. While Gorman and Cream may not be literally dead, they are figurative ghosts haunting the road with memories of the past; yet these memories do not express their suffering. Instead, by holding on to their past and scorning the present, they have isolated themselves from the modern crowd.

Both Cream's use of the word 'ruinated' and Cream and Gorman's distaste for modern technology point to their war experience. Using this word, which often refers to destruction caused by war, Cream harks back to the First and Second World Wars. Memories of these wars recur in conjunction with modern science and machinery.

When Gorman and Cream try to recollect past events and dead friends, modern technology inevitably intrudes:

Gorman   The Lootnant yes, died in 14. Wounds. (*Deafening roar of engine.*)

Cream   The bloody cars such a thing as a quiet chat I ask you.[75]

In this passage, a car's engine silences the dialogue momentarily so that it is impossible to partake in 'a quiet chat'. This is the only incident in this play when the roar of an engine is described as 'deafening'. By flooding the soundscape with a noise that deafens, Beckett shows how modern technology threatens to erase the Lieutenant's tragic death and threatens to desensitise Gorman and Cream to it while ironically calling up sounds and images of the war for the audience. The roar intrudes like tanks during a military invasion.

Theorising on the change of the storyteller's role as a result of his war experience, Benjamin explains:

A generation that had gone to school on a horse-drawn streetcar now stood under the open sky in a countryside in which nothing remained unchanged but the clouds, and beneath these clouds, in a field of force of destructive torrents and explosions, was the tiny, fragile human body.[76]

Many of Benjamin's generation could not separate new technology from how it was used. Unable to express their awe and horror at the technology which caused so much suffering and devastation, these men, Benjamin tells us, became silent:

With the [First] World War a process began to become apparent which has not halted since then. Was it not noticeable at the end of the war that men returned from the battlefield grown silent – not richer, but poorer in communicable experience?[77]

Although Benjamin notes that ten years later several books on the subject of the war flooded the market, the process of communicating stories had changed from one of healing to one of information. Indeed, when Gorman and Cream do not rail against modernity they question one another. These two estranged friends ask each other questions to gather information about each other's lives and the whereabouts of old friends and family. Additionally, they argue over small details such as the make of the first car they saw and the exact date they joined the forces to establish a concrete and precise record of the past.

The 'deafening roar' of the engine, furthermore, indirectly refers to war weaponry. Beckett merges both his Irish and European experiences and his memories of the First World War with that of the Second. While Beckett was only a child during World War One, during World War Two Beckett worked for the French Resistance and after the war he joined the Irish Red Cross. He found himself in the Normandy town of Saint-Lô where he saw for the first time the mass destruction and devastation caused by war machinery. Unlike Benjamin, who claims that the 'new form of communication is information',[78] Beckett offers another possibility.

Beckett gives us a radio play that departs from mere information. He composes a story based on the disintegration and decomposition of the modern world. In his expression of decomposition, Beckett composes. It is a tune that falters, yet does so appropriately in order to express impotence and ignorance, as he described his writing in an interview with Israel Shenker in 1956.[79]

In the face of the destruction caused by World War Two, a literature, like James Joyce's, of omniscience and omnipotence was, for Beckett, impossible. As a result of the destruction caused by war machinery, Gorman and Cream are hostile towards cars and scientific progress. Gorman thrice characterises the cars punctuating the play as threatening: 'They'd tear you to flitters with their flaming machines',[80] 'As soon as look at you, tear you to flitters'[81] and 'their flaming machines they'd tear you to shreds'.[82] His descriptions of cars could easily be applied to that of war weaponry. War weaponry consists of 'flaming machines' that tear men 'to flitters' and 'shreds'. Modern science, according to Cream and Gorman, is too concerned with creating tools of destruction, which induce more misery, instead of creating remedies to ease pain.

Gorman and Cream sneer further at modern progress when discussing atom rockets and the moon expeditions of the twentieth century. While Cream is correct in that scientists have discovered the moon prior to these moon expeditions, his assertion that 'the moon is the moon and cheese is cheese'[83] is reductive. He assumes that the signifier inherently stands for the signified. Beckett here parodies an argument in direct opposition to his own use of language. His 1937 letter to Axel Kaun reveals a distrust of language and the relationship of words to the objects they signify. This letter expresses doubts over the concreteness of language that was most likely strengthened by his experience in World War Two, which threw into question the solidity of all objects and beliefs because it showed that all could be obliterated. Despite Cream's insistence regarding the concreteness of the moon and language, his own use of language, as noted earlier, betrays his argument. By undermining Cream's authority through his use of words such as 'ruinated', Beckett does not allow the audience to find comfort in Cream's assertion.

After listening to Cream's rant against the moon expeditions, Gorman assumes that Cream is 'against progress'.[84] In reaction to Gorman's assessment, Cream tries to draw the distinction between progress and science: 'Progress, progress, progress is all very fine and grand, there's such a thing I grant you, but it's scientific, progress, scientific, the moon's not progress, lunacy, lunacy'.[85] To Gorman and Cream, modern science is 'lunacy' because instead of focusing on improving standards of living and reducing human suffering on earth, it is preoccupied with exploring the far-off moon. When Gorman complains that 'Rheumatism they never found the remedy for it yet, atom rockets is all they care about'[86] and when Cream explains that his daughter died of 'Malignant'[87] cancer, Beckett juxtaposes modern science with the ageing and suffering body.

The radio play ends with each old man returned to his former isolation. Announcing his departure, Cream says: 'The bloody cars, such a thing as a quiet chat I ask you. (*Pause*.) Well I'll be slipping along I'm holding you back from your work'.[88] Leaving Gorman in reflection, Cream aborts their bond. As a consequence, Gorman's last words, 'When you think, when you think . . .',[89] remain unfinished.

Because of the repetition of this phrase, his thought becomes paralysed in its incompletion. His inability or reluctance to finish his sentence, ironically, results in a creative silence.

At the play's conclusion, the barrel-organ's tune triumphs. The noise of modern vehicles drowns out the old tune for a moment, but the tune eventually rises above the street sounds. Gorman's tune becomes reborn after its figurative death. Regardless of the threat of modern technology, Beckett recognises that the old themes of suffering and impotence, which Gorman and Cream display even if only as information, remain important. Beckett incorporates technology to renew old tunes. He exposes the storyteller's impotence as a result of war machinery and understands that the audience listens to Gorman and Cream because they acknowledge the suffering body. They allow the audience to laugh at their own nostalgia for older art forms and their own buried discontent with modern technology.

Words and Music, Cascando, Rough for Radio I, Rough for Radio II

Beckett's radio plays produced after *The Old Tune* move towards an experimental minimalism, eliminating plot as they turn to the process of composition. Both Beckett's fourth radio play, *Words and Music* (broadcast on the BBC in 1962), and his last, *Cascando* (broadcast on the BBC in 1964), are experimental works that examine the obligation to compose a narrative using words and music. The character of Music in both radio plays is expressed by eerie, modern musical compositions. The original score for *Words and Music* was composed by the writer's cousin, John Beckett, and the original score for *Cascando* was composed by the French composer, Marcel Mihalovici.[90]

The similarities between these two radio plays make them impossible to discuss separately. What is more, Beckett's *Rough for Radio I* and *Rough for Radio II*, initially withheld from the BBC because Beckett also considered them 'rough', deal with the struggle to create. In exploring all four works together, we discover Beckett engrossed with the question he set out years previously: what is the artist's chief reason for creating? Struggling at times with his own inability to write and his desire to end the torment of writing, Beckett, in these four radio plays – all of which were written in the 1960s – echoes in one way or another his response to Georges Duthuit in their 'Three Dialogues'. The predicament of the artist is that he/she must find a way to express the 'expression that there is nothing to express, nothing with which to express, nothing from which to express, no power to express, no desire to express, together with the obligation to express'.[91]

To do this, Beckett demonstrates that authors of radio plays must rely on mechanical switches to activate previously recorded sounds. In *Rough for Radio I*, the protagonist explains to a female character, who visits him at his request, that to hear the words and music 'you must twist. (*Pause.*) To the right'.[92] Many control panels in radiophonic studios and home radios even today operate by twisting knobs.

Although the switch in *Rough for Radio I* is clearly a mechanical device, in most of these radio plays the image of the switch is either represented by the word 'On' or in a series of sounds resulting in the act of storytelling. The knob which the protagonist speaks of in *Rough for Radio I* foreshadows the function of the narrator by the name of Opener in *Cascando*.[93] Opener, likewise, figuratively opens sound channels for the listeners. John Fletcher reads Opener as a radio technician. Through his ability to open words and music, he becomes 'a kind of technician who opens and closes sound channels as if he were sitting at a kind of control panel in a radiophonic studio'.[94] More than just a radio technician, Opener represents an author creating a text in his efforts to control and shape the sounds pouring out of the radio box into the homes of the listening audience. As such, Beckett begins again with an image of technology but moves away from the image to reveal Opener's distress and struggle to control the stories he begins.

The title of the radio play can shed light here. The word 'cascando' is a Spanish gerund, no longer used today, that means to 'crack open'. In effect, Opener cracks open, pouring out his thoughts. Additionally, cascando can be used to describe a cracked, or broken voice.[95] Indeed, in the BBC première of the radio play Voice is played by Patrick Magee, the actor whose cracked voice Beckett admired. In effect, Opener releases his artistic voice but that voice is broken and cracked, struggling to tell his tale of Woburn.

When Music and Words, in *Rough for Radio I*, voice themselves, the male protagonist exclaims, 'Good God!',[96] and when Words speaks he says in a shrill voice, 'Come come! Come come!'[97] His protestations over Music and Words are ambiguous. On the one hand, he seems to be in agony over, even disgusted by, the sounds Words and Music produce. These protestations, particularly 'Come come!', which is echoed in *Cascando*, express the protagonist's desire for the text to continue.

Initially, it is not clear whether he desires their company or their completion. After speaking into the telephone, his protestations become less vague. He pleads on the phone for the doctor to come because 'they're ending . . . ENDING . . . I can't stay like that after . . . '.[98] Not only do Words and Music begin to fail, but also the telephone falls short of providing the protagonist with company. The telephone conversation merely reminds the protagonist of his loneliness because through it he learns that the doctor will not arrive until 'tomorrow noon'.[99] Even his female companion at the beginning of the play, who was apparently called for, does not offer communicative company because 'she's left me . . . ah for God's sake . . . haven't they all left me?'[100] Despite twisting the knobs to animate Music and Words, he cannot keep them from '*Together, failing*'.[101] The end of storytelling is near and, with the completion of musical and verbal texts, the protagonist finds himself alone. His agony is not only that of knowing he will be isolated, but also that he has never correctly recorded his story. His only hope is for the doctor to come and release him by either curing him of his need for company or repairing his machine.

In *Cascando*, written shortly after *Rough for Radio I*, Beckett again expresses the failure of the storyteller's communicative authority. The voice, one of the three characters in this radio play, begins:

> – story . . . if you could finish it . . . you could rest . . . sleep
> . . . not before . . . oh I know . . . the ones I've finished . . .
> thousands and one . . . all I ever did . . . in my life . . . with
> my life . . . saying to myself . . . finish this one . . . it's the right
> one . . . then rest . . . sleep . . . no more stories . . . no more
> words . . .[102]

Here the word 'story' establishes the importance of the theme of
storytelling. Yet the story told throughout this radio play is either
incorrect or insufficient to fulfil Opener's need for company. It is
worth noting that the pronoun in the above quoted moves from
'you' to 'I'. The use of the second person singular 'you' implies a
separation of voice and body, but the move to the first person
singular 'I' suggests that the breech between voice and body is, at
times, resolved. Voice recognises that he is the subject of his journey;
however, in the age where the voice is mechanically reproduced out
of a radio box, the body becomes isolated by this medium. Beckett's
radio plays operate like a camera in that they produce a 'close-up' of
the voice that dismembers the voice from the body. Furthermore, the
protagonist in *Rough for Radio I* who switches on sounds to create
the presence of a fellow communicator, Opener, is also left alone:

> But I don't answer any more.
> And they don't say anything any more.
> They have quit.[103]

All those who once criticised him, claiming that Words and Music
are merely in his head, now have stopped speaking altogether.

Rough for Radio II, written in the 1960s but not broadcast until
1976, and *Words and Music*, broadcast on the BBC in 1962, maintain
the theme of 'switching on' the mechanisms that produce narratives,
but do so with a menacing edge. In these two plays Beckett uses
violence in connection with technology and text production. Croak,
in *Words and Music*, thumps his club on the ground to begin
composing a narrative. The 'thump' is introduced so that Words and
Music will begin composing their texts on the subject of love, and

later sloth. Even though there is no physical violence to the body in *Words and Music*, when Words falters the adverb used to describe the thump of the club is '*Violent*'.[104] Croak is Words's and Music's author and master who violently beats out his orders; however, he, like the director (Animator in *Rough for Radio II*) and narrator (Opener in *Cascando*), is not all-powerful.

When Animator discovers that one of the mysterious members of his crew, Dick, is responding to orders, he demands that they get 'On!' with their story.[105] Several sounds follow his command until the storyteller, a tortured victim by the name of Fox, begins: '(*Thud with ruler.*) Do you mark me? On! (*Silence.*) Dick! (*Swish and thud of pizzle on flesh. Faint cry from Fox.*)'.[106] Through the use of the words 'functioned' and 'on' and the sequence of sounds which varies only slightly throughout the play, Beckett constructs the production of stories as a process involving several violent attacks in an ordered, mechanical manner.

Beckett's identification of the characters in *Rough for Radio II* is divided into two groups. Fox and Dick are given proper names whereas Animator and Stenographer are identified by their professions. By naming two of the characters after their professions, Beckett challenges the production process that sets the machine of radio drama in motion. In French, the language in which this work was originally written, *animateur* directly translates into 'a radio or television producer'.[107] But in its translation into English, the word takes on another definition.

The word 'animator' means one who brings to life, or even who brings *back* to life; in *Cascando* this idea of reanimation, too, appears. Opener reveals that it is the month of May, 'the reawakening',[108] as he calls it, suggesting that he has reawakened Voice and Music to complete the tale of Woburn. Together with his discourse of the switch, the word 'to animate', moreover, alludes to early uses of electricity. Like the thud of the pizzle on Fox's flesh, electrotherapy was used to stimulate patients who suffered from exhaustion. While it was thought to be therapeutic, these violent electrical shocks, which were heralded for killing off the patient's neurological confusions and pathological behaviour, also caused memory loss. An excessive amount of electricity was, and in some places still is, used to torture, and in extreme cases, execute hostages and criminals.[109] Fittingly, the audience learns that, like a hostage or a criminal held for interrogation, Fox's mouth is gagged, he is blindfolded and his ears are plugged.

Interestingly, in this rough work for radio, Beckett depicts storytelling in a similar way to that of *Play*. The telling of a story is forced on Fox as though the crew were attempting to torture him to discover something unknown to them. The violence executed upon Fox after his gag, blindfold and earplugs have been removed animates him and turns on the process of storytelling. However, Animator's authority is destabilised by Fox's inability or refusal to end the story.

In all four of these radio plays, the image of the mechanical switch falters and the machines producing texts break down. In *Rough for Radio II* the torture that activates Fox falters when Fox no longer speaks. Fox, the audience learns, 'has gone off again'.[110] The verb-phrase 'to go off' is defined as 'to go to sleep', 'to explode', 'to wear off', 'to deteriorate', 'to leave the stage' and 'to fail to fulfil'. The phrase works on all of these levels. When he begins his storytelling, Fox *explodes*, telling his tale. Fox is not the modern novelist of Benjamin's criticism, but the traditional storyteller captured in the age of mechanical reproduction. Hence, when he can no longer go on he, literally, *goes back to sleep* and because he is heard no longer, figuratively, *leaves the stage*. His authority as a storyteller has *worn off* and *deteriorated*, and he has *failed to fulfil* his task.

Once Fox has 'gone off', Animator becomes a storyteller. When he adds the phrase '*between two kisses*'[111] to Fox's text, the question arises as to whether Animator has introduced anything else to the text previously or whether he is gaining authority over Fox. This addition may be Animator's bid to re-establish his diminishing authority. On the one hand, Fox appears to be Animator's prisoner, but his inability to carry on with his text is ambiguous. The day Fox completes his tale before going off, the production crew 'may be free'.[112] By stopping his narrative, Fox defies the Animator, and as a result remains imprisoned. On the other hand, by breaking off his tale, Fox imprisons the crew. He boxes them in. When Animator adds '*between two kisses*' and when the crew physically attacks Fox's body to arouse him, they attempt to break out of their captivity. Animator and his crew, in effect, struggle to break out of the confines of storytelling by trying to force Fox into completing his tale. Fox refuses to be obliged to create and as such reverses the power structure of the interrogation.

In *Words and Music* Beckett provides an alternative response to *Rough for Radio II*. In order to free himself, the narrator in *Words and Music* reveals that not only must the theme of the story be the right one, but also that Words and Music must 'Be friends!'[113] Throughout, Words and Music work against each other, each struggling to be heard over the other. At the close of the text, when Words and Music join, Croak, curiously, lets the club fall and leaves the stage abruptly. Shocked at Croak's sudden change, Words exclaims 'My Lord!',[114] before Croak drops the club and departs.

Here, Beckett capitalises on the listener's blindness. While the audience learns Words is '*Shocked*',[115] the visual image that Words reacts to is not described nor is it clear whether Croak leaves because he is free or whether he leaves unable to bear the narrative any longer. Unable to imagine Croak's expression, the listener, too, is a prisoner of the medium of radio – imprisoned by the very need for closure.

In *Cascando*, Beckett's last and by far the most experimental radio play, the stories Voice tells are of his need to get the story right, and of Woburn, a character who continuously falls:

> – story . . . if you could finish it . . . you could rest . . . you could sleep . . . not before . . . oh I know . . . the ones I've finished . . . thousands and one . . . all I ever did . . . in my life . . . with my life . . . saying to myself . . . finish this one . . . it's the right one . . .[116]

> . . . he goes down . . . falls . . . on purpose or not . . . can't see . . . he's down . . . that's what counts . . . face in the mud . . . arms spread . . . that's the idea . . . already . . . there already . . . no not yet . . . he gets up . . . knees first . . . hands flat . . . in the mud . . . head sunk . . . then up . . . on his feet . . . huge bulk . . . come on . . . he goes on . . . he goes down . . . come on . . . [117]

Each of these utterances expresses failure, as does Opener's comment on his audience's reactions: 'They say, He opens nothing, he has nothing to open, it's in his head'.[118] The character in Voice's narrative, Woburn, becomes an ambivalent figure as the listener initially associates him with failure – he falls and lies outstretched in the mud – but his failure becomes the stuff of a story that may free Opener from the obligation to compose. Mud in Beckett's plays, after all, is a bifurcated image that signifies both waste and creation. In its depiction of failure, the Woburn story may be the right one. While Woburn falls repeatedly, he gets up again as if he is reborn out of and revived through the mud.

Indeed, only *Cascando* and *Words and Music* end with brief triumphs of storytelling. *Cascando* concludes not with another fall from Woburn but rather with Woburn out to sea, hanging on as do Voice and Music: '– this time . . . it's the right one . . . finish . . . no more stories . . . sleep . . . we're there . . . nearly . . . just a few more . . . don't let go . . . Woburn . . . he clings on . . . come on . . . come on –'.[119] Because Opener does not close the text, we are left with a cliff-hanger, clinging on as the soundscape fades into silence. The phrase 'come on' discloses their desire to be done with the text despite their inability to come to an end. Likewise, in *Words and Music* the two characters responsible for creation finally become friends to compose a song:

> Then down a little way
> Through the trash
> Towards where
> All dark no begging
> No giving no words
> No sense no need
> Through the scum
> Down a little way
> To whence one glimpse
> Of that wellhead.[120]

Their brief collaboration brings the audience back to Woburn's descent into the mud in *Cascando*. The journey to find the source of life and renewal is a descent through darkness and trash where words and meaning do not exist.

The final destination of this journey is the place where a spring breaks out of the ground. Whereas water in *Embers* is associated with the agonising mechanical sound of the sea,[121] in both *Words and Music* and *Cascando* it is associated with renewal and life. Yet their victories do not last; *Words and Music* ends with Words resigning in a '*Deep sigh*'.[122] The song depicts the journey to the wellhead, but the narrator only captures 'one glimpse' of it. The 'trash' and 'scum' are not washed away. While trying to sing, Words composes an image of having to go through the 'trash' and 'scum', past meaning and words, in order to wipe clean and begin one's story anew. The inability to wash away waste results in the failure to continue.

However, in washing away waste one also washes away language and the presence of the human voice, as seen in *Embers* as well. In *Cascando* the audience, likewise, discovers that waste in the form of mud fertilises and rebirths Woburn as well as his failures. Although it is a composition of waste, this wasteful composition, in its enterprise, becomes compost. Beckett, through these different explorations of waste production in relation to mechanical and text production, reveals that texts are composed out of refuge, trash and waste – the impotence and ignorance he spoke of with Israel Shenker in 1956.[123] The modern subject is waste – the crucial substance of the human condition. To sterilise the text is to erase its humanity.

Conclusion

All Beckett's radio plays utilise technology thematically. In *All That Fall* and *The Old Tune* the listener hears vehicles which remind them of the possible destruction technology can bring. Not only does it interrupt the conversation between Cream and Gorman, disrupting the piece, but Beckett also reveals that the technology that helps us travel outside of our communities isolate individuals in the process.

Furthermore, with the help of radio Beckett creates self-reflexive plays that comment on the artificiality of sound and the struggle to create stories. The listener is made aware that the voices speaking to us are ghosts in a machine. These ghosts are also storytellers, however. While this theme runs throughout the radio plays, Beckett becomes increasingly unconventional in the way in which this theme is explored.

In works such as *Words and Music* and *Cascando*, Beckett explores the difficulties inherent in composing original art through words and music that struggle to come together and tell a comprehensible story. The tales are often interrupted, revised and restarted, mirroring the very struggle of an author's writing process. Exploring radio, Beckett challenges the role of the storyteller and listener and, in the process, exposes the production of a narrative as a composition that ultimately decomposes before our ears. However, the decomposition of the storyteller, listener and text is necessary in order to compose a new form of narrative – a narrative which illuminates the production process of a story about the very struggle to create.

In the next chapter, we see Beckett move away from a thematic use of technology. Maturing in his understanding of the use of technology, Beckett uses a formal exploration of television and camera technology, much as he did in *Play* to incorporate the theme of storytelling with that of being haunted. On the television screen, Beckett's male narrators obsessively think about women that are no longer with them. Attempting to cope with the women of their pasts (whether by reinventing the past or forgetting it through the process of storytelling), these men are trapped by the camera lens. Beckett utilises the technology of the camera in the teleplays in daring ways.

CHAPTER 3
THE TELEPLAYS

Samuel Beckett's fifty-ninth birthday marks his journey into the world of television. He began writing his first play for television, *Eh Joe*, to be broadcast on BBC television in 1965. Shortly thereafter, Beckett was asked whether he would be interested in directing *Eh Joe* for a German audience at the Süddeutscher Rundfunk (SDR).

The SDR television crew with whom Beckett directed all of his seven teleplays first invited the Irish writer to work with them in Stuttgart, Germany, in 1965 – three years after he wrote his last play for radio, *Cascando*. During this time, the studio had invited many German authors to write for television. The Artistic Director of the SDR, Reinhart Müller-Freienfels's bold vision gave him the courage to ask his friend, art historian Werner Spies, who was living in Paris and was acquainted with Beckett, to extend this invitation to the Irish writer. What Müller-Freienfels was pleasantly unprepared for but rewarded with was his subsequent long-standing friendship with Beckett.

Agreeing to direct a television piece he had originally written for the BBC, but not accepting the honorarium offered by the SDR,[1] Beckett took on the task and would thereafter return to the SDR eight times to direct seven plays written for television.[2] Of these seven plays, four (*Ghost Trio*, *. . .but the clouds . . .*, *Nacht und Träume* and *Quad*) were written specifically for the SDR and one (*What Where*) was adapted from the stage to the small screen for the studio.

Müller-Freienfels, in his lecture of 6 February 1988 to commemorate Beckett's work at the SDR, recalls the moment he first laid eyes on a manuscript copy of *He Joe* (the German translation of *Eh Joe*): 'Here the elements of the television medium were being utilised in a fully new and unusual manner'.[3] While Beckett's vision was completely original, Müller-Freienfels was quick to point out that, despite Beckett's innovation and his never having worked in the medium of television, Beckett's piece was written so precisely it could only have been written for television; it was not theatrical or cinematic: 'Here had someone, from whom we had not awaited this from, an intense understanding for and interest in working with the possibilities of the small screen'.[4] Indeed, Müller-Freienfels was 'surprised at how accurately Beckett had envisioned each camera position, the light and the method of recording sound'.[5]

Beckett's explorations of the technological possibilities offered by the camera were remarkable experiments. The camera in Beckett's teleplays is predominately fixed. By only using a dolly minimally in *Eh Joe* and increasingly fixing the camera, working primarily with techniques that require the lens in his subsequent teleplays, Beckett distances the machine from human interference. While there is always a cameraman behind the camera, manoeuvring this tool, Beckett's teleplays alienate the audience from this fact to transform the camera into a self-serving machine.

Yet, despite erasing the presence of the cameraman, Beckett continues to create highly self-reflexive works through techniques such as close-ups, zooms and fades, among others. As such the camera becomes an inquisitive spectator, threatening to mechanise the individuals filmed. The protagonists in his teleplays, furthermore, find themselves entangled in the act of reproduction and repetition. In each repetition, the protagonists try to inscribe meaning into their past in order to break out of the patterns that imprison them in the present. Yet, when caught by the camera eye, these protagonists suffer because they cannot take on the role of the subject inscribing meaning into their past or present. They do, to some extent, escape the patterns imprisoning them, but their escape is not liberating. Instead, they break one set of patterns merely to construct another.

Eh Joe

Samuel Beckett's first teleplay, *Eh Joe*, opens into a bare room. Joe, a lonely old man in his fifties or sixties, inspects his room, looking out of the windows, through the doors and under the bed, before settling on his bed. Once seated, the voice of a former lover begins to recall the past for him. As he listens, he is slowly attacked by the camera and the voice.

In essence, Joe has missed one perceiver, the camera eye, which initially is situated behind him, but as he sits down the camera positions itself in front of him. Although Joe does not see the camera eye, the third being in this dramatic text, he recognises the voice as perceiving his past and his inner turmoil. It is important to recognise that the voice and the camera are distinctly separate, as most scholars have argued, but they work together to haunt Joe.[6] Beckett writes: '*Each move [of the camera] is stopped by voice resuming, never camera move and voice together*'.[7] As the camera inches towards Joe's face, the voice becomes increasingly '*remote*'[8] until she '*drops to whisper, almost inaudible*'.[9] However separate the voice and the camera may seem, the camera's movement and the voice are clearly in '*pursuit*'[10] of Joe. The camera attacks Joe's face, the external surface seen on screen, and the voice attacks his unconscious, the internal space unsuccessfully protected by the external surface of the face. 'Perception in *Eh Joe*', Graley Herren notes, 'is highly predatory'.[11] The voice pries deeper into Joe's unconscious by bringing to light for the audience his unfilmed past, and the camera moves in closer recording his present state and reactions to the memories that are conjured up.

By isolating the moves of the camera from the voice, Beckett confronts his audience with the conventions of television. His most striking experiment involves television's trademark – the close-up. Throughout this play for television, the voice pauses, and during her three-second silence the camera zooms in, intensifying both Joe's agony and the viewer's experience as voyeur. Unlike conventional television that uses the zoom always in conjunction with dialogue, narrative or music, Beckett isolates each element – the zoom and sound – to awaken the viewers to the camera's movement. While viewing *Eh Joe*, the spectators are struck by their awareness of the camera's movement forward, although it only moves '*four inches*'[12] each time. Additionally, the viewers are stunned by Joe's inability to dodge the camera eye. His face remains '*Practically motionless throughout*'[13] perhaps because the movement is so minute.

The camera's purpose, as Beckett constructs it, is to expose the audience's desire to reduce the distance between itself and the object projected on screen. The audience *looks* to read, and in the process, understands the image. This confrontation with the desire to bring the object closer is linked to the audience's desire for information. Striving for information transforms the work of art into a piece of evidence.

Still photographs, Susan Sontag explains, furnish viewers with the evidence they desire: 'A photograph passes for incontrovertible proof that a given thing has happened'.[14] Sontag traces this desire back to one of the earliest uses of photography. As early as the 1800s, photography was used by the Parisian police as a tool to survey and control crime scenes. In the postmodern age video cameras have allowed even greater opportunities for surveillance. A still photograph positions viewers as archaeologists, digging into images for evidence of what has happened, whereas the video camera associated with television positions the spectators as voyeurs waiting and searching in the present for something to happen. Beckett's television programmes, produced for British and German audiences, invite both possible readings. As the camera in *Eh Joe* zooms in on Joe, it compiles evidence of the past. The camera peers into Joe's present conscience, digging up the past while surveying him for any change. Is the audience not searching Joe's face for remorse and regret, or has his heart crumbled – 'Dry rotten at last'?[15]

Surveying the object, the camera takes on the form of the peeping Tom. 'Beckett called television "peephole art"', Toby Zinman points out. She goes on to describe *Eh Joe* as

> utterly 'peephole', especially if we stop to remember that peepholes have two sides; the person peeping (with those implications of voyeurism, auto-eroticism, isolation, and the insularity of self-absorption) and the person peeped at (with those implications of paranoia, commodification, and surveillance).[16]

Likewise, Clas Zilliacus understands *Eh Joe* as 'keyhole peep', explaining that the 'surest sign that the camera is a peeping Tom, not an illustrating device, is – for the viewer unfamiliar with the author's written directions – its firm refusal to translate any of the voice's rich verbal stimuli into pictures'.[17]

In addition, Beckett's teleplays were, for the most part, broadcast late at night. Some were shown as late as midnight, adding to the atmosphere of peeping into the private bedroom of an old man. Zinman and Zilliacus are correct in their analysis of this teleplay as an exploration of the medium in relation to voyeurism. However, both personify the camera lens as a thinking perceiver rather than a mechanical device that records and projects the image onto television screens. Rather, the camera functions as a prosthetic situated between the home viewer and Joe. A peeping Tom watches from a fixed distance, usually in the dark, whereas in this teleplay, the camera is able to move closer as if there were no barrier between the viewer and Joe. The camera zooms in as the voice provides the voyeurs at home with a prelude to Joe's current state and his past love affairs.[18] She taunts Joe with, 'Anyone living love you now, Joe? . . . Anyone living sorry for you now? . . . That slut that comes on Saturday, you pay her, don't you?'[19] Joe remains silent. Joe lacks the ability to stop the voice with his own voice.

In television programmes, as well as films, 'the spectator has no alternative but to identify with the camera as the only available perspective'.[20] The angle of the camera gives the impression that the object filmed is seen through a particular set of eyes. By establishing a subject–object relationship, the point of view reveals the power structures that are in place, and through the identification of these power structures, they can be challenged. Along these lines, Beckett has subverted the gender roles of the gaze. Unlike *Happy Days*, in which Winnie is the object of the male gaze, Joe is the object of the scrutinising eye of the camera. Brought closer to the viewers through the camera eye, Joe is consequently caged in by this technology. Like a caged beast (an echo from *Embers*), he is completely deprived of his power; he is at the whim of this gaze.

Joe's former power was tied to his ability to smooth-talk his way into and out of romance. The audience learns that Joe seduced women with his words. As an old man, however, his inability to revitalise his former self results in his reliance on money to attempt to assert his sexual virility. The one woman Joe can still have, according to the voice, is the one he pays. However, this economic exchange further reduces Joe's power over women. His love-making has become a cold and cheapened exchange.

As in *Play*, Beckett's stage play of 1962, in which he draws on a clichéd romantic love scenario, here Beckett draws on the theme of parting lovers to explore the medium's technology. In the voice's description of the way Joe prepares to leave each of his lovers, she reveals much more than the mere plot of the tale:

The best's to come, you said, that last time . . . Hurrying me into my coat . . . Last I was favoured with from you . . .[21]

The best's to come, you said . . . Bundling her into her Avoca sack . . . Her fingers fumbling with the big horn buttons . . . Ticket in your pocket for the first morning flight . . . You've had her, haven't you? . . . You've laid her? . . . Of course he has . . . She went young . . . No more old lip from her.[22]

Repeating the same line and actions, Joe's seductive powers are a mere habit and thus have become dead – as Didi reflects, 'But habit is a great deadener'.[23] Joe's repetitive actions, especially that of saying the same phrase ('The best's to come') to each woman as he helps her into her coat the day he prepares to leave her, results in death. Joe's actions, ultimately, propels one young woman into committing suicide. During the suicide revelation, the voice taunts Joe by using imperatives to instruct both Joe and the spectator to 'Imagine what [was] in her mind to make her do that',[24] to 'Imagine' the dying young woman. She even goes so far as to attempt to get Joe to 'Say it'.[25] The word 'imagine' is repeated, emphasising the images the audience should imagine. Although the television screen shows Joe to the audience, a second screen – the audience's minds – imagines the hands, eyes and lips of the young woman as she dies.

What is more, the voice functions as a camera when she says, 'Cut a long story short' and 'Cut another long story short'.[26] On the one hand, the word 'cut' refers to the young woman's death (her life has been 'cut short'). On the other hand, it reflects the technology used in television. 'Cut' in visual media means to edit, to stop filming or recording and to go quickly to another shot. More generally, this word also refers to switching a machine off. All these possible definitions imply a removing or excluding of material, whether through switching off the camera or editing out a scene. Similarly here, the voice cuts from the scene in which the young woman 'lies down with her face in the wash' to she 'Gets up in the end'; and from 'Get out the Gillette . . . Takes the blade from the holder and lies down at the edge on her side' to she 'Tears a strip from the slip and ties it round the scratch'.[27]

Like the camera that only captures Joe's face, the voice commands the audience's attention and projects selected images of the past outward through her words. However, the voice is losing strength: 'I was strong myself when I started . . . In on you . . . Wasn't I, Joe? . . . Normal strength'.[28] The current Voice is below normal strength and recognises that she, too, will fade out like the other voices recalling unpleasant memories.

In contrast to the published text in which the voice and image fade out together, in the BBC and SDR productions the teleplay ends with an extreme, grotesque close-up of Joe's face – the close-up is so close Joe's eyes occupy the screen – lingering after the voice has gone out. The emphasis is on the face, and the concluding close-up can be understood in terms of Gilles Deleuze and Félix Guattari's metaphor of the white wall/black hole.

The French philosophers use this image to explain that meaning is read through both the words spoken and the automatic, unconscious facial expressions that accompany both the speaker and the one spoken to. The surface of the face becomes a white wall which reflects the appropriate facial expression, and the black holes are the eyes and mouth which absorb meaning.[29]

Deleuze and Guattari, however, remind their readers that this system of faciality is much more complex. While meaning is constructed by reading surfaces, we can only read what we already know. Viewers are programmed to read and express themselves in culturally and socially predetermined ways. In effect, the white wall becomes a barrier and the black holes become prisons because inscribing meaning limits other possibilities.

To bring the matter back to Beckett, Deleuze and Guattari give the audience a way to read Beckett's teleplays – a way in which the audience can allow for the unknown. *Eh Joe* presents its viewers with a face that they constantly struggle to read. Although the audience sees Joe's face reflect the *'mounting tension of* listening'[30] as well as regret, remorse and agony, perhaps even trauma, Beckett asks the spectators to question how much they project onto Joe's face, and how many black holes they seal in the process of inscribing significance to this teleplay.

Ghost Trio

Ghost Trio, completed in 1976, eleven years after *Eh Joe*, stages the process of interpretation to a greater extent than Beckett's first teleplay. In these plays for television the protagonists are both narrators and readers, and as such they are implicated in attempts to ascribe meaning.

In *Ghost Trio*, the protagonist, designated as F, struggles to defy the confining pattern established by a female voice, designated as V, in order to gain control of his environment. Although he succeeds in breaking out of the confines of V's pattern, he does not free himself from the camera recording his face. *Ghost Trio* not only 'dramatizes the construction of a pattern, but it also dramatizes a power struggle to control, and even to deconstruct, its own formal framework'.[31]

Working against a tradition of scholarship that maintains that in *Ghost Trio* 'the text is, as it were, merely there to introduce the image and then to fade away',[32] Herren insightfully shows F's subtle rebellion against the repetitions V establishes. This rebellion propels the teleplay towards an unravelling of V's authorial strategies. Herren's argument is thorough and persuasive. However, he does not question what the implications are regarding V's and the camera's position as authorial structures in relation to the mechanisms that tempt the spectators into inscribing meaning. By creating a line of authority, Beckett constructs a work reflecting the audience's process of reading the visual images on screen.

Initially, one perceives V as controlling the camera, the spectator and a 'sole sign of life'[33] – the strange, ghostlike man on the screen. Although V does not appear to recognise the audience as a sign of life, perhaps because the viewer is absent from the view of the camera's threatening gaze, V eventually speaks to the viewer: 'Good evening. Mine is a faint voice. Kindly tune accordingly. (*Pause.*) Good evening. Mine is a faint voice. Kindly tune accordingly. (*Pause.*) It will not be raised, nor lowered, whatever happens',[34] but then commands them to 'Keep that sound down'.[35]

V's power, ironically, is solely one of convention. Viewers can raise the volume throughout the teleplay after their initial adjustment. In effect, her request to adjust the sound, spoken twice, and her warning, directs the gaze at the technology that brings the performance into the viewers' homes. At the movies, viewers cannot adjust the volume to their preference, but in front of their television sets they certainly can. She cannot hold the audience to this command; V's authority is faltering. Her voice is 'faint', implying that her power to communicate is fading away. She, like the voice in *Eh Joe*, is weakening, and by extension so is her power.

To further illustrate her loss of power, neither F nor the camera obeys her commands. James Knowlson argues that

> The whole status of the speaker in the play is highly ambiguous. She appears able to instruct the camera as to what it should reveal. Yet it seems to move independently of her too, as if free to change the closeness or the remoteness of its 'stare'.[36]

The camera is not a mere tool she manipulates; it is the machine that documents F's rebellion by surveying him. At the conclusion of part two, when V orders F 'Now to door', he goes instead '*to stool, takes up cassette player, sits*'.[37] By recording his rebellion, however, the camera threatens F's freedom and existence because it positions him as an object. Despite his struggle to break away from these machines, F remains caught by the staring eye – he remains a mere shadow on-screen. The camera, in essence, reduces F's existence to that of a ghost, perhaps one attempting to break out of purgatory.

The image of the ghost is extremely important to this teleplay. Beckett himself credited the title to the music he incorporated into the play – the Largo of Beethoven's Fifth Piano Trio also known as *The Ghost*.[38] The image of the ghost, furthermore, recalls modernist accounts of photography. Early photographs have often been described as capturing ghosts because only a trace of the object photographed is captured in the print. The print reveals how someone looked (the past) or wished to look (a constructed dream) but never how someone looks (the present). It is either a record of a vanished moment or a mask. According to the nineteenth-century photographer Nadar, his contemporary, the novelist Balzac, had a dread of being photographed because he believed:

[E]very body in its natural state was made up of a series of ghostly images superimposed in layers to infinity, wrapped in infinitesimal films. . . . Man never having been able to create, that is to make something material from an apparition, from something impalpable, or to make from nothing, an object – each Daguerreian operation was therefore going to lay hold of, detach, and use up one of the layers of the body on which it focused.[39]

Nadar's recollection of Balzac's fear reveals that the layers of the individual filmed can be stripped away by the intrusive camera eye. The proof of one's decomposition lies in the ghostly image captured on the print.

In this teleplay, however, Beckett depicts the struggle to compose images despite the continual disintegration of them. The camera presents a threat in its ability to transform F into a ghost through a decomposition of F's reproduction onto the television screen. F, by defying V, tries to make his ghostly image into something material. However, the mechanical reproduction of the camera and the audience's identification with it further plunges the object caught in the gaze into depths of nothingness.

The repetition of the opening of *Ghost Trio* reflects the medium of television as a machine that mechanically reproduces images. That which is being performed has been performed previously, and V repeats verbally what the viewers see visually. Of her description of the 'familiar chamber', V states 'the obvious'[40]; not only is her description obvious because the audience sees the room with the help of the camera but also because the chamber reflects the television screen.

Televisions of the 1960s and 1970s – the time when Beckett writes and directs for the medium – are 'The colour grey'[41] when switched off. The emphasis on grey rectangles in the room – a repetition of bland images – reflects V's desire for control. On the one hand, V desires control over the images reproduced. On the other hand, the repetition distils the image into static death. All the objects here, Knowlson argues, 'recall the shape of a coffin'.[42] The television screen, thus, is a death chamber as the camera slowly dematerialises the objects filmed. Working against the viewer's expectations of colour images, Beckett employs 'Shades of grey'[43] to suggest that, through filming, objects lose their lustre.

Structured on the repetition of three parts, each of which contains exact repetitions, this teleplay comes alive in its representation of the machine as a power structure and in its questioning of mechanical reproduction. Repetition is a key feature in television; it helps to stabilise itself as a meaningful art form.

Although television has traditionally maintained distance from prescribing authorship to its programmes, nevertheless, its use of repetition assures an audience's return. Most weekly programmes implement a pattern that reassures the audience that they will be entertained by repetition with slight variations in form. Playing on this convention, Beckett heads each section with the word 'action': Pre-action, Action and Re-action.[44] The sub-heading of part three, Re-action, reveals that the action is happening again; however, it is also a 'reaction' to the camera's role in the decomposition of the object. Indeed, V ends part two with the command: 'Repeat'.[45] V wishes the repeat to be one that does not defy her authority as part two does when F looks in the mirror and goes to the stool rather than the door. Nonetheless, the repeat is a repetition of F's defiance. In his subtle revolt, the television monitor begins to materialise into a richer picture. And yet, F's revolt, like that of Animator's in *Rough for Radio II*, does not free him. He remains locked into the television monitor. The camera both imprisons F in television and continues to threaten to transform him into a ghost.

Like the camera, the cassette player functions as a mechanical trigger, and by doing so it decomposes the medium of television and the mechanics that go into teleproductions. It is curious that the music heard in the teleplay is only heard when the camera is close enough to the cassette player. As the camera slowly moves in, the music grows '*slightly louder*',[46] and the reverse is true when the camera pulls back. The camera and microphone initially point to the music's possible source (the cassette player), yet F is never seen switching the cassette player on or off, and the musical score of Beethoven's *The Ghost* is not played in progressive order, both of which suggest that the music is displaced from its source. Thus, the music and cassette player are crucial to the difficulty of inscribing meaning to the teleplay.

The BBC's production includes a close-up from above of the cassette player.[47] The close-up of the cassette player, a primitive-looking gadget, reflects a blank rectangle with two dark knobs. Additionally, F's posture over the cassette player recalls Krapp's closeness to his tape recorder as discussed in Chapter 1. Perhaps F, too, longs for a love lost. If so, F's return to the cassette player is an attempt to inscribe meaning – to make the mysterious woman appear.

Because his cassette player does not actually emit music (the source of the music remains out of view), F's mechanical prop and the music heard are ghosts tied to the memory of some woman. Caught in a cycle of habit in order to trigger the memory that might bring the awaited woman back to life, F is stuck in his mechanised existence. Each time after F thinks he hears her and checks the door and window, he returns to his cassette player.

Herren points out that, despite F's rebellion, he nevertheless is 'a creature of habit' who 'does not abandon V's pattern entirely'.[48] Indeed, like Krapp, F attempts to transform the machine into a mechanical bride. However, because his memory of the woman remains mechanised in habit, she remains an apparition in his mind. When he thinks he hears her, F makes a sudden movement that cannot be described as naturalistic. Beckett's actors do not follow Stanislavski's method of acting. F's sudden movement, *'raises head sharply, turns still crouched to door, fleeting face, tense pose'*,[49] is repeated four times. Beckett referenced Heinrich Kleist's 'Über das Marionettentheater' ('On the Marionette Theatre') as a source for this movement as Knowlson recalls from his conversations with Beckett. However, I would like to offer another possible reading for F's movement that is also linked to German Romanticism.

In German Romantic literature both the marionette and the automaton became important images of mechanisation. F's initial movement is that of the jerk of a string, but the pattern that follows reveals that this lack of awareness and memory launches F into mechanised acts. It is as if, with the jerk of the string, a switch is turned on. Like an automaton, F is mechanised by memory as he is controlled by the puppet-masters identified as the camera and V. 'A puppet cannot animate itself', Herren observes. 'While more graceful than its human counterpart, a marionette possesses no freedom of movement nor interpretation and is totally dependent on its operator to activate its grace'.[50] Both images become important in terms of power constructions in the mechanical age. Control is maintained by more than just pulling the strings; it is maintained through the mechanisms of habit and memory.

This teleplay ends with F raising his head so that his *'Face [is] seen clearly for [a] second time'*,[51] yet this time it is seen without the aid of the mirror. In the SDR production, 'Klaus Herm's darkened eyes and blackened lips', Herren observes, produces 'the disturbing impression of a grinning corpse'.[52] This final image recalls the haunting ghosts of Beckett's stage plays of the 1960s and 1970s. The audience is left with the task of inscribing meaning onto this death-mask, as it is in Beckett's stage play *That Time*.

From the very beginning V composes the teleplay on repetition even in her '(*Surprised*.) Ah!'[53] which is later reproduced in the creaking of the door and window in part three. F fills in the grey areas by adding sound, a corridor, rain and a boy. However, none of these images provides an escape or rebirth. Instead of an image of renewal, the rain is menacing and gloomy in the darkness. The corridor is equally menacing, and, although the boy comes with a message, that message is one of negation; he shakes his head twice. The boy cancels out V's earlier command that 'No one'[54] is at the door, but he represents a crippled image as the taps of his feet sound like a crutch.[55] Even the music, which is no longer at the mercy of the camera's microphone, swells into doom. Although F strives to break out of the confines of television by breaking patterns and opening the dark holes of the door and window, he merely creates more unreadable ghosts.

. . . but the clouds . . .

The protagonist of *. . . but the clouds . . .* , like F in *Ghost Trio*, wants to verify his existence and rematerialise a companion. However, unlike *Ghost Trio*, in which, at least initially, the ghostly protagonist is mechanised by a woman's cold mechanical voice, in *. . . but the clouds . . .* the male protagonist, designated as M, narrates and stages his own tale of his daily goings-on. Throughout his narrative, M refers to routine, memory and mathematics, perhaps to provide his narrative with a sense of precision. Yet these mechanical triggers fail to help M inscribe meaning into the ghostly image of his lost love, designated as W, whose face appears on screen in the upper right-hand corner. Increasingly mechanised by the camera and his narrative strategies, M, instead, plunges into 'deepening shades'.[56]

M will attempt to be the author of his story as does Opener in *Cascando* (see Chapter 2), but instead of a pencil or pen marking the page, the writing instrument in *. . . but the clouds . . .* is that of a camera lens[57] which perceives images as they enter the frame. The camera is fixed in three positions: (1) dissolving from the near shot of M; (2) the set in which the audience sees the protagonist, now designated as M1, walking into and out of the playing field; and (3) a close-up of W's face.

The fixed camera can be understood in relation to a telescope or microscope. The lens concentrates on a specific area and allows the individual to peer into the mysteries that the naked eye cannot see. In M1, the 'maximum light at centre'[58] and the positioning of the camera slightly above the set creates the illusion that M has placed himself under a microscope. He does not merely narrate his story; he attempts to treat himself as a specimen of study. By positioning himself in the dual role of scientist and specimen, M tries to take on the role of an author.

In his scientific scrutiny he becomes the object of his own mechanical gaze. Yet, despite trying to take on an authorial role by inspecting his narrative, M remains further mechanised by his choice of words. When M says, 'Such had long been my use and wont',[59] he refers not only to his desire for W but also to his accustomed practice or procedure of recalling her image. The expression 'use and wont' is rarely used in contemporary English; hence, like Maddy Rooney in *All That Fall*, M struggles with a dead language.

Indeed, throughout the teleplay, M uses archaic phrases. For example, he says: 'to issue forth'[60] instead of *to set out*, 'exhibiting the other outline'[61] instead of *turning around*, and 'shed robe and skull, resume my hat and greatcoat'[62] instead of *take off the robe and cap and put on the hat and coat*. As such, Richard Bruce Kirkley claims that in this teleplay 'language controls the image: the words provide a contextual frame in which the images acquire significant meaning'.[63] The meaning created in this teleplay, then, is one of a narrator struggling with a dead image. W's appearance is that of an apparition. When M begins 'to beg, of her, to appear',[64] he struggles to conjure up the image of W, and when he speaks the words she inaudibly utters, he tries to reanimate her.

With the repetitions in M's narrative, Beckett further explores mechanisation and technology. M's narrative includes three types of repetition: the repetition of phrases, M's repeated journey and the intertextuality of W.B. Yeats's poem 'The Tower'. Repeating words and phrases, M is stuck in an endless cycle of trying to reanimate W's ghost – a task linked to television. Historical and news programmes, especially, work to reanimate the past. Only through the camera can the audience view those moments or individuals, dead or gone, as being alive on the small screen. However, as seen earlier, the line 'my use and wont' represents repetition as a 'great deadener'[65] paralysing perception, and, in this case, M's cycle of remembering.

In addition to the repeated words and phrases, Beckett's repetitious staging of M's daily routine reveals that his journey is a Sisyphean cycle. M moves in a circle always returning to the same spot to begin walking the roads again:

> M1 *in hat and greatcoat emerges from west shadow, advances five steps and stands facing east shadow. 2 seconds. He advances five steps to disappear in east shadow. 2 seconds. He emerges in robe and skullcap from east shadow, advances five steps and stands facing west shadow. 2 seconds. He turns right and advances five steps to disappear in north shadow.*[66]

Moving eastward, that is, in the opposite direction of the sun, M 'brought night home',[67] creating, in his return home, his own cycle of return and rebirth. The possibility of W appearing is renewed at the end of the day and with it his narrative is reborn. While each night is identified with a rebirth, each day is cursed with death. In trying to bring W back, M attempts to 'open' the closed holes of the text in order to undo the process of disintegration, but his task is futile. Rather than opening up the text, M's habit of narration closes off the possibilities for renewal. The new day represents another day of being mechanised:

> M1 *in robe and skullcap emerges from north shadow, advances five steps and stands facing camera. 2 seconds. He turns left and advances five steps to disappear in east shadow. 2 seconds. He emerges in hat and greatcoat from east shadow, advances five steps and stands facing west shadow. 2 seconds. He advances five steps to disappear in west shadow.*[68]

Only at night, not caught by the daily routine of walking the roads until the break of day, can M dream of W. His dream of W, however, has become a habit and as such is mechanised. With its distinction between night and day and the reversal of the setting of the sun as rebirth and its rising as death, Beckett blurs the boundaries between the dream world and the waking world. Likewise, in Beckett's *Nacht und Träume* the dream, while offering an escape from the mechanised daylight hours, becomes mechanised by its repetition.

Another form of repetition is found in the teleplay's use of intertextuality. Beckett incorporates several lines of W.B. Yeats's 'The Tower'. 'The persistence of snatches of language in the memory, learned perhaps by rote and reinforced perhaps by rhyme', Daniel Katz reveals, 'are a perfect example of memory's mechanical ability to function and preserve signs and images in the absence of the meaning, presence, truth, or power they are meant to signify'.[69] Yeats's poem, remembered by rote, is only half-remembered, however. M's memory, Beckett suggests here as in *Happy Days*, is flawed. Fragments of the poem are repeated to preserve images, but their significance has long since been forgotten.

What is more, the intertextuality of 'The Tower' is not typographically reproduced with line breaks, but instead split up by ellipses and, at times, these ellipses create pauses that do not exist in the original: '. . . clouds . . . but the clouds . . . of the sky . . .'[70] and '. . . but the clouds of the sky . . . when the horizon fades . . . or a bird's sleepy cry . . . among the deepening shades . . .'.[71] Beckett, in effect, visually restructures the poem.[72] Although Katz suggests that the vocalisation of Yeats's and W's lines is an empty repetition and a part of M's daily habit, this intertextuality rather functions as a decomposition of Yeats's poem. In these reproduced fragments, new significance emerges from 'The Tower'. In reconstructing Yeats's poem as a fragment, Beckett challenges Yeats's authority over the lines, and, ironically, challenges the ethics involved in remaking and adapting another writer's work.

As has been well-documented, Beckett struggled to maintain strict control over productions of his texts, even to the point of halting stage productions which grossly disregarded his script.[73] *. . . but the clouds . . .* , however, expresses the author's lack of control over the text once it is in the public domain. Along these lines, the ending becomes increasingly important. To explore the significance of the ending, one must note that the concluding images in the BBC and SDR productions vary greatly.

In the published text, and the SDR production which Beckett directed, the teleplay concludes with the image of M in his sanctum while he speaks Yeats's lines a final time. He is, in other words, struggling to call forth the image of W once more. The SDR production thus concludes with M's failure; his desired object remains absent. At the BBC, however, the play concludes with these lines uttered by M while the camera frames W as she mimes the words. In this production, the audience never loses sight of the fact that these words belong to W. She may not voice them, but she does mouth the words, giving the language of the poem an absence that must be filled in. Beckett positions M as a spectator who must inscribe his reading onto the image. When M '*murmur[s], synchronous with lips*'[74] of W as she utters inaudibly '. . . but the clouds of the sky . . . when the horizon fades . . . or a bird's sleepy cry . . . among the deepening shades . . .',[75] M fills in the missing sound and, as such, inscribes meaning to the text and image that embodies his authorial voice rather than hers.

Drawing attention to an additional case in an early typescript of *. . . but the clouds . . .*, where W appears and speaks in her own voice, Stan Douglas argues that by speaking the words of W's inaudible utterings, M 'projects the task of melancholy onto this woman, in his attempt, not to remember "her", but to remember and reclaim the pleasure of how he had once remembered "her"'.[76] When M projects onto W by speaking the words she mimes, M fills in the black holes, struggling to position W as the subject of the narrative, yet he is unsuccessful by the very nature of the fact that he voices her unspoken words.

As M's voice supplements W's absent one, W becomes even more ghostly, recalling modernist reactions against sound film. 'One set of objections', Tim Armstrong explains, was 'to the way in which the body reappears traumatically in sound cinema, as a maimed or aggressive object: a ventriloquist's dummy, a statue throwing stones'.[77] He adds that the voice in sound film was perceived by feminist thinkers such as Dorothy Richardson, who wrote for the film journal *Close Up*, as an image of patriarchal authority imposing itself onto the democratic image.

While this may be so in the historical debate surrounding sound film, in Beckett's teleplay the male patriarchy, in spite of narrating the images, is a figure depleted of authority. Beckett's teleplay does not stage W as M's ventriloquist dummy; M does not master his material. Even though she may remain a statue or ghost, seeing nothing and emitting no sound, by forming the words W keeps M from taking on the role of an author; he merely repeats rather than creates. M's vocalisation of W's words is M's attempt to disrupt the very dreamlike quality of W; he wishes to bring her back to 'life'. However, M fails and W remains the object of remembrance. Although M takes on a role similar to that of the camera and, in the process, objectifies himself, he, nonetheless, becomes one of the ghostly images he tries to rematerialise through the act of reproduction. M remains mechanised in the medium and the teleplay remains full of gaps.

In his attempts to rematerialise W from an object to a subject, M reveals his own desire for precision and authority. Like many of Beckett's protagonists (as discussed in previous chapters), M is concerned with getting his narrative right. He corrects himself in the opening: 'No, that is not right'.[78] The phrase 'When I thought of her it was always night'[79] constructs W as a phantom in the mind. Herren explains that 'M controls his present perception by controlling the selection process of memory. In order to do so, he does not passively wait for the past to return to him; rather, he actively returns to the past, selecting, condensing and redirecting his actions on the stage of memory'.[80] M tries to make W into more than a memory. He corrects himself by claiming: 'When she appeared it was always night',[81] echoing the description of himself when returning from walking the roads. Appearing, ironically, both implies that she, like M, can take on a life of her own and that she is a ghost mysteriously appearing out of nowhere.

Having corrected his narrative, M replays it to 'make sure we have got it right'.[82] Yet through this repetition, M's narrative is threatened. In the act of repeating the narrative, the danger that it will be reduced to nothingness arises. Repetition brings with it the possibility of a form of habit which results in paralysis, in death. Indeed, M reveals that his pleading for W usually is in vain:

> There was of course a fourth case, or a case nought as I pleased to call it, by far the most commonest, in the proportion say of nine hundred and ninety-nine to one, or nine hundred and ninety-eight to two.[83]

When W fails to appear, M busies himself with either 'something else, more rewarding, such as . . . such as . . . cube roots', a mathematical diversion, 'or with nothing'.[84]

In his reference to cube roots, M discloses his need for precision, yet Beckett undermines mathematical precision by embedding the text in uncertainty. Firstly, his calculations of how often W appears is an estimation. Not only does he qualify his statement with 'say', but he does not know for certain whether W appears only 0.01 or 0.02 per cent of the time. Secondly, the 'such as . . . such as . . .' functions as a repetition announcing M's search for 'something more rewarding', that is, something that can assist him in his project to make his and W's existence concrete. In its repetition, however, that something is decomposed into nothing. Thirdly, the conjunctive 'or' both constructs 'nothing' as the binary opposition of 'cube roots' and positions it as an alternative to mathematics, establishing cube roots and the very act of precision as a waste of time.

Immediately following the statement, 'busied myself with nothing', M curiously says: 'that MINE'.[85] 'Beckett's 'MINE' is doubly ambiguous', Enoch Brater perceptively notes: 'In one sense it is a rich source of supply, but in another it is a pit from which all resources have been taken, as well as an encased weapon designed to destroy'.[86] Crouched in his sanctum, M attempts to busy himself with something more rewarding to keep his 'desire and wont' from exploding into a chaotic, uncontrolled memory. He strives to compose a precise narrative because by narrating it 'perfectly' he controls the memory of her. Once the narrative is completed, M may be free of the memory of W.

Beckett once again supplies his viewers with an extreme close-up, at least in the BBC production, this time of a *woman's face reduced as far as possible to eyes and mouth*.[87] W's face does not respond to the images before her. Neither does she speak to M nor does she look at him. Her eyes are 'unseeing',[88] reflecting and absorbing nothing, not unlike nineteenth-century portrait photography in which the person photographed was often held still by a metal brace. Theorising on such portraits, Roland Barthes explains that the subject in the photograph is of someone already dead because the identity and moment photographed has passed.[89] Unlike the close-up of Joe in *Eh Joe* or F in *Ghost Trio*, the close-up of W appears 'as a transparent shot superimposed on another video image'.[90] Not only does this close-up provide the viewer with a ghostly image, but also the empty unseeing eyes and emotionless face of W offers the audience black holes and a white wall to read in accordance to Gilles Deleuze and Félix Guattari's system of faciality. Any inscription onto W is a vocalisation of that which is not present. The audience cannot animate the image of W into anything other than that of a ghost.

Nacht und Träume

Although some scholars have argued that Samuel Beckett's teleplays are as sentimental as *Krapp's Last Tape* (the teleplays consistently feature men longing for some type of connection with a woman), Beckett's television works simultaneously blur the distinction between the ghostly world on screen and the viewer's reality.

Beckett's teleplay *Nacht und Träume* is a prime example of this motif. Written and produced for the German broadcasting system, SDR, in April 1982, *Nacht und Träume* radically breaks from the conventions of television by denying the viewer dialogue, plot, action and colour images. The printed text of *Nacht und Träume* is an outline or 'blueprint' which must be deciphered by the television technicians in order to be fully realised.[91]

While the reader may opt to view the piece to catch the words sung, this has its limitations because these bars are so 'Softly sung'[92] that the words are nearly impossible to make out. More so here than in *What Where*, Beckett's stage play of 1983 which he later transferred to television in 1985, the line 'Make sense who may'[93] is appropriate. As *Nacht und Träume* begins, an elderly man, identified in the text as dreamer, with long white hair, head bowed and both hands resting on the table at which he is seated, is illuminated by evening light. He softly sings Schubert's Lied. As the light fades and he falls asleep, an image of the dreamer's dreamt self appears, lit by a 'kinder light'[94] and situated slightly above and to the left of the dreamer. In the dream a hand appears, conveying a cup gently to the dreamt self's lips. Thereafter, the hand gently wipes his brow and finally takes the dreamt self's hand. This scenario occurs twice.

Strange as these images may appear, the sense that can be made of the teleplay is of the struggle to decipher that which viewers do not understand. This play for television transforms the viewers into seekers of sense and uses the camera to obscure meaning by blurring the barrier between the waking world and the dreamt world. Through the techniques of fade and zoom, Beckett decomposes the wall separating these binaries, allowing them to bleed into each other. The disintegration between the real and the dream challenges the audience's attempts to decipher the work.

In much psychoanalytic writing, most notably Sigmund Freud's *The Interpretation of Dreams*, dreams are thought to offer a symbolic network to unlock the hidden desires and anxieties of the individual dreaming. Yet in staging the inability to read these symbols, Beckett does not allow the dream to unlock the mysteries of the dreamer or the teleplay itself. On the contrary, the dream plunges the audience into a cycle in which by closing off one hole another is opened. Hence, a Freudian model fails to illuminate the teleplay.[95] Instead, the equally perplexing work, Jean Cocteau's 1946 film *La belle et la bête* (*Beauty and the Beast*), can offer ways into Beckett's very difficult play for television. Both Cocteau's and Beckett's works draw distinctions between the dream world and the real world, not in the Freudian sense of using the dream to understand the waking world, but rather to reconstruct and possibly comment on the viewer's attempts to decode the dream.

Although it is tempting to read the teleplay in relationship to Gilles Deleuze's essay 'The Exhausted' which was included with the 1992 Minuit volume of Beckett's teleplays (*Quad, Ghost Trio, . . . but the clouds . . .*, and *Nacht und Träume*), crucial to *Nacht und Träume* is Gilles Deleuze and Félix Guattari's system of the white wall/black hole which is mapped out in their philosophical work, *A Thousand Plateaus*, originally published in 1980, shortly before Beckett wrote and directed *Nacht und Träume*.

Through the metaphor of the white wall/black hole, Deleuze and Guattari argue, as outlined earlier in this chapter, that meaning is constructed by filling in gaps and inscribing onto surfaces. Their model provides readers of Beckett with an understanding of his works that does not erase Beckett's comment on the limitations of interpretation. *Nacht und Träume* ultimately stages these limitations. Reflected on the wall of the set is a slightly lighter grey rectangle which Beckett describes as 'a window set high in back wall' which is 'lit only by evening light'.[96] When this barely perceptible window subtly goes dark – 'Fade out evening light'[97] – the dreamer falls asleep and his dream becomes a new window: 'Fade up on B on an invisible podium about 4 feet above floor level, middle ground, well right of centre'.[98] As the light from the window diminishes, the hole is sealed. However, the audience is not left with a wall without holes. The dream creates another hole – the window to the dreamer's mind. Through this new hole, the viewer attempts to fill in the meaning of the teleplay.

Employing a fixed camera, Beckett provides the viewer with the ability to survey the protagonist. The audience peers into the chamber of his mind as night falls. As the dreamer dreams, the spectator's eyes pry deeper as the dream opens and is brought closer with the help of a zoom. Closing in on the object and invading his dream, Beckett uses the camera's gaze, and by extension the audience's, to decompose the object. In bringing the object closer so that the audience can devour it, Beckett figuratively uses the photographic process of enlarging a negative onto a print. The image of the dream loses distinction as a photographic image does when the selected image of the negative is enlarged. The result is an image with less sharpness, and thus is less readable. Hence, as Beckett suggests in his late novella of 1983,

Worstward Ho, contrary to the desire to see better by seeing the object closer, the audience sees 'better worse'.[99]

Unlike standard contemporary television and cinematic images, the set of this teleplay is 'minimally lit' and the dreamer 'remains just visible throughout dream'.[100] The dark quality of this short piece is suggestive of images reproduced as an artefact. This teleplay places its audience in a peculiar position. Beckett's viewers find themselves playing the role of the sole voyeur, digging holes, or, in other words, digging for answers.

The viewers are both waiting for something to happen and, as the archaeologist does, attempting to piece together the dug-up artefacts. Indeed, the dreamer's dream, while providing company, is one of fragmentation. The dreamt hands are disembodied, appearing and disappearing from out of the darkness. A similar image appears in Jean Cocteau's surrealist film. While there is no record of Beckett's impressions of Cocteau or his film *La belle et la bête,* Beckett would certainly have been aware of Cocteau's work – Roger Blin, Beckett's friend and the first director of *En attendant Godot,* worked with Cocteau and acted in his 1950 film *Orphée.*

The parallels between *Nacht und Träume* and *La belle et la bête* are interesting in that both Cocteau and Beckett use fragmented hands to create two distinct worlds. In *La belle et la bête* the dream-like fantasy world is represented in the Beast's castle and the waking world is represented in the bourgeois home and village where the Beauty lives. Cocteau, like Beckett, was interested in fragmentation and the blurring of these spaces. In *La belle et la bête*, the Beast's castle is enchanted with magic. The corridors are lined with hands holding candles that light magically as the characters in the film walk towards them. They assist the father, the Beauty and the cinema audience, who are all viewers of the mysterious castle. In essence, the hands illuminate the way for those entering the dream-like world of the Beast, and thus tempt them to inscribe meaning onto the mysterious images. The dining room is, likewise, lit and the diner is given drink and food by these disembodied hands – similar to the image of the dreamt self in *Nacht und Träume* – providing the diner with morsels which will help to fill in the mystery.

In *Nacht und Träume*, the dreamt hands help the dreamt self by touching the dreamt self's head, appearing with a cup and conveying it gently to his lips, wiping his brow gently and taking his right hand. The cup can be read as a chalice, and the hand offering the dreamer a drink as encouraging him to gain some spiritual insight, as James Knowlson and Graley Herren suggest.

Knowlson points to Beckett's acknowledgement that the image is rooted in religious paintings.[101] Hence, the chalice represents divine knowledge, but the viewer and the dreamer once awoken are not privileged with this knowledge. In other words, although the audience can read the cup as embodying religious significance, what that significance is remains 'One of our numerous teasers'.[102] Knowlson notes that Beckett insisted the gender of the dreamt hands should not be distinguishable in the production. He told Müller-Freienfels that the uncertainty of the gender will remain 'One of our numerous teasers'. The whole teleplay is a teaser as none of the images come together. Despite the spectator's attempt to bring the images together as the dreamt hand joins with the dreamer's hand, the images remain fragmented and, consequently, indecipherable.

Herren, unlike Knowlson, is able to examine the religious iconography Beckett employs without sealing the holes left for the audience to puzzle over. Herren argues that although the legend of Veronica, wiping Christ's brow on his way to the cross, may be a direct source for the teleplay, Beckett ultimately deconstructs the icon. No longer is Veronica an emblem of 'truth', but rather this icon is a fragment in the dreamer's rubble heap, and ultimately the dreamer 'must content himself with rearranging the fragments of his ruin into various aesthetically pleasing forms'.[103] In *Nacht und Träume*, then, fragments and the division between the dream and the non-dream are used to expose the viewer's attempt to solve the unsolvable and thus the teleplay positions the dreamer as a failed author as he, too, struggles to recreate a narrative, even if this act is only possible in his dream.

In *La belle et la bête*, the father's world is on the brink of financial ruin as he is faced with having to repay his debts. The financial worries, the petty bourgeois siblings and the unrequited lover of the Beauty, are compared to the wealth and mystery of the Beast's castle. These worlds can only join once the curse that separates them is broken. When this happens, the Beast takes on the appearance of Beauty's unrequited lover who, in the process of breaking the curse, dies.

Through the Beast's transformation, the viewer recognises that the distinction of these two worlds is an artificial one – their separation is a human construct. Beckett, too, initially separates the dream from the non-dream to expose the separation as a fiction, which is reinforced through the camera and the desire to inscribe meaning onto the inexplicable. Beckett's dream world is a repetition of the waking world. The dreamt self 'is seated at a table in the same posture as [the dreamer] dreaming, bowed head resting on hands, but left profile, faintly lit by kinder light'.[104] The only difference in the dream is that the dreamer is in the presence of dreamt hands.

Despite the dream containing these hands, Beckett questions whether it should be constituted as an illusion or fantasy. Through trick photography, Enoch Brater suggests, 'Not only do we see [the dreamt self] invade [the dreamer's] territory, but we also see how a dream *becomes* the video reality'.[105] Although the dream invades the territory of the non-dream, the viewer does not lose sight of which image is categorised as the dream. Rather, we are made aware of the arbitrary construction of the distinction between fantasy and reality. Both the dream and the non-dream are, to use Brater's words, a 'video reality', but ironically this reality remains a mystery for the viewers, almost constituting reality and dreams as both being unreal.

In *Nacht und Träume*, Beckett points to a very 'real' concern – that of the struggle to decode the seemingly dreamlike reality. Deleuze and Guattari argue that 'reality' is built on the process of how we read and interpret the unknown, but reveal that our understanding of the world is ultimately based on an act of assigning meaning in order to shut out the gaping horrors of the unknowable. For Deleuze and Guattari the ultimate unknowable is death. They explain that the face of death is, in fact, a white wall with black holes; the dead have white faces with expressionless eyes and gaping mouths, much like O's expression when confronted by the camera in Beckett's 1974 cinematic project, *Film*. The act of closing the mouth and eyes, and in some cultures incorporating a death-mask into burial rituals, according to Deleuze and Guattari, is an attempt to explain the mystery of death.

Unlike most of Beckett's other teleplays, *Nacht und Träume* does not, however, conclude with a ghostly close-up of a corpse-like face. Regardless, its protagonist is yet another ghostly figure re-enacting an unexplainable haunting that exposes the need for an explanation. The dreamer is haunted by the need for another, and the dream and the dreamer haunt the viewer who is unable to provide the dreamer with the answers sought for. However, Beckett's ideal viewers are not those who, like Bam in *What Where*, 'switch off'[106] their pre-programmed answers to allow for the nothingness to seep through meaning. Rather, Beckett's ideal viewers search for meaning despite the futility of it all. It is the process of searching, not the answers found, that Beckett repeatedly stages.

Quad

The admiration of the SDR's crew for Samuel Beckett's precision continued each time they received a new manuscript from him. However, this precision would also lead to the frustration of the crew and even more so of Beckett. The genesis of *Quad* attests to this frustration. Much more complicated than any of his previous work for television, this 'still crazier invention for TV' (as Beckett called it in his letter, containing the *Quad* manuscript, to Müller-Freienfels on 30 January 1980)[107] includes a bizarre geometric diagram, and is relentless in its vision of movement and sound.

Despite its seemingly monotonous action of four robed figures walking counter-clockwise and towards the centre, but always avoiding the centre, this piece proved the most difficult to produce. Nonetheless, the 'fieberhafte Monotonie' ('feverish monotony') as Beckett expressed it to Müller-Freienfels was achieved.[108] Anyone who has seen this work can attest to its hellish monotony; some scholars and television technicians have even recalled Beckett's interest in Dante when discussing this teleplay.[109]

Gogo Gensch, who worked with Beckett at the SDR as the production manager for the filming of *Quad 1* and *Quad 2*, recalled Beckett's frustration with *Quad 1*, attributing one of the main difficulties to the fact that the teleplay was to be filmed without editing shorter shots together, which meant that each time a dancer[110] or a musician made an error the whole piece had to be re-filmed.[111] In addition, the dancers and musicians were recorded live and simultaneously. There was no thought of either prerecording the percussions and synchronising them to the dancers' movements or of prerecording the dancers and adding a live musical recording to the action. As such, everything had to be timed perfectly.[112]

It is remarkable, then, to observe the monotony of the piece considering how it was, in fact, anything but technically monotonous to produce. What can be understood with this need for precision is that Beckett was creating a machine. In one of the earliest investigations of *Quad*'s mechanical nature, Hans Hiebel notes that 'The most obvious characteristic of the movements of the four protagonists is mathematical precision and geometrical exactness'.[113] Elizabeth Klaver too comments on this precision, interpreting both *Quad* and Beckett's stage play of 1982, *Ohio Impromptu*, in relation to computerised 'image-processing machine[s] in which the same textualised memory revolves with slight distortions through its code'.[114]

Both scholars point to the precision that was achieved in the work and both point to Beckett's use of the camera as a new writing technology. What the audience witnesses in *Quad 1* and *Quad 2* is that, although the movements of machines may seem habitual to the untrained eye, the act of putting the machine together so that everything runs smoothly is an enormous task. All the cogs must be in place, all the movements must go on as planned – any hiccups would result in the machine going haywire, much like the feeding machine in Charlie Chaplin's 1936 film *Modern Times* does.[115] For Beckett, ultimately, writing is a technological production which the writer must be constantly maintaining and fine-tuning.

This need to maintain and fine-tune the technology of writing often left Beckett feeling isolated and trapped in creating new works. Throughout his biography of Beckett, Knowlson points to the playwright's frustration with his struggle to create new texts, especially texts that were requested by others. Even in his letters to Müller-Freienfels, who Beckett regarded highly as a friend and colleague, he expressed the impossibility, or near impossibility, of creating new inventions for television. Yet each time Beckett surprised both himself and those expecting a new work from him, with a unique manuscript. In a letter to Müller-Freienfels, partially reprinted in Knowlson's biography, Beckett wrote: 'I'm quite lost in TV technicalities and shall never write again for that medium',[116] but only a few months later was working on his next invention for television – *Nacht und Träume*. Perhaps he was fulfilling the very dilemma of the artist that he sketched out in his 1958 conversation with Georges Duthuit:

> I know that all that is required now, in order to bring even this horrible matter to an acceptable conclusion, is to make of this submission, this admission, this fidelity to failure, a new occasion, a new term of relation, and of the act which, unable to act, obliged to act, he [Bram van Velde] makes, an expressive act, even if only of itself, of its impossibility, of its obligation.[117]

In *Quad 1* and *Quad 2* there is a sense of being obligated and thus trapped by the technology recording the protagonists on screen. This entrapment is carried out by the camera. Surveying the objects, the camera in these teleplays, as discussed earlier in this chapter, takes on the form of the peeping Tom. The imprisonment of the protagonists in *Quad 1* and *Quad 2* works differently than it does in Beckett's previous teleplays. The audience is put in the position of struggling to read the images before them – images that are unlike anything they have ever experienced before. Indeed, many have argued that Beckett's teleplays present the audience with ghosts, and the titles of several of his works for television (*Ghost Trio* and *Nacht und Träume*, for example) support this reading.[118]

However, the protagonists of *Quad 1* and *Quad 2* are not being closed in on as the protagonists in Beckett's other teleplays are. Instead, they reside in a prison of sorts, an eternal state, filmed from a position slightly above them (recalling Michel Foucault's analysis of Jeremy Bentham's panopticon in *Discipline and Punish: The Birth of the Prison*) so that the viewers can see the quad on which these ghostly dancers move about.[119] They are trapped in a quad and, in their very movements, forced to repeat the same motions.

Quad 2, a slowed-down, black-and-white version of the previous work – as though exhausted and drained of any life left in the colourfully robed figures of *Quad 1* – testifies to their entrapment. The figures are never released; they keep moving even when drained of their livelier existence. In fact, Beckett said to Müller-Freienfels that the time that has lapsed between *Quad 1* and *Quad 2* is 'ten thousand years'.[120]

Ultimately, the completion of any writing, for Beckett, is not a release. Rather he returns to the same themes, reworking techniques, fine-tuning them, exhausting them without coming to an end. Like many of his protagonists who struggle, but cannot end (as do Opener in his radio play *Cascando* and Animator in *Rough for Radio II*, both of which are discussed in Chapter 2), Beckett perhaps saw himself as obliged to express the inexpressible. '[B]ecause he is an artist', Graley Herren notes,

> Beckett cannot resist the urge to eff the canvas – with colour no less. What exactly this ineffable gesture is meant to signify is unnameable by its performers and directors and unknowable by its critics (and probably by its author, too).[121]

What most if not all of Beckett's work for television and radio have in common is a sense that even if all technological structures break down, escape or liberation from technological structures is unattainable. Modern civilisation, Beckett seems to say, would not fare better without technology even though it is at times destructive. *Quad 2*, the worn-down version of *Quad 1* – in which the viewers witness the dancers 'ten thousand years later' still in a 'feverish monotony' although their pace has been radically slowed down, their colourful robes have been turned into shades of grey, and now instead of the sound of percussions we hear only their footsteps –

echoes Beckett's stage plays of earlier decades, such as *Footfalls*, *Come and Go* and even *Krapp's Last Tape*. That which haunts the figures in *Quad 1* and *Quad 2* – which sets them in their purgatorial pacing cycles – is absent, buried perhaps in some poor mind. This machine never comes to an end; its poor souls are never released from their paths, and Beckett was never completely satisfied with either *Quad 1* or *Quad 2*. According to those who worked with him, he seemed almost haunted with the technical difficulties.

Where does this investigation of Beckett's writing technologies leave us? What remains when plays with their endless cycles wear down? Perhaps the answers lie in Beckett's extremely brief stage play of 1969, *Breath*. In this play, a faint light illuminates a stage 'littered with miscellaneous rubbish'.[122] After about five seconds, a faint cry is heard. Not surprisingly, this action repeats itself once more. What is the rubbish? The audience is not told. Whose cry is it? The audience is not told. I like to imagine that the junkyard of *Breath* holds artefacts of modern civilisation – much of which is technological. In any junkyard, one finds old cars, televisions and other technological gadgets that are no longer restorable. However, unlike these broken-down implements, Beckett's teleplays never seem to come to a resolved closure; instead they linger and wear down only to be revived. Better than most, Beckett understood the junkyard of academia.[123] Archives house the worn sheets of paper written on by famous men and women and hold recordings on odd-looking tapes that are no longer used in the modern world. Beckett understood that writing technologies remain even if only as hauntings of the past.

What Where

The coming-into-being of Beckett's last teleplay, *Was Wo* (*What Where*), is unusual as it is one of the few works that Beckett allowed to be transferred from one medium (theatre) to another (television). Originally, *What Where* was conceived of as a stage play, but two years after its première in 1983 Beckett undertook a production of it for the SDR under the title *Was Wo*. When entering into a discussion about Beckett's position on the transference of texts into an alternate medium, most scholars quote Beckett's letter to his American publisher Barney Rosset. In this letter of 27 August 1957 Beckett writes that to stage his radio play *All That Fall* would be 'to kill it'[124] because it was a play written for voices, not bodies.

Despite his strong refusal to stage *All That Fall* and his disapproval of other such projects, nonetheless Beckett did grant some friends and artists whose work he respected permission to experiment with his works in different media. The most notable of these are David Warrilow's staging of Beckett's short story *The Lost Ones*, Jean Reavey and Alan Schneider's staging of Beckett's teleplay *Eh Joe* and Billie Whitelaw's remarkable television performance of Beckett's stage play *Not I*. Whereas the texts of *The Lost Ones* and *Eh Joe* remained identical to their original productions, and *Not I* was altered only slightly (the Auditor was eliminated), Beckett completely reworked the visual image and drastically reduced the spoken text of *What Where* when transferring it to television.

Both the stage play and the teleplay have a narrator, the Voice of Bam, who recalls the interrogation of Bem, Bim, Bom and himself. On stage, the Voice of Bam is depicted by a megaphone, situated as if Bam were holding it to his mouth, and the actors are made to resemble each other as much as possible, wearing long grey gowns and long grey hair. On the television screen, the image has been changed – Beckett keeps the narrative function, but now the voice of Bam is a distorted floating head and the other B-ms are faces with no hair or clothing showing. What information the interrogation seeks to uncover is unknown; the audience is left never discovering what, if anything, the B-ms know.

In her illuminating essay '"Everything Out but the Faces": Beckett's Reshaping of *What Where* for Television', Martha Fehsenfeld, reflecting back to her reactions to the première of the staged production of *What Where* and later the televised version, speculates that Beckett 'had the small restricted place of the television screen in mind as the setting for this play' from the outset, and claims that the overt repetitions on the vast and empty stage produced 'an unexpected element of comedy' which was resolved in the televisual image.[125]

Beckett's own struggle to reconceptualise the play for television suggests a much more complicated genesis of the work which perhaps can never be fully understood. As such, I will analyse how in each version of the play technology is incorporated in the work in order to produce a text critical of the politics of inscription. Technology, in the stage play and teleplay, interrogate the spectator's role in the production of political narratives. Beckett concludes his work in television and theatre with an exploration of the way in which the technology of writing becomes aligned with the senseless politics of torture.

Fehsenfeld is one of the few Beckett scholars to consider the mechanical imagery in this work. Sharing her experience as an audience member, she describes the première of *What Where* as being hindered by mechanical images: 'I wanted to "go in" to the story of the play, and I was constantly being "pulled out" by the megaphone and by this intrusive comic quality – both of them external, mechanical hindrances'.[126] She goes on to speculate that these 'mechanical hindrances' probably contributed to Beckett's choice to move the play from the stage to the television screen.

Yet, although Beckett eliminated the megaphone and freed the B-ms from their bodies, which Fehsenfeld believes saved the play from being 'too mechanical', Beckett did not want to eliminate the mechanical effect on-screen. In an interview, Jim Lewis, Beckett's cameraman for the SDR production of *Was Wo*, explains that Beckett initially wanted 'every movement to be rigid – a kind of mechanical ballet'.[127] Walter Asmus, the German director who often worked with Beckett to produce his stage plays, defends the mechanical movement on the stage, although he is not convinced of its effectiveness. He explains that in the stage play and, more successfully, in the teleplay, Beckett presents his audience with 'the tension between the animate and the inanimate'.[128] Indeed, on stage the inanimate is present in both the 'robotlike quality',[129] as Asmus described the entrances and exits of the characters, which mocks the conventions of theatre, and in the megaphone, reminiscent of a circus.

The circus metaphor, achieved in the play through the megaphone, recalls, for Graley Herren, W.B. Yeats's poem 'The Circus Animals'

Desertion'. He suggests that, like Yeats's poem, Beckett's play is a return to old themes:

> 'What can I but enumerate old themes?' Yeats asked in 'The Circus Animals' Desertion', a lament reiterated by Beckett in his last play. Memory, identity, and spectatorship are all 'given the works' one more time. Beckett's *œuvre* is remarkably consistent, but it is never redundant. In the play *What Where* he hauls the usual suspects out on stage for interrogation. But he varies his formal methods of questioning, shedding new light on the 'old themes'.[130]

The circus is a type of theatre, constructed around a series of entrances and exits that are announced by a ringmaster, usually using a megaphone – an object that appears on stage as the voice of Bam. Beckett not only alludes to Yeats but also parallels circus theatrics with political rituals and performance.

By mocking theatrical and circus conventions in these cycles of torture, Beckett asks the spectators to interrogate his play, and what they are asked to question within the play is their own role within this political structure. Ironically, however, by actively questioning the works, the spectator becomes one of the inquisitors. For Beckett, existing outside the system is impossible. The spectator is never innocent. On the contrary, even the passive spectator is inscribed into the system by his or her complicity in the inquisition, as seen in Beckett's 1982 stage play *Catastrophe*, when the tortured protagonist looks up at the audience during the canned applause. The applause dies down and the lights go out. The viewers in the auditorium are meant to ponder whether or not they should applaud the catastrophe they have just witnessed.

Both the teleplay and stage play of *What Where* successfully attempt to activate, or in Beckett's words, 'switch on',[131] the audience's awareness of its role in political structures. Through the megaphone and its efforts to turn on the interrogation, Beckett draws together memory and habit with the politics of torture. The torturer subjects the torturee to 'the works' until he 'confesses' – his confession acts as the inscription which the black hole of the megaphone tries to absorb in order to break out of this mechanical structure. The act of remembering is an act of personal and political interrogation. As a circus ringmaster, the megaphone is Bam's mind recollecting and decomposing memories. When V, the voice of Bam, twice says 'I switch on',[132] he activates the cycles of torture to recall the memories of 'anything',[133] 'it'[134] and 'where'[135] in the staged version, and 'what' and 'where'[136] in the revised text for television. *What* is the story, and *where* does it take place are probably the two most crucial questions for any play on stage or screen. As such, Beckett likens a political inquisition with performance. These memories, like the information that Bam tries to extract from Bem, Bim, Bom and himself, however, are locked into Bam's mind represented in the 'lampblack'[137] hole of the megaphone.

The mechanical structure of politics depicted in this play imprisons its participants. V's narrative provides slight variations from its repetitions, but these deviations are manifestations of V's struggle to get his narrative right, like so many of Beckett's narrators. This narrative struggle manifests V's endeavour to gain authority over his past and his present situation. In other words, V's narrative production is both a political system of torture and an attempt to inscribe meaning into this political dead-end without becoming a political subject to be inscribed upon. V's attempt to break the cycle through his highly repetitive narrative, however, simultaneously locks him and the other B-ms into it. As Herren posits, 'As each suspect becomes "free", Bam enlists him to torture one of the failed interrogators'.[138]

According to several critics, pointing to the text's repetitions and V's attention to the seasons at the onset of each new cycle, *What Where*, like Beckett's *Quad 1* and *Quad 2*, is another example of an endless cycle.[139] Nevertheless, while the repetition and mention of the seasons suggest a continuity, unlike the cycles in his previous work this cycle does end, but in ending becomes enveloped in a shroud of darkness, emitting no light, no matter, no information: 'It is winter/Without journey'.[140] The black hole of the megaphone on the stage, while emitting a voice, pulls into it all possible meaning.

Caught in this whirlpool, the B-ms become absorbed inside the black hole.[141]

What is more, the textual loop in *What Where*, Elizabeth Klaver convincingly argues, revolves 'through series of signs and images [which] also inscribe the technological properties of television'.[142] Beckett is hyper-aware of the technological properties and conventions of television, as demonstrated in the repetitions and (even more so) in his reduction of the visual image onstage from the ghostly figures in long grey gowns with long grey hair to television's trademark – the close-up of their faces.

Beckett further eliminated all marks that might distinguish these faces from one another. With the use of make-up and by cutting a small hole in pieces of cardboard later placed in front of each of the four cameras,[143] Beckett, with the help of Jim Lewis, created the illusion that these faces fade in and out like floating specks refusing to be fixed onto the black backdrop.

On the one hand, Beckett has reversed the white wall/black hole system of faciality. What the audience sees is a black wall/white holes. While the black backdrop suggests that the wall cannot be inscribed upon and the white faces suggest that these holes cannot absorb subjectivity, the faces themselves reflect white walls that seek inscription. Indeed, with the elimination of the megaphone and the emphasis on the faces, Beckett's television version of the play prioritises the white wall represented in the close-ups over that of the black hole. 'We stare straight at the screen to see talking heads, face-forward, never looking at one another, always staring straight back at us', Herren observes. He goes on to note:

> We see them asking for one another the same questions that we ask of them: Who are these people? Where is this supposed to take place? What is going on here? How can it be resolved? When will this end? And, like V, we are guaranteed little success in providing answers to these questions. Not that this keeps the hordes of Beckettians from trying. Yet even these desperate attempts to make sense are reflected on screen.[144]

In television, the close-up functions as an indicator of emotion and psychological development within the character; however, Beckett's faces remain disturbingly impassive, and as such position the spectators within a struggle to make sense of what they see. The audience struggles but cannot read these impenetrable faces.

Fehsenfeld recalls Beckett mentioning to her that 'the faces were like masks – death masks',[145] and V's distorted face particularly gives this impression.[146] Jim Lewis comments that 'The image of Bam in the beyond or beyond the grave or whatever you want to call it – the *death-mask* thing that wasn't originally planned at all – that gave us the biggest trouble'.[147]

This metaphor of the death-mask recalls Deleuze and Guattari. For them, the death-mask represents the ultimate white wall/black hole system. Unlike the process of sealing all the gaps in the face of a dead person to keep from being absorbed into the horror of the face, the death-mask invites inscription. Whereas in rituals the death-mask helps to animate a narrative around death, in Beckett's teleplay these death-masks function to expose the production of narrative, like this cycle of torture, as mechanical and ineffectual. The faces and voices of the B-ms remain emotionless, and the information of what and where, which is needed to break out of the stifling cycle, remains obscured. The death-mask veils 'the things (or the Nothingness) behind it' in much the same way that Beckett accuses language of doing in his letter to Axel Kaun. While Beckett once strove to tear off the veil and bore holes into language to discover what lies underneath the shroud,[148] here Beckett seems more interested in the permanence of the mask. In other words, through the image of the death-mask as a white wall, Beckett points to the inability of revealing and uncovering meaning.

V's final words 'Make sense who may/I switch off'[149] invite the audience to puzzle out the play, provided they bring their own aspirin,[150] but before any certainties can be inscribed onto the face, page and screen, V deactivates the machine of faciality by switching off.

V's position is ambiguous. On the one hand, V inscribes the B-ms into a political structure – he pins them to the black backdrop that does not allow for free inscription. On the other hand, in both inscribing the B-ms into a position of torture and by keeping his eyes shut throughout, he tries to keep them from becoming subjectified into the engulfing and inescapable black hole.[151] He struggles to keep them from becoming political subjects consumed within a higher authority. It is through this tension between the white wall/black hole and the animate/inanimate that Beckett suggests that the production of politics is a narrative production that must be interrogated.

Conclusion

From 1965 to 1985 Samuel Beckett wrote five plays and one adaptation of his stage play *What Where* for television, all of which were broadcast on the BBC and SDR. What is more, he frequently travelled to Stuttgart, Germany, during these years to direct his teleplays for the Süddeutscher Rundfunk. He was obviously intrigued by the creative possibilities of the small studio space and the camera. Television allowed Beckett to further explore the ways the past haunts us, the ways we attempt to tell our life histories, and the ways we are trapped by endless repetitions of voyeurism and subject–object relations.

In the early teleplays, Beckett uses the technology to explore male characters attempting to recapture or erase a past that they regret. Joe tries to erase the memories of the past that remind him of his destructive tendencies in *Eh Joe*. He is trapped by his memories as he is trapped by the Voice and camera. In *Ghost Trio* and . . . *but the clouds* . . . , Beckett's protagonists struggle to remake their past by remembering lost loved ones. However, again, they fail to gain control over the haunting memories.

In the later teleplays, Beckett becomes increasingly minimalistic in order to examine the process of storytelling. It is the process, or the struggle, not the story itself, that we discover in works like *Nacht und Träume*, *What Where* and *Quad*. In the process, Beckett reveals that much of the stories told are fiction – that which we do not understand and which we cannot read – we invent. However invention, Beckett reveals, fails to satisfy.

CHAPTER 4
CRITICAL PERSPECTIVES

Professor Emeritus in the Department of Theatre at the University of Maryland, Baltimore County, **Xerxes Mehta** *is best known for his work as a director of Beckett's short plays. His productions of* Not I, Play, That Time *and* Ohio Impromptu *have toured to Beckett festivals in Strasbourg, France, and Berlin, Germany. In addition to his work in the theatre, Mehta has published several essays in the* Journal of Beckett Studies, Samuel Beckett Today/Aujourd'hui *and in books dedicated to Beckett. The essay below first appeared in Lois Oppenheim's collection of interviews and essays,* Directing Beckett *(Ann Arbor: University of Michigan Press, 1994).*

Ghosts: Chaos and Freedom in Beckett's Spectral Theatre

The prescriptiveness of Beckett's stage directions, especially in the short plays he wrote toward the end of his life, appears to leave the director with little to do. This is, in fact, an illusion. The deeper the director, designers, and performers venture into these works, the more they realise that almost everything is unknown, and perhaps unknowable. What follows, therefore, is offered tentatively, and with humility, as one director's experience of an art whose power and intractability, grandeur and mystery, are inseparable.

Eye

In my view, Beckett's stage works since *Play* are ghost-plays, haunting, their spectral quality lying at the heart of their power. What the spectator sees appears to come swimming out of blackness, near yet far, floating yet fixed, obsessively present in the manner of visions and nightmares. To achieve this quality requires control of darkness and light. Darkness in these late, short works is, I suggest, of a different order than the normal theatrical blackout. Darkness here is a part of the weave of the work, the most important single element of the image. It should be as absolute as can be managed. Darkness at this level becomes a form of sense deprivation. Its effect is to cancel the group existence of theatre; to cancel the awareness of surrounding space, to throw the spectator into a physical void, and thus to create in the spectator a psychological dependency on the image that finally appears. If that image, then, is itself disturbing, unbalancing, assaultive, or recessive, the spectator topples into a world of nightmares, will-less to resist, on the edge of sanity.

The image that finally appears is spectral, wraithlike – from the floating heads and funeral urns in *Play*, to the floating mouth in *Not I*, to the lower-body apparition in *Footfalls*, to the white heads and hands in *Ohio Impromptu*, to the residual skull in *Rockaby*. These images immediately reinforce the assault on reason: the heads in *Play* appear and disappear with bewildering speed and randomness; the mouth in *Not I*, eight feet off the ground and thus decisively dematerialised from any possible connection to a human form, seems to move around in a kind of optical illusion, although it is in fact quite fixed; the rocker in *Rockaby* starts to rock on its own, silently, without apparent human agency. All of these images float. All are white or grey, except for the red of the mouth in *Not I*. Finally, all are fixed, with a fixedness that goes far beyond their fixedness onstage. They have the force of the unchanging, the eternal, there before the light finds them, there after the light departs, there as in nightmares, with no beginning and no end.

In the effort to summon such dreadful ministers – in rehearsals, in design sessions, in private communing – the production team begins to intuit their sources of power. Our quotidian nightmares attack us when we are most vulnerable – in sleep, in exhaustion, depression, or weakness. Therefore, to successfully subvert an alert and normally sanguine theatre audience Beckett's ghosts must first create states of susceptibility. As already suggested, the ghost's first great weapon is its inky domain, a blackness that, if held long enough, will destroy time, place, and community and force each spectator into herself. Abetting inwardness and further loosening her grip on reality is her inability to ground the image. Her eye cannot find its source or complete its outline. Even such apparently solid objects as the rocker or the white table and chairs fade into the night, their lower parts invisible, they and their occupants suspended in dim and fitful light. Light, in turn, intensifies destabilisation by offering the viewer little comfort or guidance. Beckett light does not shape action, define space, cue mood change, or focus meaning; nor does it collaboratively lead the viewer through the work's ebb and flow, beginnings and endings. Not only does it not help the viewer to receive, respond to, or understand the image; it seems to have no source outside the image. It seems, in fact, to emanate from the image toward the viewer, rather than the reverse. The result is that Beckett's ghosts glow in the dark, dimly or blindingly, and when they cease to glow one is left with the near certainty that they are still there, near us, always with us, capable of reappearing at any moment, as in *Play* and *Footfalls* they do.

Brought low by radically original and ruthlessly assaultive treatments of darkness and light, the viewer now drifts into timeless realms. The burning image begins to be felt as unshakable. Time stops. Pressed in by a seemingly endless and hellish present, the viewer is without control, without rescue, desperate for rest but unable to wake up. This experience, of course, exactly mirrors the experience of the performer, of the 'he' or 'she' ghosting that being, of the whispers, rustles, and murmurs ghosting the 'he' or 'she', and so on across 'all the dead voices' to the beginning of time. I shall return to some of the implications of this extraordinary equation. For now perhaps it is enough to dwell briefly on one other aspect of the image, as I see it.

It is intellectually nonconvertible. By this I mean that it cannot be understood, and thereby denatured, with reference to something else. The image does not enter, exit, move, change, interact with other images, or partake of larger symbolic visual patterns. It does not draw from our image bank or our well of cultural memory and so cannot be assimilated to visual habit or tamed through visual association. By forcing confrontation with itself and nothing else, it defeats meaning. It is just there. It *is*.

Ear

So far I have spoken only of the visual image in Beckett's later short plays. The sonic image is, if anything, even more problematic and terrifying than the visual, grounded in silence as the visual is in darkness – the silence both a threatening presence and a palpable absence, again destroying communion, concentrating being, yawning like a pit, creating extreme anxiety, and giving the sound that finally breaks it a mythological force. These sounds tend to be one of two kinds. Like the visual image, the sonic image is either assaultive or recessive. Sound is either used in furious and relentless attack, as a kind of racing, dazzling, shrieking, laughing, mesmerising logorrhoea, or it is used as a receding presence, an evanescence, a slow, quiet, even, toneless murmur, like the wraiths that twist through grief-stricken dreams, leaving traces on the heart but not on the memory.

Sound coalesces into language, and the language is of the simplest kind – unliterary, stripped of rhetoric, without metaphysics, with barely a nod to the great tradition, uninterested in ideas or ideals. In concrete words of one or two syllables the plays speak of love lost, love never gained, abandonment, death, the search for self, the torment of consciousness, childhood memories, the yearning for rest. But Beckett asks his performers to speak of these things without expressed feeling, and I would now like to offer a few thoughts on his request.

'Voices toneless. . . . Rapid tempo'. This direction, for *Play*, also sets the pattern for the works that follow it. Beckett's wishes are not always made clear on the page; sometimes they have to be discovered from the production history. In every case, however, it becomes apparent that the voice the audience hears, whether live or taped, is to speak faster than normal or slower than normal and is to remain – brief, specified moments excepted – 'toneless' or 'expressionless'. I think the success of the plays depends on these directions being respected. Whether one agrees with this view or not, it is undeniable that such drastic limitations evoke anxiety in performers, shock in audiences, and confusion in critics, perhaps because they fly in the face of the central performance tradition of Western theatre, the expressive actor.

The first comment I would make about imperatives such as 'expressionless' and 'toneless' is that they are less absolute and less lucid than they seem. Just as no person can rest a perfectly neutral gaze on another's face, no speech can be perfectly toneless, if only because there are two subjectivities involved. Similarly, *rapid* and *slow* are elastic terms. In order not to lose itself in a maze of seemingly equally valid rehearsal choices, the production team must therefore ask itself what these rather clumsy directions are trying to achieve.

As more productions have emerged and our experience with these plays has grown, the answer to this question becomes clearer. I think that Beckett is moving toward a treatment of *sound-as-image* that will exactly parallel and complement the visual image that each play sets before us. Sound-as-image should be distinguished from the notion of text-as-music, commonly used to describe Beckett's language. The latter carries with it overtones of cost-free eroticism, and, while eros is amply present in these works, it is not cost free, nor does it stem from a direct response to the performer's voice but, rather, from the sense of surrender that the inescapability of the work, as a whole, compels in the spectator. In my view the core purpose of Beckett's use of sound is to strike ear and brain with a sonic image as hard, fixed, and relentless as the visual image that accompanies it. Sound becomes an icon.

To realise the icon the performer's verbal delivery must acquire three characteristics: it must become an abstraction; it must be felt as possessing enormous magnitude; and it must cancel the audience's sentimental response to individual suffering. Sonic abstraction is achieved in one of two ways: through delivery so constantly rapid that it is initially unintelligible (*Not I*, *Play*) or through an even, unchanging rhythm slightly slower than normal (*Footfalls*, *Ohio Impromptu*, *Rockaby*). Magnitude is achieved more variously: the assaultive amplification in *Not I*; the unlocalised voice from the dark that becomes a racial memory of loss and desire; the instantaneous, puppetlike response to the demonic light in *Play*; and, in several works, the stillness and catastrophic silences that make us cling to sound as to a lifeline. Finally, even as the spectator begins to understand and react to the ghastly human story bleeding through each work's formal brilliance, the icon's relentless rhythms and underinflected voice enforce distance, reject sympathy for the speaker's plight (strictly, for the plight of the creature the speaker is describing), and so turn grief that is flowing toward the stage back upon the sender. In the process, sound-as-image/sound-as-icon desentimentalises, universalises, and focuses suffering, and therefore the awareness of suffering, away from a particular and perhaps dismissible life onto the life that each of us holds most precious, that each of us is condemned to live.

Once these essential structural dynamics are intuited in rehearsal it is not difficult for director and performer to arrive at decisions about intonation and tempo. A key to such decision making is the gradual awareness, more instinctive than deductive, that the scripts are misleading us by asking for a negativity in the performer – absence of expression/tone – whereas what Beckett is after is a positive and active creation, a mask of diamondlike hardness, brilliance, depth, and mystery.

The type of alienation achieved by this mask is, in my view, entirely original in the history of our medium. Unlike Brecht's distancing devices, which gather strength in proportion to the clarity and breadth of social vision and judgement they solicit from the viewer, Beckett's masks lead us inexorably inward and downward into darkness and personal chaos. How this sense of chaos is achieved I will speculate on in a moment. For now it is enough to see that, by first using image and narrative to invite sympathy for human distress and then, by formal means, blocking the release of that emotion, Beckett locks the spectator to his own consciousness. The spectator falls into a kind of horrified trance, trapped in a world not of his making but one in which he is absolutely implicated.

Chaos

Nightmares, by nature, are ambiguous, mysterious, threatening, obsessive – personifications of our desires and repositories of our deepest fears. What they are not are discursive, linear, explicit, and moralistic. Crowning his lifelong pursuit of a form that 'admits the chaos', Beckett finally arrives at works that successfully join the intense subjectivity of personal experience to a shape that 'accommodates the mess' and yet survives the demands of a gross and public medium.

How gather a ghost? How harness a haunting? Based only on my own experience with these plays, and offered most tentatively, I suggest a response along the following lines. Chaos is achieved in two interwoven and mutually reinforcing ways, which for argument's sake I will separate out. First, eye and ear subvert each other. Second, the art object self-destructs, forcing performer and spectator to confront each other personally in their unaccommodated nakedness.

Eye versus Ear

Extended darkness and silence break the communal bond and, by turning the spectator inward, isolate her. When the ghost finally appears it does so with such force that the spectator, condemned to deal with it alone, immediately admits it into her inner sanctum. As time passes, the apparition – itself unchanging, fixed, and monomaniacal but increasingly saturated with the play's tonal values of terror, grief, and loss – acquires the quality of an icon, starkly emblematic of one view of the human condition. I suggest it is at this stage, roughly two or three minutes into the performance, when the emblem is at the height of its power, that, paradoxically, the play is also in greatest peril of failure. For the spectator's conscious mind, having absorbed the shock, having noted with relief that sight and sound show no sign of changing, moves to defang the haunting – either by retreating into reductiveness and intellectualising the emblem down to 'a point of view' or by rejecting the feelings it evokes and so denying the validity of the emblem altogether. But it is also at this moment, I suggest, that Beckett's ghosts show just how malign they can be. The spectator becomes uneasily aware that sight and sound seem to be diverging, and that ground he had assumed to be stable is in fact shifting under his feet. In *Not I*, for example, the brilliance of Mouth burns the audience's eye from start to finish. First moment to last, all vision in the theatre is focused on that twelve square inches of palpitating redness. At first the accompanying sound is heard as babble, drone, buzz, clamour – sound and sight all of a piece. But gradually, as the ear adjusts to the furious pace, individual words detach themselves; patterns of repetition begin to register; screams, laughs, increasing panic, increasing vehemence begin to be subliminally absorbed, 'faster and faster' becomes clearer and clearer, until, miraculously, *both* the unitary impression of sound-as-image, words-as-babble, *and* the ghastly human story bleeding through are somehow suspended together in the spectator's shrinking soul.

The early stages of comprehension yield something like this: abandoned old woman, wretched life, lost her mind, poor thing, delusional, obsessive, that's life, poor thing. Very quickly, however, and in no particular order, Beckett's telegraphic spirals of repetition throw up clouds of questions. Who is 'she'? Who is the interlocutor whom 'she' can hear but who we cannot, who knows all about 'she', and who corrects, prompts, and asks 'she' unanswerable questions? This interlocutor is not 'she's' thoughts, for 'she' refers to and recounts her thoughts. Who is the one who laughs? Certainly not 'she', for 'she' makes it clear that her attempts at screams resulted in 'no sound of any kind . . . all silent as the grave'. If not 'she', then, is Mouth the laugher/screamer? If Mouth knows all about 'she', including the content of the unheard interlocutor's innermost promptings, how does Mouth achieve the distance necessary to mock 'she's' illusions and general ineptitude, and why is Mouth unable to demystify the 'buzzing', the 'dull roar' that torment 'she'? 'She's' 'stream of words' and 'beam . . . ferreting around' obviously echo what we hear and see. So is the visual/sonic stage image the inside of 'she's' mind?

Who, then, are we in the audience, we who also are 'straining to hear . . . make something of it', we who also have 'something begging in the brain . . . begging the mouth to stop', we who also make a 'quick grab and on . . . nothing there . . . on to the next', we who also keep 'trying to make sense of it . . . or make it stop', we who also have no idea, finally, 'what to try'? The gigantic and barely visible figure on stage who listens to Mouth and reacts first with anger and later despair to Mouth's failure to say, presumably, 'I', seems telepathically to be soliciting a different answer. Is this listener transmitting to Mouth or to 'she'? Is this listener a ghost of 'she's' interlocutor? Since we respond to Mouth's failures as the listener does, does the listener also embody us? Is Mouth 'she's' mouth as well as the performer's mouth? Is the expressionless performer, then, to be supposed to be personifying 'she', presenting Mouth, representing 'she', acting Mouth, being 'she', or none of the above? These are only a few of the questions that beat at us as we race to keep up with the ghosts before us. The pressure of the questions' accumulation, coupled with our intuition that they are unanswerable and the work unknowable, lead to fresh spirals of terror, terror now stemming less from the wretched simplicities of the life on view and more from the inescapable equation developing between 'she' and 'we'. The sonic image horrifies through its unrelenting fixity, even as it horrifies through its simultaneous self-destruction. Words spew out ceaselessly as a hedge against the dark, a lifeline to sanity, a bridge over chaos, even as they lead us inexorably into darkness, insanity, and chaos.

This example from *Not I* shows only one of the ways in which Beckett plays with the tension between the fixed and the dynamic. It is possible, in fact, that every one of these works uses it differently. In *Ohio Impromptu*, for example, I suggest that it is the sonic image that takes on the emblem's stony cast. Although a narrative, and therefore dynamic by definition, the slow, even telling of the inner story of deprivation and grief is so inexorable in its progress and so ineluctable in its outcome, that it acquires the force of a parable, the exemplary permanence of one of those bedtime stories that sum up the human condition. The visual image at first seems to parallel the sonic one – a still life of two identical old men at a table, in the heart of darkness, one reading out, the other listening to the story being told. Both images, the visual and the sonic, appear emblematic of a single vision, a black but nonetheless coherent and intelligible view of life. At the very end of the work, however, after all sound has ceased, the two ashen ghosts before us lift their heads from their hands and look directly at each other. It is on this tableau that darkness finally descends.

This mirror move, which is quite shocking in performance, acts like the opening of a dam, releasing in the spectators all the half-formed ambivalences and insecurities that they have suppressed under the melancholy spell of the narrative and the formal spell of an almost motionless *pas-de-deux*. Among the thoughts that flood the mind are: Are there two present at all? Is there not, rather, one? Is the reader an invention of the listener, called up to make fictional what would otherwise be an unendurable torment? Is the listener the suffering 'he' of the tale? Does the listener stand in the same relation to Beckett as the 'he' stands in relation to the listener? Is the work, then, about art rather than life, about the creative process itself, in keeping with the tradition of the Impromptu? If so, 'where are all these corpses from', whence these feelings of intense personal melancholy expressed by many members of the audience, why do we still see 'the dear face' and hear 'the unspoken words'? I suggest, in short, that the visual image at the end of *Ohio Impromptu*, one of the most powerful in the Beckett canon, subverts the play's emblematic dimension by once again dropping us into that floating world in which all we can cling to is the intuition that the less these works clarify the more nakedly and profoundly we respond to them.

Staying with this contradiction for a moment, I think it is precisely the tension between sight and sound, between the fixed and the dynamic, between emblem and chaos, that lifts Beckett out of the company of didacts into the realm of the greatest artists. But the trick succeeds by only a hair's breadth. Were both what one hears and what one sees to feel static (as they do, for example, when the plays are done at the wrong speed), were the emblem to hold firm, the works would not only feel too long, despite their brevity, but they could also be written off as hectoring moralisms, much in the manner of those medieval sermons with their cautionary death's-heads and pseudoprofound abstractions used to beat away life's complexities.

Being Perceived

The treachery between eye and ear is, in my view, one of the ways in which Beckett 'accommodates the mess' by finding a form for chaos. Another way, bound to the first, is through fictions that consume themselves and so bring performer and spectator into a unique and unbearable confrontation. Since this issue is of overriding concern to the performer, I will discuss it here from the performer's perspective.

The central performance dilemma of these plays, as I understand it, is the necessity for the performer to face an audience without any stable identity to rest upon. The performer does not know whether he or she is an actor, a character, or some form of transparency for an unknowable other. All that can be known with certainty is that a being in front of the stage is looking at and listening to a being on the stage. Nothing else can be asserted unequivocally, least of all the identity or function of the being on the stage, the being perceived.

The performer has no character to represent. The performer is asked only to look a certain way, sound a certain way, and, in that created and anonymous persona, tell a story about another being who is not present. Sometimes this absent being hears a voice, which, the story tells us, is the voice of still another, who in turn is absent even to the absent one, although the voice is heard by all – the absent one, the anonymous stage being, the performer, and the audience. After a few days at these altitudes performer and director feel the strongest urge to reclaim their sanity by assuming that there is a character there after all, a character without a name but playable all the same, that this character is none other than the 'he' or 'she' of the story, that the anonymous persona with 'the look' and 'the voice' is merely a disguise, and that the character's recourse to the third person is no more than a transparent effort to avoid implication in the pain of his or her own life. Unfortunately, these assumptions cannot be made. Even as one admits the suspicion that such an obvious psychologism as the last is far removed from the level of invention on display elsewhere in these pieces, one also makes the miserable discovery that the circular and self-consuming nature of each work's inner narrative is expressly designed to frustrate the assertion of identity. *Not I* thus comes into focus as the title of a play; a map of its physical workings (eye looking at mouth, not eye); a description of an obsession of the 'she' in its story; *and* a clear professional warning from playwright to performer that nothing is assumable.

The performer is now faced with the dilemma of having to live in public on several levels of selfhood without knowing what those levels are, how to gain access to them, or what they will do to the performer or to one another. This, of course, is also the dilemma faced by the anonymous onstage speaker, by the 'she'/'he' of the fiction, and, through extension and implication, by every receding level of consciousness, every ghost, present in the place of performance.

Among the implications of this equation of dilemmas are, I suggest, the following. Since the search for identity is the core action of tragedy; since the performer, the anonymous stage being, and the fictional 'he'/'she' are all involved in the search for identity; and since, by the nature of things and by the narrative shape of these plays, their search is steeped in suffering, all three partake of the tragic impulse and live in the tragic world. (This said despite Beckett's obvious distance from several defining characteristics of the traditional genre.) Second, because the search is the same for all three, the distinction between the real world (of the performer) and the world of the fiction is cancelled. Reality and imagination become indistinguishable, with the further implication that the inner world is all. Finally, and paradoxically, there is the strong indication that the opposite is also true, that, since selfhood is not achieved at the innermost level, a failure that radiates outward to the performer, the performer can never reach an accommodation with her doppelganger, the mysterious stage being who lives in her body and speaks through her voice.

Of course, none of this is understood in this way in rehearsal. Much of it is not understood at all. What *is* sensed by every performer I have directed in these extraordinary works is the centrality of the issue of identity – the performer's identity. Who am I? Let us now suppose that means are found to create the visual and verbal images necessary to summon Beckett's ghosts. The nightmare begins; the 'old terror of night' lays hold on us again. The performer, at full tilt, in mid-flight, is now doing the following things, all more or less simultaneously: spinning out the sonic patterns of tempo, volume, and pitch that most securely walk the tightrope between subliminal intelligibility and sound-as-image, sound-as-'buzzing'; opening psychic doors to the narrative's spell so that body and voice will accurately and organically respond to the play's 'charge'; conversely, keeping psychic distance between self and the stranger occupying self; in consequence, successfully sustaining the mask of blank face and unvarying delivery, except where specified; and, finally, picking up visual cues – number of steps, curve of body, swing of turn (*Footfalls*), upward angle of mouth for audience sight line (*Not I*), absolutely motionless head

(*Play*), varying speed and force of hand movement (*Ohio Impromptu*), rate and distance of head drop (*Rockaby*), rate and distance of head lift (*Ohio Impromptu*), painful maintenance of unblinking gaze for specified and extended intervals (several plays), and so on.

Skilled performers can do all of these things, despite the very great psychic and physical toll they exact. The central performance issue is not a technical one. Rather it is structural, having to do with the basic architecture of these plays, and, not surprisingly, it stays focused on the unresolvable dilemma of the performer's identity. Briefly, it is my view that the bedrock purpose of Beckett's final body of work is to expose the nakedness and terror of human existence by exposing a naked and terrified human being on a stage. Since the only human being on the stage is the performer, it is the performer who is the final focus of each work. I think that the stripping of the performer is done like this.

First, Beckett denies the performer a character to impersonate, a fictional identity. The performer is therefore immediately aware at some level that the audience will be looking at and listening to him personally. He reacts with anxiety, fear. Beckett anticipates this and offers him a mask that slightly abstracts him, providing minimal privacy: his face is not visible, or parts of his body are not visible, or his face becomes a mask, or his voice becomes a mask. The performer feels a bit safer and, although still uneasy, recognises the trappings of art and takes the bait. Beckett now asks the masked performer to tell a story about another person's life. This story is full of grief but so simple, so typical, and so seemingly ineluctable that performer and audience adopt its emotional field as their own. And yet the performer's mask and the *fact* of the narrative keep the whole thing within the precincts of culture, of aesthetic consumption, of fictional suffering shaped by form and filtered through art. Very soon, however, the story begins to disintegrate. It turns inward and consumes itself, or it accelerates toward the point of flying apart, or it declines toward the point of stasis or death.

In every case the fictional inner being, the subject of the story, threatens to disappear or die. I suspect that the performer senses this looming disaster before the spectator does. The performer now bends every effort to prevent an outcome that would not only signal his professional demise, for he would have nothing to send to the audience, but that would also, in some obscurely sensed fashion, implicate him personally in the nightmare he has been ghosting, by removing the prop of art. As the nightmare advances, therefore, the performer's refusal to relinquish the third-person voice becomes felt as an act of will, necessary to the *performer*'s sanity. Instead of the performer remaining a transparency for 'he's' or 'she's' nightmare, the nightmare becomes a transparency for the performer's suffering. Once this shift has taken place the content of the interior narrative becomes unimportant; almost anything will do. The audience's focus has now shifted from the 'he' or 'she' of the story to the actual suffering being onstage in front of it. A consequence of this shift is that both performer and spectator are stripped of fiction's camouflage. The performer is now spiritually and psychologically naked; the spectator is now an enforced voyeur of a human being in extremis. The horror for the performer is the exposure of his nakedness and terror to the spectator. The horror for the spectator is the exposure of his own nakedness and terror himself.

Freedom

There is the belief among many theatre people that Beckett's plays are uninteresting to embark on because the prescriptiveness of his stage directions places unacceptable limits on artists' creativity. It is true that Beckett, particularly in his final body of work, robs us of certain freedoms. But I think it is also true that in exchange he offers us other freedoms, which not only liberate performers and spectators but also, by profoundly recasting the relationship between them, liberate the core energies of theatre itself. Therefore, I approach the recent controversy pitting directors' prerogatives against writers' rights less for its intrinsic importance than for the light it can shed on the seemingly inexhaustible possibilities of these marvellous and revolutionary works.

Does a director have the right to ignore Beckett's stage directions? This issue reached an apotheosis of sorts in the recent donnybrook in Boston over *Endgame*. Apparent even at the time of this bitter dispute was the writer's desperate but inevitable futile attempt to claim ownership of a theatrical *event* after the *script* or that event had left his hands. I think that such a claim cannot be sustained and therefore that, in principle, the theatre was quite within its rights to stage *Endgame* as it saw fit. A script is not a theatrical event. It is a blueprint for an event. Art is not engineering. Artists are not machines. The animation of the blueprint involves hundreds, thousands, of acts of cocreation by director, designer, performer, each such act being inevitably conditioned by the differing personalities and life histories of the artists involved, by the circumstances of performance, by the pressure of the cultural moment, and so on. To say so much is to dwell in truisms; so, let us leave this level and move from the issue of ownership to the issue of intention.

Are a writer's performance intentions knowable? Can Beckett's own productions of his works be duplicated by other production teams? Was Beckett necessarily the best director of his own plays? I suggest that the answer to each of these questions is no. Even directors with the best will in the world, who study a work (and its surrounding literature), who examine tapes of Beckett's own approaches to it and talk to people who remember what Beckett did to it in rehearsal, come out at the end knowing little more about bringing it to life than they did when they read the script initially. This is not to say that this kind of preparation need not be done; it should. It can broaden context, give insight, save rehearsal time, and forestall performance errors (the approach to tempo in *Not I*, for example, crucial to that work's life, is not indicated in the script but is discoverable from the criticism and from the play's production history). Rather, it is only to suggest that the word on the page carries the stamp of failure the moment it leaves the writer's pen, for it is already an imperfect reflection of the maelstrom in the mind that gave it birth; that that maelstrom is irrecoverable, the word its only trace; that those words, if they are to find embodiment, must create fresh turbulence in the minds of the cocreating performers; that that turbulence will be different in every particular, and in every performer, from the original but will partake of its essence; that the embodied stage vision will create new turmoil in the audience; that

that turmoil will be different for each spectator; and that it is in that final transaction – single being to single being – that all value resides. The distance between this end and the first mover crosses many generations of intervening activity. It is a great distance, which no amount of 'fidelity', 'accuracy', or appeal to 'original' versions can reduce. It is a distance that is part and parcel of the theatrical process, inherent in the act of theatre. Our only defences against intolerable outcomes – dead, reductive, stupid, self-regarding outcomes – are what they have always been: sensitivity, culture, openness, discernment, and, in the case of Beckett, those prior deposits in our blood that expel pretenders. There are no shortcuts.

That said, it is necessary to add that I have seen no production of *Play* or any work written after it that has been improved by a significant departure from the writer's wishes. The reason for this, in my view, is unique to late Beckett, unique to the nature of these particular works.

While directors and performers have no option but to respond freshly and personally to any script, they encounter in these scripts formal and structural devices that are, as far as I know, entirely new in the history of theatre. The central difference, as I see it, is that in theatre as we have known it so far, including Beckett's own before *Play*, reality onstage is coextensive with reality offstage, the reality of the world, whereas in late Beckett reality onstage is itself and nothing else, sealed off from the world. Characters do not enter from somewhere and leave to go somewhere else; stage space does not connect in the mind's eye with the world's space; stage sight and sound are not experienced as fragments of, referents to, or even symbolic stand-ins for, the sights and sounds of the world. On the contrary, the visual and sonic images that appear in late Beckett seem to me to be the first wholly successful examples in theatre of the great modernist project: to make art that, in formal terms, is not about life but, rather, in Flaubert's words, 'about nothing but itself'. These images – parts of the human body, light, darkness, sound, silence – appear to us as flat, opaque, non-referential, defiant of interpretation and void of meaning. They are simply and completely *present*, sealed with the audience in the here and now.

If one accepts this view, its most obvious implication is that the stage directions, which solicit the images, *are* the play and that a director or performer who adds to, subtracts from, or alters them in any appreciable way is not tinkering with interpretation but, rather, creating something different, not by Beckett. So, certain prerogatives are undeniably sacrificed. However, far profounder in my view than such a loss of freedom are the new freedoms Beckett offers in exchange, freedoms that flow from the type of interdependence between performer and spectator that he enforces, an interdependence that I think has no parallel in modern theatre and that lies not only at the core of these works but at the core of theatre itself.

Implicated in an emotional field of suffering, loss, terror, and death – denied release of those feelings, stripped of character, stripped of identity, stripped even of the act of imitation, yet condemned to remain exposed in front of another – the performer lives only through the spectator.

Hallucinatedly fixed on shimmering ghosts, forbidden under-standing by self-consuming narratives, cut off from community by darkness or silence, unbalanced by the sub-rosa treachery between sight and sound, prevented from thinking through, with, or about the work, denied any form of message, extractable idea, or separable content, locked to the image in an inescapable embrace, the spectator lives only through the performer.

Performer and spectator experience each other viscerally, sensually, intuitively, immediately, and profoundly intimately. Able to survive only through each other, always alone yet always 'tied', performer and spectator finally discover what it means to be human. This experience, like the opening of a furnace door, is the heart of our art form, theatre's blazing core. Beckett arrived at it at the end of his life, walked into the flames, and, like alchemists of old, transmuted chaos, grief, and failure into a kind of joy.

Assistant Professor in Drama at Trinity College Dublin and co-founder and deputy director of the Samuel Beckett Summer School, **Nicholas Johnson** *has published in the* Journal of Beckett Studies, Forum Modernes Theater, Theatre Research International, *and* Museum Ireland. *He has also directed and translated the work of German writers Ernst Toller, Franz Kafka and Max Frisch.*

A Spectrum of Fidelity, an Ethic of Impossibility: Directing Beckett

Among his many distinguishing features, Samuel Beckett is notable for the wide range of genres in which he wrote, often redefining the rules of each form as he worked. The student or scholar who wished to approach him comprehensively would be expected to work with, or at least be aware of, his literary criticism, poetry, short prose, novels, plays, radio scripts, film and television plays, and now his letters (which he seemed to treat as an art in and of themselves). The emphasis among scholars in recent years has unmistakably been on an archival Beckett and the so-called 'grey canon',[1] with the publication of the first volumes of his collected letters, the launch of the Beckett Digital Manuscript Project, and the publication of some of his notebooks. Even the new Faber editions of his collected works draw on the archives and draft materials for 'authoritative' revisions to previously published editions, contributing hugely to the clarity of texts on which future scholarship will be based. This field-defining work has emanated mainly from departments of literature, sometimes in English and sometimes in French, and it has benefited from disciplines as diverse as Philosophy, Religion, Comparative Literature, History, and Media Studies. Drama departments and practitioners of Beckett's theatre, although dominant in the first generation of Beckett scholars and still visible in the research field, are clearly a minority in the conferences and publications of recent decades.

This scholarly focus on the prose and manuscripts does not change the fact that for the wider public, Beckett became and remains a household name largely because of his work in drama, in particular

Waiting for Godot; his identity as a novelist is secondary, if known to the average playgoer at all. This creates a disjunction between the academic discussion and the public perception of Beckett, and this gap remains a central problematic of his legacy. The director, as a figure who researches in scholarly and textual material from the past but then selects, frames, and disseminates Beckett to an audience in the now, inhabits a zone where these academic and public perceptions intersect. This essay will position the director as a guide who can help us to explore some of the theoretical and practical tensions that animate these texts as a result. While the discussion will move freely across genre and draw on some historical examples and past scholarship in this area, the main focus will be on issues arising from the present *event* of Beckett in performance, not the *object* of the texts. Indeed, it will show that this division – between object and event – remains central to the cultural reception of Beckett, both in and out of the academic discourse, not least because it illuminates an elemental conflict within late capitalist society.[2]

Aside from this appeal to the public consciousness of Beckett as dramatist, I will argue at a deeper level that the Beckett we all encounter today is itself a performance, unavoidably bounded within and changing with time. Reception, whether achieved through reading a book or hearing a talk, is a lived and embodied experience. This means that to focus solely on the origin of texts, to seek a 'definitive' at all, mistakenly assigns a stability that Beckett's art constantly undermines at every level. It is a truism in performance studies that there can be no original version of a theatre production and that repetition is impossible. I wish to extend this argument to novel and film as well. We mistakenly expect that their status as physical objects or experiences within the user's control renders them somehow more fixed or constant than a play. The problem with this view is not only that other variations exist (as the new editions show us), but also that the reader is changing, along with the time and place that condition the reader's encounter with the text. The text can never be read the same way twice. It is this mutability that performance of Beckett's prose and other trans-generic adaptations draw on, using the theatre as a resonator for an instability already inscribed in Beckett's narrative approach. It is for this reason that performance should be thought of as more than something that applies narrowly to Beckett's drama: performance is a philosophical tool that illuminates the ways in which text continues to live through praxis, through encounters that happen between bodies, spaces, and time.

The Director's Role

To understand the Virgil who will lead us in this purgatorial terrain, it is also necessary to define what is meant by the term 'director'. This task is not simple; there is little agreement on the director's proper role across or within theatre cultures. Historically, the single director as a unifying creative force is a product of the twentieth century, overturning prior models of the actor/manager or producer/patron. At one level, this change was borne of convenience, given the increase of theatrical technologies (especially electric light) and the resulting need for an overseeing manager of the expanding potential choices. At another level, this central figure manifests an impulse that recurs throughout aesthetic modernism: the neo-Romantic earnestness of the visionary 'new man', legible to different degrees in the manifestos of the Futurists, Symbolists, Surrealists, and Expressionists. The rise of the *auteur* in the post-war New Wave cinema cemented the change of the director from a purely functional organiser to an artist.[3] It is telling that specific training for theatre directors did not enter university education until the second half of the twentieth century, and that it continues to be taught largely through apprenticeship, particularly in Europe. The difficulties that Beckett had with directors as his career progressed mirrored this broader change in the discipline, as more directors asserted their prerogatives as interpretive artists in their own right and naturally came into conflict with authorial stricture. This tendency toward conflict is built into the modern idea of direction. The fact that most theatre at a professional scale requires the labour of multiple artists means that the director is always in the role of a negotiator, and that the skill set of personnel management and communication is at least as important as an artistic objective; there are also unavoidable power dynamics in play that can exacerbate conflicts that arise within every process.

My working definition of direction is twofold: first, that it is a necessary stage of *mediation* between author and audience; second, that the director is the maker of a *conceptual process*. This paradigm retains the interpretive artistry of the director, but it weights the tasks of vision and articulation equally. When I teach directing, I recommend that each choice be judged in terms of its 'why' and its 'how'. I have found that many young directors prioritise either the role of creativity or the role of control, while the challenge is to integrate them. There is a further temptation, connected again to the triumph of object over event, to focus on the product rather than the process. The French term for 'director' that was most commonly used in Beckett's era was *metteur en scène*, a term that suggests a link to painting: the director's task is that of making an image by *putting* things in the scene. Unlike brushes and oils, however, actors can talk back. Directors who have a clear idea of 'how they want it to look at the end' often find that the challenge occurs in explaining why, or in communicating to actors how they might achieve a desired state or effect. This is why the second part of my definition, the 'conceptual process', is essential: the ethics of dealing with living artists as material demands that conditions, rules, expectations, and methods are internally consistent throughout a rehearsal period, if the director is not merely to become a kind of dictator. The directors who might be grouped under the rubric of the postmodern are often the makers of systems or games in which actors inhabit a process and – at least in theory, although notably not always in practice – retain a large degree of freedom in creation. There is a natural friction between this contemporary conception of the director and the more high modernist, precise, and writerly tendencies of Beckett.

This writer unmistakably has a reputation, sustained and extended by the Beckett Estate after his death, as problematic for directors who see their main role toward text as the obligation to innovate. Although it was not the first such controversy in Beckett's career, the struggle with the American Repertory Theatre in 1984 over JoAnne Akalaitis's production of *Endgame* is an emblematic one. Beckett's stage directions call for a *'Bare interior. Grey light. Left and right back, high up, two small windows, curtains drawn. Front right, a door*.[4] The 1984 production, designed by Douglas Stein, was set much more specifically in the remnants of an underground tunnel, with large steel girders implying windows and two life-size burnt-out subway cars. In spite of the addition of music by Philip Glass, a further sticking point in the legal wrangling that followed an attempted injunction by Grove Press, the dialogue (including pauses) was rigorously accurate with Beckett's text. Like an ancient tribal trauma, this public fight has mutated the DNA of all Beckett directors, because it introduced a binarism that cannot now be revoked. The language of the programme insert, agreed as an out-of-court settlement and distributed to audiences with the first page of Beckett's play, is striking in its emotional and personal tone. It continues to colour the contemporary debate as one notionally about fidelity. Beckett wrote, in part:

> Any production of *Endgame* which ignores my stage directions is completely unacceptable to me. My play requires an empty room and two small windows. The American Repertory Theatre production which dismisses my directions is a complete parody of the play as conceived by me. Anybody who cares for the work couldn't fail to be disgusted by this.

Robert Brustein, artistic director of the theatre, wrote his rebuttal on the same page, a portion of which reads:

> To threaten any deviations from a purist rendering of this or any other play – to insist on strict adherence to each parenthesis of the published text – not only robs collaborating artists of their interpretive freedom but threatens to turn the theatre into a waxworks. Mr Beckett's agents do no service either to theatrical art or to the great artist they represent by pursuing such rigorous controls.[5]

This represented an origin moment for two camps of Beckettians, each claiming to be more faithful to Beckett than the other: one group stands up for the object (the published text), and one for the event (the moment of performance). It is often forgotten that Beckett knew everything about this production from hearsay, and never saw it; the actual agents in the legal fight were the publisher and the producer, the solitary stability of the book against the collaborative, messy live.

A Spectrum of Fidelity

It is at this dense crossroads – between the publishers and producers, the scholars and the public, the book and the play, the past and the future – that the director of Beckett stands, with loyalty divided between a private experience of Beckett's vision and the demands of a present, living actor or audience. To put this conflict a different way: for the director there might be an impulse to create that remains in the free realm of thought, but in the constraints of the real world of theatrical production, there is an imperative to communicate that thought (not to mention the quotidian demands that one must finish on time and under budget). In my own directing practice, I have called this space of decision the 'spectrum of fidelity'.

Author  Audience

Figure 1: The spectrum of fidelity

It is not impossible to be faithful both to the original author and to the present audience. It is helpful to see each performance as a compromise along this continuum, pulled by both poles, and to use this spectrum as a means of describing more precisely what we mean by a functional or successful performance. We can imagine a performance that attempts complete authorial fidelity, but like so much in Beckett's universe, this attempt is an *a priori* failure. We can also imagine a 'pure innovation' performance that attempts to discard the past, and focus on the present audience alone. This too would be of questionable value, and at its extremity would suggest a departure from Beckett altogether. In popular consciousness and the legal history of cases brought by the Beckett Estate or the publishers, this challenge may seem to manifest as the difference between 'faithful' and 'unfaithful' iterations, or perhaps more accurately *adaptations*, of Beckett's drama. I eschew this terminology in part because I don't see a difference on this spectrum between faithful or unfaithful, both of which are oriented exclusively in relation to the author and to the text as fixed object. I wish to allow the possibility, aligned with the tradition of Brustein and 'Beckett as event', that a piece being unfaithful to tradition might be faithful to innovation at the same time, and that these two are inseparably and dialectically linked, what Beckett might have called a pseudocouple. This introduces another way of seeing the director's task, which is to place the living text along a spectrum of time:

Tradition ◄━━━━━━━━━━━━━━━━━━━━━━━━► Innovation

Figure 2: The spectrum of time

Tradition rests upon the past, while innovation creates development focused on the future. Performance, however, occurs in the now, in a continuously advancing and ungraspable present. For the director, the moment of performance forces a choice that could be expressed as a balance, an uneasy coexistence, of tradition and innovation.

It is worth noting as well that the borderland between tradition and innovation is highly patrolled by competing interests, whether individuals or cultural authorities. Collaboration, practicality, and artistic exigencies will always transform a play as it enters the public discourse, a fact that Beckett understood well when he was directing his own plays.[6] As manuscript, it is private; as play, it becomes public, and at this moment 'the terms of its ownership alter and are contested'.[7] The Beckett Estate has made it extremely clear where it stands on the question of legal versus aesthetic ownership. Edward Beckett, the writer's nephew and head of the Estate, uses the metaphor of music to make the case for his protective ethos:

> There are more than fifteen recordings of Beethoven's late string quartets in the catalogue, every interpretation different, one from the next, but they are all based on the same notes, tonalities, dynamic and tempo markings. We feel justified in asking the same measure of respect from Samuel Beckett's plays.[8]

This statement is deeply revealing of the text-based ontology put forward by the estate, a vision of the drama – or even the performed prose – which ignores the phenomenology of the event. The analogy to music, although one to which Beckett often had recourse and one that can only be said to help a director, cannot be probed very deeply until it falls apart. The question has never been about whether changes from the original document will occur. Not only are such changes the essence of performative aesthetics, whether in music or theatre, but there is also no such original. The published texts, protected although they are by copyright law, are not mutually consistent, so no analogue exists to the Beethoven score of this example. The extensive body of research into Beckett's drafting and self-translation process, to say nothing of the changes introduced when he was directing himself, leave each interpreter an enormous number of possible 'faithful' choices within tradition, before even entering the realm of innovation.

It is here that the final dialectic of the director comes into play on a spectrum of methodology, responding to the issues raised by genre and the twenty-first century Beckett Studies community with which this essay began. Mirroring the oscillations along the continuum of past and future is an internal disciplinary debate that posits a type of binary of methodologies, often making what has been a vibrant and complicated symbiosis in the history of the field into a more explicitly confrontational and simple binary:

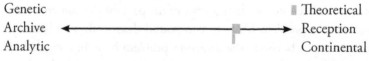

Genetic		Theoretical
Archive	⟵————————⟶	Reception
Analytic		Continental

Figure 3: The spectrum of methodology

On the one side, this thinking goes, there is a genetic approach based in archival and empirical analysis. This group comes often from English departments, focuses more on prose, and has a great deal to say about the specifics of origins of Beckett's writing. Some adherents of the archival approach have expressed its superiority in terms of Analytic philosophy.[9] On the other side, there is a language-based,

usually Continental philosophical approach, somewhat more concerned with theoretical description and deconstruction, in which
– although it rarely describes itself this way – a concern with cultural
reception over textual production is visible. This is more common in
drama departments, among those who study the plays and films, and
of course among practitioners.

Again, however, it is the figure of the director who reveals just how
layered and linked these apparent 'camps' remain, because the task
of making a play demands equal facility across the spectrum. Absent
any research in the archival Beckett, a director reduces the calling
of this task to a set of arbitrary decisions; fixation on this history,
however, attenuates the contemporary expression and thereby the
audience experience. The director must hold a dual consciousness
in order to make a play that happens *in the present*. Nowhere
is this more evident than in the plays that have a technological
dimension. The clearest example is in *Krapp's Last Tape*, which calls
unmistakably for a reel-to-reel recorder (cutting-edge when the play
was written), but the first stage direction of which is 'A late evening
in the future'.[10] If this were a novel or a film, fixed in text alone, an
audience would tolerate a version of the future which is now the past,
as it does with Orwell's *1984* or Kubrick's *2001*. But theatre does
not have the liberty that comes from textual stability; a theatrical
future is *always* the future, constantly being reinterpreted so that
the audience of now understands it as the future. The analogue
technology of *Krapp's Last Tape*, impossible to excise from the
script, has become a faulty signifier of the past for the contemporary
audience, a problem likely to compound drastically in a hundred
more years or beyond. The director's problem here, in a nutshell, is
about fidelity: one must either disrupt the time in which the play is
set, or disrupt the prop that is called for, as the two become more
and more incompatible. Ideally a solution will be discovered that
answers both issues, but this clearly requires interventions of the
kind that a purely authorial fidelity or text-focused methodology
cannot allow.[11] What is required, in fact, is the assertion of certain
freedoms: to experiment, to fail, to interpret, to choose. If there is
an ethics for a Beckett director, a set of right actions that precede

the practical choices of time, space, bodies, narration, or style, these verbs might be a good place to begin.

An Ethic of Impossibility

At this point it may begin to seem that being a Beckett director is not unlike being a Beckett character: trapped between contradictory or unreachable alternatives, surrounded by troublesome objects, grasping for the ideal but condemned to live in the material, drifting into consolations of music or mathematics – anything to escape habit, the 'great deadener'. In the face of these genuine difficulties, it would not be unheard of to say, as Didi and so many others do, 'I can't go on'. But let us remember that Beckett's terrain is purgatorial, not infernal, and that there is always the troublesome comma that follows 'I can't go on', right before the words 'I'll go on'.[12] The solutions to going on are, in fact, innumerable (if unnamable), and in the act of pushing ahead after impossibility has been admitted, the director of Beckett is enacting a uniquely Beckettian logic.

This riddle is posed by director Xerxes Mehta, in the midst of the volume *Directing Beckett*, an indispensable collection of interviews and essays with practitioners from around the world:

> The prescriptiveness of Beckett's stage directions, especially in the short plays he wrote toward the end of his life, appear to leave the director with little to do. This is, in fact, an illusion. The deeper the director, designers, and performers venture into these works, the more they realise that almost everything is unknown, and perhaps unknowable.[13]

Mehta's insight reveals more than just the mathematical and philosophical fact that precise limits can contain boundless freedom. It shows an understanding of performance as a philosophical tool that Beckett was wielding in service of his wider vision, with stunning specificity that did not waver even as it crossed so many genres. No matter what practical difficulties arise when one attempts to direct Beckett, there seems to be an indomitable will among those artists drawn to Beckett to witness his thought, even though it means weeks of grappling with minutely detailed stage directions and demanding text. Especially in the late plays, actors are forced into frightening and uncomfortable human experiences not dissimilar from those lived by their characters. Analogously, the Beckett director is pressed into circumstances not unlike the author, as revealed through his archival notebooks: trying but failing to count steps, sketch bodies, and shape light. All the human struggles in black boxes and university studios and grand houses and national theatres around the world, the aftershocks of Beckett's own 'siege in the room', exist solely to make the *event* of his thought live for a present audience. The problem of 'how' is hard enough without figuring out 'why' one might do this, but because the director has already been defined as the one who must ask (if not answer) both questions, the remaining discussion will attempt to articulate a *reason* for directing Beckett in the theatre.

As clearly emerges from the history of controversies over stage directions or casting choices, Beckett's favourite directors (Roger Blin, Alan Schneider) were strongly on the authorial end of the fidelity spectrum. Beckett had a much lower opinion of those who, in his view, deviated from his instructions. He is quoted by Jonathan Kalb as saying in conversation, 'I detest this modern school of directing', for the reason that 'to these directors the text is just a pretext for their own ingenuity'.[14] This critique reflects an anxiety with the deconstructive literary theory that surrounded Beckett in post-war Paris, as well as a rejection of the 'death of the author' posited by Roland Barthes, although by the 1980s (when this conversation took place) it was almost an article of faith. Now that the author is actually dead, what has changed?

According to Herbert Blau, the founder of the San Quentin Drama Workshop and one of the most innovative directors who was close to Beckett, not as much as one might expect: Despite all theory, a lot of people still have this incredible investment in the Master's voice. This Master has given us, however, the conceptual ground for doing precisely what he didn't want us to do.[15] Following from Blau, if a director properly understands Beckett's project as one of the most radically interventionist and innovative *oeuvres* of the century, it is difficult to be content with repetition. If a director understands the depth of his critiques of order, unity, language, violence, and complicity, emerging as they did from the weight of radical evil in the European twentieth century, this is a hard lesson to forget. Finally, if a director understands the theatre itself, then he or she will know that it is impossible *not* to intervene, and innovation (etymologically, to 'make new') is a phenomenological fact of the live. Here again the director is presented with a contradiction well aligned with Beckett's own aesthetics. Beckett wrote in 1949 that instead of going 'a little further along a dreary road', he preferred 'the expression that there is nothing to express, nothing with which to express, nothing from which to express, no power to express, no desire to express, together with the obligation to express'.[16] The properly 'Beckettian' director, then, is the director who has internalised the obligation to express, together with the impossibility of expression. It is the director who wishes, like the painters that Beckett admired, to depart from the 'plane of the feasible' and go on. Each work by Beckett is, in fact, a portal into the abyss. The director's task is merely to teach a cast how to guide an audience into this chasm, into 'another compartment', to give to others the sense that there is, as Gogo has it, 'no lack of void'.[17] This void should not be viewed as a negative category, nor as a lack or absence of something positive, nor as 'absurd', as so many have mistakenly classified it in the Anglophone world. The void here, as Alain Badiou calls it in his philosophy, is 'the proper name of being'.[18] It is the high calling of the director to devise an occasion in which this insight can be imparted to others, in a one-on-one conversation with hundreds of people at once.

The future trajectory of directing Beckett is unmistakably toward the audience end of the spectrum of fidelity, flowing toward greater openness to experimentation in service to the living and changing thought of Beckett. Indeed, an experimental stream has been active since the works first came to be, and it is clearly a myth that the author, the Beckett Estate, or the texts themselves are fundamentally anti-innovation. More tragically, perhaps, the restrictions remain as inconsistent and mercurial as Beckett was in his lifetime, affecting some of the work some of the time. This will likely remain a natural feature of the landscape in the years before 2059, when (according to the current laws, which are not guaranteed to stand) Beckett enters the public domain. Even now, however, the plays are produced in new contexts and new languages, for new bodies and with new meanings that accrue easily precisely because Beckett left so much open. Adaptations have flourished, even if some of it stays underground, with many artists taking Beckett's prose and film to the stage, others taking stage to film, and still others experimenting radically with digital space and art installation. Events that take account of a fluid, moving Beckett are beginning to multiply, with a large community of Beckett scholars attending conferences, the creation of a Samuel Beckett Summer School, and the nascent Enniskillen Festival and Samuel Beckett Laboratory in Ireland. These events have already begun to form a substantial community of interest around a living idea of this writer.

The challenge of directing Beckett today is that one does so in a society heavily weighted toward the object and away from the event, with legal rights heavily weighted toward those who own the object. Theatre's lasting power is precisely its apparent weakness: that it cannot be distributed or reproduced, and therefore cannot be wholly commodified. Theatre is founded on empty spaces, ghosts, and traces, and thus remains an exceptionally powerful resonator for Beckett's thought.

Professor of English at Xavier University, **Graley Herren** *is the author of* Samuel Beckett's Plays on Film and Television *(Palgrave/Macmillan, 2007). In addition to his excellent study of Beckett's teleplays, Herren has published numerous articles on Beckett and other modern playwrights and novelists. He serves on the executive board for the Samuel Beckett Society, and edits the Society's newsletter,* The Beckett Circle.

Beckett on Television, Beckett on Love: A Response to Badiou

Throughout his career Samuel Beckett issued some exceedingly grim pronouncements on love. In his first book he praised Proust's work for its unsparing depiction of love: 'Surely in the whole of literature there is no study of that desert of loneliness and recrimination that men call love posed and developed with such diabolical unscrupulousness'.[19] Elsewhere in the same book, he remorselessly asserts, 'We are alone. We cannot know and we cannot be known'.[20] Beckett's own early fiction strives to out-Proust Proust in its diabolical depiction of love, with character after character condemned to solitude following their failed attempts to know and to be known. Even in a novella with the nominally encouraging title *First Love*, the narrator declares, 'What goes by the name of love is banishment'.[21] The outlook remains equally discouraging in Beckett's dramatic works. When it comes to love, the stage characters – whether bottled in ashbins, buried in mounds, or stuffed in urns, and despite clinging to tape machines, pacing floors, and rocking in chairs – are all consigned to a remarkably singular fate: as Mouth sums it up in *Not I*, 'no love . . . spared that'.[22]

Yet still they persist. If anything, the longing for love becomes even more plaintive in Beckett's later work, and nowhere is this more evident than in his plays for television. Although Beckett denounced the whole business of love as a sucker's game from the start, the tantalising lure that it might somehow be achieved continually motivates his protagonists. No sooner is the possibility closed by one character than it is reopened by the next, picking the scab off an old wound that refuses to heal. Oblivious to the unremitting failure of their predecessors on page and stage, the teleplay protagonists express their desperate desire with special urgency. Taken as a whole, the teleplays constitute a compact but densely suggestive meditation on the problem of love. Guided by rigorous philosophical standards of interrogation, Beckett uses his teleplays as an innovative forum for reconsidering (to borrow Raymond Carver's famous phrase) 'what we talk about when we talk about love'. These pieces dramatise fundamental questions posed by love: What relationship is possible and desirable between self and other? To what lengths will one go in pursuit of the elusive other? What obstacles lie in the path? How viable are the chances for success? In trying to answer these questions, the teleplays offer small but potent samples of the bitter love potions Beckett spent a career distilling.

It is beyond my present scope to provide a thorough overview of Beckett's background in philosophy or the various philosophical problems to which his work responds. A brief explanation of one especially key concept is important at the outset, however, to appreciate the philosophical context for his treatment of love: the concept of 'the Other'. One can begin by thinking of the Other as that which lies beyond the Self, but this rudimentary definition only takes us so far; a full portrait of the Other in modern and postmodern discourse is far more complex. Although the term is rooted in actual interactions with another person or group, its conceptual (capitalised) form always encompasses broader ideas governing all interactions, real or hypothetical, with all persons, known or unknown. Some psychological formulations of the Other understand it primarily as an imaginary construct, based upon the external world but then internalised within the Self, and there shaping identity and behaviour (e.g., Sigmund Freud's 'super-ego', Melanie Klein's 'internal objects', and Jacques Lacan's 'imago'). More political formulations, like Edward Said's 'Orientalism', emphasise the Other as an ideological construct by one powerful group in an attempt to demonise or belittle another group, thereby asserting the former's perceived superiority and justifying its domination over the latter, as in the West's centuries-long distortions of the East. From still another perspective, postmodern ethicists like Emmanuel Lévinas and the later Jacques Derrida emphasise the Other's unassailable 'alterity' (that is, its absolute 'otherness'). By this understanding the Self can never fully know or assimilate the Other, in other words, can never convert the Other into 'the Same'. Nonetheless, the Self remains bound in an indebted position of responsibility to the Other, a relationship sometimes referred to as the 'ethics of alterity'. As should be obvious from even this cursory introduction, different theoretical approaches ascribe distinctly different functions to the Other. All of these diverse schools of thought agree, however, that the Other plays an integral role in the composition of the Self. For better or worse, Self and Other are inextricably linked through their ceaseless oscillating interactions. This primary encounter determines the parameters of personal identity, social interaction, political engagement, ethical responsibility – and love.

The French philosopher Alain Badiou has recently stirred up a great deal of critical debate in Beckett studies along these very lines. In 2003, he published *On Beckett*, a collection of several essays written over a period of years. Badiou seeks to rescue Beckett's work from what he regards as a long critical tradition of nihilistic misinterpretation. Rather than accepting the conventional view of Beckett as poet laureate of despair and failure, he stakes a provocative parallax view of Beckett as exemplar of love and heroic resilience. Badiou fully concedes that his claim does not pertain to Beckett's early writing, although those works do serve as indispensable stepping stones toward the mature theme of love. He describes the early fiction as increasingly self-obsessed and self-contained, leading by the late 1950s to an unsustainable impasse, 'the endless torture of the solipsistic *cogito*'.[23] This phrase may need some unpacking. The '*cogito*' refers to René Descartes's philosophy, built upon his bedrock first principle, *cogito ergo sum* ('I think, therefore I am'). For Descartes, one might cast reasonable doubt upon the concrete existence of almost everything, but the fact that one is capable of thinking the thought 'I think' at least confirms that the mind exists. Pressed to a Beckettian extreme, however, the *cogito* tends to incarcerate the thinker inside his mind, confining him to 'solipsism' (the notion that nothing exists outside the mind, that everything else that appears to exist is merely a by-product of the mind). This is the dead-end logic Beckett finds himself stuck in, according to Badiou, until a breakthrough around 1960. Beginning with *How It Is*, Badiou detects a radical transvaluation in Beckett's writing where 'the centre of gravity shifts to the question of the Same and the Other, and, in particular, to that of the existence – whether real or potential – of the Other'.[24] Badiou uses shorthand terms to isolate two alternatives. On the one hand, 'One' or 'the Same' refers to the mind as detached from everything else and turned in upon itself, along with the accompanying impulse to collapse all differences into a single unified sameness (i.e., 'the solipsistic *cogito*'). On the other hand, 'Two' or 'the Other' means recognising the existence of beings outside the mind, according respect for difference, and acknowledging the imperative to forge relationships. Badiou locates these concerns at the heart of Beckett's work throughout the latter half of his career: 'This is the question that ultimately ties together all of Beckett's work. Is an effective Two possible, a Two that would be in excess of solipsism? We might also say that this is the question of love'.[25]

Badiou clearly believes not only that an effective Two is possible, but also that Beckett guides the way for how to pursue such a relationship: 'Beckett's evolution goes from a programme of the One – obstinate trajectory or interminable soliloquy – to the pregnant theme of the Two, which opens out onto infinity'.[26] So, one might well ask, how does Beckett conceive and deliver this pregnant theme? Through love, answers Badiou. But Badiou's understanding of love is decidedly unconventional, unsexy, and unromantic. What he talks about when he talks about Beckett's love is serious business: 'Beckett never reduces love to the amalgam of sentimentality and sexuality endorsed by common opinion. Love as a matter of *truth* (and not of opinion) depends upon a pure event: an encounter whose strength radically exceeds both sentimentality and sexuality'.[27] Badiou plots the truth encounter of love with the mathematical dispassion of intersecting lines on a grid. A student of Beckett may be reminded of *Quad*'s crisscrossing patterns in this description of love: 'Whilst Beckett's fables are subject to a number of variations, one feature remains unchanged: love begins in a pure encounter, which is neither destined nor predestined, except by the chance crossing of two trajectories. Prior to this meeting, only solitude obtains. [. . .] The encounter is the originary power of the Two, and therefore of love itself'.[28] Panting and petting seem conspicuously missing from this definition of love; but absent too are domination, forced assimilation, erasure – in other words, all the sinister strategies postmodern ethicists (more specifically post-Holocaust ethicists) associate with the One. Viewed from this vantage point, the One is distrusted and demonised for its monolithic refusal to respect alterity and its insistence upon co-opting the Other into the Same. In contrast, for Badiou's Beckett, 'In no way does love turn a pre-existing Two into a One; this is the romantic version of love that Beckett never ceases to deride. Love is never either fusion or effusion. Rather, it is the often painstaking condition required for the Two to exist as Two'.[29] Badiou contends that being open to a true encounter with the Other, an encounter that preserves the differences of both partners, constitutes a heroic gesture of risk and hope. More specifically, he sees this kind of love as Beckett's exit out of torturous solipsism: 'This Two constitutes a passage, or authorises the pass, from the One of solipsism [. . .] to the infinity of beings and of experience. The Two of love is a hazardous and chance-laden mediation for alterity in general. It elicits a rupture or a severance of the *cogito*'s One'.[30] This breaking up of 'the *cogito*'s One' is not regarded by Badiou as destructive but as constructive, a necessary precondition for opening up 'to the infinity of beings and of experience', namely the experience of love. 'There is a crack in everything', as Leonard Cohen sings in more straightforward terms, 'That's how the light gets in'.[31]

Badiou illustrates his theories chiefly through reference to Beckett's fiction. However, the teleplays offer an equally rich testing ground for Badiou's interpretations, steeped as they are in painstaking considerations of love. Beckett's first teleplay, *Eh Joe*, immediately raises questions about Badiou's thesis. Who could be less open, more closed off from others, than Joe? Rather than pursuing love, Joe retreats into his private bunker. His only 'companions' there are voices. Joe intently, mutely listens as Voice, a droning feminine murmur identifying herself as a former lover, mocks his deficiencies and berates his past infidelities. Although Voice provides the sole soundtrack on this particular night, we are informed that she is only the latest in a series of voices, beginning with his father and mother and including subsequent loved ones, who have haunted Joe for years in his lonely cell: 'Others . . . All the others . . . Such love he got . . . God knows why . . . Pitying love'.[32] Voice invokes a vivid image of 'that penny farthing hell you call your mind',[33] referring to those old-fashioned bicycles with the giant front wheels ('penny farthings') and suggesting that Joe, like May in *Footfalls*, will never have done 'revolving it all' in his 'poor mind'.[34] Each night Joe is guided by voices to return imaginatively to the scenes of his crimes against love. He was inconstant in his devotions during the lives of these loved ones, and, when they return as ghostly visitations, he exerts his mental efforts to silencing them, 'Throttling the dead in his head'.[35] Joe's record with love becomes more complicated, however, when Voice turns her attention to the 'green one'.[36] This is another former lover (her solitaire suggests they may have been engaged to marry), who apparently killed herself after being jilted by Joe. Voice enthrals Joe with a riveting (and necessarily hypothetical) account of the green girl's suicide. Elsewhere, in *Samuel Beckett's Plays on Film and Television*, I provide a detailed interpretation of this imagined suicide, both as a televisual treatment of Freudian theories on mourning and as Joe's virtual rehearsal for his own suicide. In the present context, the salient point is Joe's deep identification with the green girl, collapsing of distinctions into a mirror-like reflection of sameness, unity. It might be tempting to read Joe's apparent sympathy with the green girl as a sign that he is open to a true encounter with love, both her fatal love for him and his undying love for her. But insofar as her experiences are contained solely within the penny farthing hell of his mind, and so long as the green girl's suicide functions primarily as a sadistic fantasy of punishment or a masochistic fantasy of self-annihilation, then it is difficult to see how Joe ever really passes beyond 'the endless torture of the solipsistic *cogito*'[37] to achieve 'the originary power of the Two, and therefore of love itself'.[38]

The other teleplays likewise raise objections to Badiou's thesis. *Ghost Trio* once again features a silent male figure (F) sequestered in his room and a faint female voice-over (V). F crouches over a cassette recording (occasionally bars from Beethoven's 'Ghost Trio' are audible), habitually waiting for an anonymous 'her' to appear (the teleplay's working title, 'Tryst', implies a romantic rendezvous). Despite occasionally thinking he hears her, and looking out the door and window multiple times for her arrival, the anticipated 'crossing of two trajectories'[39] never materialises. As if to confirm the (seemingly infinite) deferral of the tryst, a messenger boy arrives, silently shakes his head no, and recedes back into the netherworld. Where the boy comes from and where he's going, where the elusive 'her' is keeping herself and when (or if) she will ever arrive, is not known and cannot be known by F, who never risks leaving the hermetically sealed sanctuary of his 'familiar chamber'.[40]

His counterpart in . . . *but the clouds* . . ., M (male figure), has certain advantages over F. M does at least leave his 'little sanctum' each day to 'walk the roads'.[41] The love connection he pursues is not out in the day world, however, but in the night world of his dark imagination. Each night he crouches in his sanctum and devoutly applies himself to 'a begging of the mind, to her, to appear, to me'.[42] And to his credit, M in . . . *but the clouds* . . . meets with better success than F in *Ghost Trio*. He manages on occasion (once or twice every thousand nights, so he says) to conjure up a brief image of his beloved, W (woman's face). However, her appearances are always fleeting and silent, despite his pleas for her to 'Look at me' and 'Speak to me'.[43] Again, 'the infinity of beings and of experience' promised by Badiou's love[44] hardly seems fulfilled in . . . *but the clouds* . . ., where M focuses finitely on the same being and the same repeated experience night after night, to little avail.

By any standard of measurement, the teleplay that comes closest to Badiou's originary power of love as pure encounter is *Nacht und Träume*, arguably the least ironic depiction of love in the entire Beckett canon. A solitary dreamer (A) hums and then sings a verse from Schubert's Lied 'Nacht und Träume': 'Holde Träume, kehret wieder! [Sweet dreams, come back again!]'.[45] He then falls asleep and envisions his dreamt self (B) being ministered by a pair of helping hands. The hands descend from above (i.e., out of frame, above screen) to pat B's head, wipe his brow with a cloth, give him a drink from a cup, and finally clasp him in an embrace. The dream is later repeated, the second time in close-up and at a slower pace, indulging the fantasy with still greater intensity. The dream in itself is a perfect consummation of love – spiritual, maternal, and Badiouian alike. The problem, of course, is that it is only a dream. The dreamer begins and ends alone in darkness, and the loving encounter he imagines so movingly gains no purchase in the real world outside his dreamscape.

The impenetrable *Quad* always defies interpretation, as if the 'supposed danger zone' at the centre (E) of its square were a black hole, sucking in all light and intellection [$E=mc^2$?] and emitting nothing but dark inscrutability. Be that as it may, there is some sense of commensurability between *Quad* and Badiou's mathematics of love. Math actually plays a crucial role in Badiou's broader philosophy, but that issue lies beyond my present parameters. With respect to Beckett on love, and specifically *Quad* on love, Badiou's earlier formula bears repeating: 'love begins in a pure encounter, which is neither destined nor predestined, except by the chance crossing of two trajectories'.[46] While their shared geometrical rhetoric might initially suggest an affinity between Badiou and *Quad*, in fact the telemime graphically invalidates Badiou's love calculations at every turn. First of all, contra Badiou, everything is predetermined and nothing left to chance in *Quad*'s numerous encounters. With a level of exactitude bordering on the autistic, Beckett plots out every permutation of the courses followed by each of the four players.[47] Secondly, and even more importantly, there really are no 'encounters' in *Quad* as defined by Badiou because no two trajectories ever exactly cross. That is the whole point of carefully choreographing all the players' courses, so that each can avoid colliding in the path of another. With hooded heads cast downwards, and precise sidestepping at the centre to avoid any crashes, the players go about their business in the square, never looking, never touching, never so much as acknowledging the presence of the others, as if each were pushing his/her own Sisyphean boulder up the mountain alone. *Quad* is perfectly designed to prevent the very kind of encounter Badiou tells us we should find in late Beckett. The 'pregnant theme of the Two' – or Three, or Four, in this case – which Badiou leads us to believe 'opens out onto infinity' in Beckett,[48] remains stillborn in *Quad*. Beckett emphasises the point in his German television production by appending a stripped-down sequel, suggesting that, even were they to continue on their courses for 'ten thousand years',[49] the practical isolation of each player would remain essentially unchanged.

One could counter in Badiou's defence that his notion of love depends no more on success than on wine and roses, so that individual failures do not invalidate the overall generative power of the larger process. What matters for Badiou foremost is openness to love, the willingness to risk an encounter with the Other. Such openness is by its very nature a gesture of hope, an admission pass into infinity. Failure may be the standard price of admission, but as Beckett famously asserts in his final novel, *Worstward Ho*, 'Ever tried. Ever failed. No matter. Try again. Fail again. Fail better'.[50] Do the attempts to 'fail better' in the teleplays rise to Badiou's threshold of love? I still don't think so. Consider once again the linchpin of Badiou's argument: 'This Two constitutes a passage, or authorises the pass, from the One of solipsism [. . .] to the infinity of beings and of experience. The Two of love is a hazardous and chance-laden mediation for alterity in general. It elicits a rupture or a severance of the *cogito*'s One'.[51] Do Beckett's teleplay protagonists really ever pass beyond solipsism in their encounters with the Other? In a word: No. Perhaps they once did, long ago, in the back-story prior to the situations dramatised in the teleplays, 'Like those summer evenings in the Green' remembered by Voice in *Eh Joe*, 'In the early days . . . Of our idyll'.[52] But by the time we meet these haggard shut-ins, they are no longer capable of, or at any rate no longer interested in, reaching outside their rooms or even outside their minds to any real external others. If they ever once had legitimate love encounters like those valued by Badiou, those have long since receded on separate trajectories into the distant past. Furthermore, Beckett chooses not to dramatise the love encounters themselves but only their after effects. Whether wounded irreparably by 'a rupture or a severance of the *cogito*'s One', or whether constitutionally incapable of accepting the alterity of the Other in the first place, the teleplay protagonists retreat into solipsism, licking their wounds in private, replaying past encounters or inventing new ones, but always within the closed confines of the *cogito*'s One.

The most thorough response so far to Badiou's interpretations of Beckett has been offered by Andrew Gibson. In his 2006 book *Beckett and Badiou: The Pathos of Intermittency*, Gibson concedes from the start that he finds Badiou by turns inspiring, provocative, and misguided. He dedicates his book to the philosopher, but in the introduction he also admits, 'The more thought I gave to Badiou's writings, the more it seemed to me that his accounts of Beckett both worked and didn't work. [. . .] Some of Badiou's explications seemed to me compelling, some less so'.[53] I share both Gibson's admiration and his scepticism with respect to Badiou's reading of Beckett. But Gibson and I draw our lines of disagreement with Badiou in different places. For instance, he seems to agree both with Badiou's characterisation of love as an impulse counter to solipsism, and with Badiou's recognition of this same impulse in Beckett. As Gibson puts it,

> Yet if the truth of love is more mundane than the other truths, in a sense, it is also paradigmatic of them. I mean this as rigorously and unsentimentally as Beckett and Badiou. The point is emphatically not, for example, that the truth of love breeds fellow-feeling or solidarity, that it spreads irresistibly from the loved one to the many. Rather, however precariously, the truth of love is the avenue out of solipsism and towards the endless possibilities for renewal.[54]

Maybe that is indeed how love operates, maybe love should point the way out of solipsism – but this is *not* what happens in Beckett's teleplays. On the contrary, the promise or memory or dream of love functions instead as the avenue whereby the teleplay protagonists arrive back where they started. What passes for love is merely an escape alley away from the world and back into the room and the mind. These unreformed solipsists shut their doors, cut their losses, and voluntarily condemn themselves to solitary confinement, choosing the One over the Two, the Same over the Other, finitude over infinity, longing for love over loving. In short, individually and collectively, the teleplays dramatise the *failure of love*. I suppose one might congratulate these characters' endurance in continuing to pursue their idiosyncratic simulacra of love despite countless failures. To endow such meagre efforts with the bravery, hope, and redemption that Badiou associates with love, however, is to burden them with more philosophical weight than they can bear. The teleplays are particularly ruthless in depicting love devotionals that have stultified into Habit – that banal bogeyman Beckett never tires of flogging. These habits desecrate love, reducing it to pathological, narcissistic, masochistic rituals wherein the Other is merely an expedient lash for self-flagellation.

'Put bluntly', writes Shane Weller in *Beckett, Literature, and the Ethics of Alterity*, 'the history of post-Holocaust thought is the history of the attempt to think a saving alterity'.[55] Alain Badiou offers one of the most committed attempts in contemporary philosophy 'to think a saving alterity'. His vehicle for that salvation is love, and the literary saviour he anoints as most exemplary of ethical love is Samuel Beckett. But who is saved in or by Beckett? Simon Critchley's more modest claims seem closer to the mark. Critchley argues in *Very Little . . . Almost Nothing* that, rather than offering redemption, Beckett offers 'a redemption from redemption':

> His work continually frustrates our desire to ascend from the flatlands of language and ordinary experience into the stratosphere of meaning. As is all too easily seen in both contemporary New Age sophism, crude scientism, and the return to increasingly reactionary forms of religious fundamentalism, there is an almost irresistible desire to stuff the world full of meaning and sign up to one or more salvific narratives of redemption. Beckett's work, in my view, is absolutely exemplary in redeeming us from the temptations of redemption.[56]

Critchley might have numbered among his catalogue of 'salvific narratives of redemption' certain postmodern discourses on the 'ethics of alterity'. Indeed, in a later article, 'On the Ethics of Alain Badiou', Critchley specifically lodges his suspicions about the love laurels Badiou places on Beckett's head: 'There seems to be a residual heroism at work in Badiou, the heroism of resistance and militant activism. [. . .] But this does not seem to be Beckett's world, filled as it is with antiheroic personages, a gallery of moribunds who seem riveted to the spot, unable to move'.[57] Instead, Critchley emphasises Beckett's 'syntax of weakness', 'a self-undoing language that cannot go on and cannot but go on, that continues *in* its failure, and continues *as* that failure'.[58] This dimension of failure seems airbrushed out of Badiou's Beckett. It is true, for instance, that the teleplay protagonists remain exercised (although never exorcised) by questions of love, and it is also true that, fuelled by these questions, they keep continuing onward in their fashion (even when sitting perfectly still). It is a mistake, however, to conclude from this that they are continuing forward in a positive trajectory toward a true love encounter with the Other. Their trajectories only lead to failure on Badiou's terms because they are never directed outward but always inward, never linear but always cyclical, never avenues of passage toward the Other but always solipsistic cul-de-sacs for doing yet another lap on the penny farthing of the mind.

Given this theme of cyclical failure, perhaps it is appropriate to close by returning to the beginning. Although he was only twenty-four at the time he wrote *Proust*, many of Beckett's core doubts about the saving power of love were already firmly entrenched. Discussing someone else's work freed him to voice his opinions much more directly than he did in his later creative literature. His pronouncements about love in Proust reveal even more about Beckett than about Proust, and the same can be said of Badiou's pronouncements about love in Beckett. For Beckett's Proust, 'Love, he insists, can only coexist with a state of dissatisfaction, whether born of jealousy or its predecessor – desire. It represents our demand for a whole'. Its inception and its continuance imply the consciousness that something is lacking. 'One only loves that which one does not possess entirely'.[59] Insofar as this critique emphasises the futility of seeking wholeness, unification, assimilation, or possession through love, Beckett's position here is perfectly compatible with Badiou's insistence, 'In no way does love turn a pre-existing Two into a One [. . .]. Love is never either fusion or effusion'.[60] Where Beckett and Badiou crucially part company is on the question, 'Is an effective Two possible, a Two that would be in excess of solipsism?'[61] For Beckett's Proust, the question itself is gauche because the answer is so obviously, emphatically 'No!'

> But if love, for Proust, is a function of man's sadness, friendship is a function of his cowardice; and, if neither can be realised because of the impenetrability (isolation) of all that is not 'cosa mentale', at least the failure to possess may have the nobility of that which is tragic, whereas the attempt to communicate where no communication is possible is merely a simian vulgarity, or horribly comic, like the madness that holds a conversation with the furniture. Friendship, according to Proust, is the negation of that irremediable solitude to which every human being is condemned.[62]

There's not only love for you, but also friendship and human communication of any kind. Badiou acknowledges the predominance of the 'cosa mentale', the 'mental thing', in Beckett's early work, but he claims that the centre of gravity shifted in the late work toward a risky, heroic openness to a true encounter of love, a turn away from the solipsistic finitude of the One toward the infinitude of the Two. The evidence of the teleplays suggests otherwise. The protagonists in *Eh Joe, Ghost Trio, . . . but the clouds . . .*, and *Nacht und Träume* (maybe *Quad*, too, although that's harder to say) are motivated by something resembling love. But as it plays out in their respective minds – and only in their minds – what results is not a meaningful, sustainable, open love connection with another person. Instead, the teleplays dramatise the failure of love, ultimately reaffirming Beckett's initial diagnosis of 'that irremediable solitude to which every human being is condemned'.

Dustin Anderson *is an Assistant Professor in the Department of Literature and Philosophy at Georgia Southern University. His research in Irish Literature crosses recent developments in national modernisms, literatures and critical theory, with an emphasis on how the writings of Joyce and Beckett complicate received discourses on cognition. Anderson also served as Associate Editor for the* Journal of Beckett Studies *from 2005 to 2010. His books,* Their Synaptic Selves: Memory and Language in Joyce and Beckett, *and* Transnational Beckett *(edited along with S.E. Gontarski, William Cloonan and Alec Hargreaves) both appeared in 2008. He has recently been solicited to contribute to an upcoming volume on Henri Bergson, and is currently working on his next book manuscript, tentatively entitled Beckett's* Novel Neurology.

Krapp's Last Tape and Mapping Modern Memory

As a Nobel Prize-winning author, Beckett has long been known for his contributions to existentialism, minimalism, and the Theatre of the Absurd, but he has also recently been noted for influencing the way we think about numerous aspects of our culture. Think about it this way: what do Johnny Depp, Yves Saint-Laurent, Sean Connery, David Bowie, and *Outkast*'s Andre 3000 have in common with Beckett? *Style*. According to *GQ*, Beckett is one of the most stylish men of the twentieth century. As far as influence is concerned, the magazine states:

> Any writer who denies fantasizing about being Samuel Beckett is either lying or not a writer. To roam the Paris streets as an expat, to join the French Resistance, to meet fans in the café of the Hotel St. Jacques – and that's just the man himself. His work, more worshiped than appraised, strips characters of everything from plots to scenery, leaving them to face the nothingness from where they came. Beckett himself looked like something from the void. A timeless figure, both ancient and modern, traditional and (whether he liked it or not) hip . . .'[63]

This certainly isn't Beckett's first posthumous encounter with popular brand names. In 1997, *Apple* unveiled a new advertising campaign featuring *iconic* images of trend-setting humanitarians 'who do' things to make a change. Among those named were: Dalai Lama, Martin Luther King Jr, Mahatma Gandhi, Charles Darwin, Albert Einstein, Amelia Earhart, Bob Dylan, John Lennon, Muhammad Ali, Salvador Dalí, Alfred Hitchcock, Jim Henson, and Samuel Beckett.

Beckett clearly saw things differently, and to such an extent that we, as a culture, have pervasively incorporated an experimental playwright into the larger fabric of our popular culture from chic fashion magazines to computer branding. Beckett is certainly not exempt from that phenomenon of those, as *Apple* says, 'who do', that inspire many to emulate, recreate, and appropriate.

More importantly than how we see him influencing pop-culture, his work can now be understood for its contributions to studies of memory and the modern conception of the mind that developed in both his plays and, more fully, in his novels which have largely gone unrecognised. By examining *Krapp's Last Tape*, we can see how this Irish ex-patriot adapts the burgeoning discussion of neurology and memory studies in Paris into an innovative exploration of the mind. The situations that Beckett creates anticipate much of what the current neuroscience community is only now exploring, and speaks as strongly to our generation of video-bloggers as it did to the pioneers of postmodern theatre. With Beckett, it is never what you remember, but how you remember it.

Both his experiences as a college student and as an adult in Paris inform how Beckett looks at what memory is and what it does for us. As a student he read and wrote on both Marcel Proust – in many ways the birth of the modernist trope of stream-of-consciousness – and another Nobel Prize winner, Henri Bergson. By literally preforming the type of memories that Bergson theorised at the beginning of the twentieth century, Beckett, in *Krapp's Last Tape*, anticipates both the exploration of memory by contemporary cognitive scientists, and the replication of Krapp's engagement with memory that our generation of digital natives has begun on *YouTube*.

The character, Krapp, is caught somewhere between J. Alfred Prufrock and Marcel Proust. He is more isolated than Eliot's wistful voyeur, and more alone with his thoughts than Proust's Marcel. Like both of these characters, Krapp is measuring out his life – not in coffee spoons or madeleine cakes, but on stage with bananas and whiskey and, more importantly, a tape recorder and a collection of audio diary entries. His interaction with the tape recorder is what makes this play *so* innovative, and *so* prescient to memory studies. Of course, Beckett's work continually revisits the theme of what James Joyce calls in *Ulysses* the 'ineluctable modalities' of sensory perception, and their collection and storage (e.g. the reels of tapes in *Krapp's Last Tape*, Morvan and Bertram's file folders in *Rough for Theatre II*, Malone's notebook in *Malone Dies*, and so on). Krapp, however, uses Bergson's metaphor of duration to show us the actual interaction between mind and body that Beckett is driving at.

Much of Beckett's work focuses on memory, but little of it depicts memory in such a literal fashion. Unlike *What Where* or *Eh Joe*, we know where the disembodied voice is coming from, and who the speaker is in *Krapp's Last Tape*. The plot is spartan: an old man sits in his den, has a banana and a couple of drinks, listens to recorded diary entries he made in the past, and makes a new entry before listening to the rest of the tape. In *Krapp*, Beckett is able to take a seemingly solipsistic situation (a man alone with his memories), and develop it into an intersubjective experiment in memory studies. To do this Beckett calls upon Bergson's metaphor of analogue tape spools for our accumulative memory. By looking at the image that Beckett chooses to represent memory from Bergson we can see how Beckett actualises what a memory event might look like onstage.

Beckett bases his depictions of memory on Bergson's concept of duration (or *durée*) and two of Bergson's images to illustrate memory as duration. Bergson begins the discussion of duration in *Time and Free Will*, and continues it through *The Creative Mind* and *Matter and Memory*. At each juncture Bergson's concept of duration evolves. Initially, in *Time and Free Will*, duration is a qualitative, not quantitative, multiplicity. He provides a number of examples of quantitative multiplicities, such as a homogeneous flock of sheep – where we can count the sheep, despite their homogeneity, because each sheep is spatially separated from the rest where each occupies a specific spatial location. Quantitative multiplicities are always represented by homogeneous and spatial symbols like the sheep.[64] Qualitative multiplicities, as in duration, are always already heterogeneous and temporal. Bergson explains this via our moral feeling of sympathy. This complex feeling incorporates a number of concurrent although potentially adverse emotions: empathy, horror, pity, pain, and humility. Bergson calls this feeling 'a qualitative progress', which takes place as a 'transition from repugnance to fear, from fear to sympathy, and from sympathy itself to humility'.[65] This feeling illustrates the heterogeneity of feelings or experiences without one negating or excluding the other.

In *The Creative Mind,* the primary example that Bergson uses is a reel-to-reel tape spool. While Bergson's metaphor isn't perfect, it is close to how we understand memory perception in contemporary science. The left side of the tape spool is our perception of the present. The *presentness* is always connected to the perceptions of the past (on the right side of the spool). As the tape spool grows on the right or larger side (our past) it begins overlapping. These memories begin to overlay one another. The memories are not simply stationary points that can be accessed on their own. We must scroll through the tape to find what we are looking for, and thereby re-engaging all of the surrounding and associated memories. In this metaphor, we must experience the memory through the filter or layer of the surrounding tape. In an age where most of us simply skip tracks, it is harder to visualise this spooling up of memory.

With this example, Bergson intends to explain that while memory conserves the past we change those memories as well. Each time we remember we add that immediate moment of remembering, which means that we experience that older memory differently (both as we originally perceived it, and through the filter of a more experienced self). The new experience does not necessarily change the original event, but it will henceforth change the way that we perceive or remember that event. Likewise, Krapp re-experiences his memory simultaneously with the event of hearing the memory (along with his other intermediate memories that are part of the recorded voice's future and Krapp's past). Every new experience of a memory is added to the older experiences, and the next experience is added onto all the other old ones plus the one that came immediately before. This accumulative image is not unlike the growing boxes of tapes that Krapp accrues between his thirty-ninth and sixty-ninth birthdays. The past is larger at the current moment than it was at the previous moment. This spooling image should imply that duration is memory, specifically the mobility and connected prolongation of the past into the present. This image, however, is always incomplete. Bergson claims that no image can represent duration, because the image is immobile, while duration is 'pure mobility'.[66] These images and their representative concepts – 'the unrolling of our duration in certain aspects resembles the unity of a movement which progresses, in others, a multiplicity of states spreading out'[67] – show us that duration actually has as much to do with unity as it does multiplicity. Patrick McNamara's reading of Bergsonian memory, in *Mind and Variability*, is most helpful with characters like Krapp. He says, 'every instance of a spontaneous remembering is composed of a series of phases'.[68] McNamara's notion implicitly situates duration within memory.

Bergson sees the word *memory* as a mixture of two distinct types of memories: the 'habit-memory', which, through repetition, establishes certain automatic behaviours or sensory-motor mechanisms; and 'pure memory', which is unconscious personal memories. That is, 'habit-memory' is aligned with bodily perception, while 'pure memory' is something we encounter. Bergson illustrates 'pure memory' with the image of the memory cone in *Matter and Memory*.

The plane, *P*, is what Bergson calls the 'plane of my actual representation of the universe'.[69] The cone, *SAB*, is supposed to represent pure memory (or what Gilles Deleuze refers to as regressive memory) that deals with a perception and a sequence of memories that we associate with that perception. At the cone's base, *AB*, are unconscious memories, which emerge spontaneously, such as dreams. As the cone narrows, there are indefinite numbers of different individual memories of the past ordered by their distance or nearness to the present, as we can see in the horizontal lines,

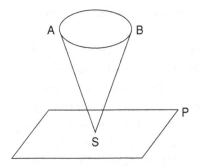
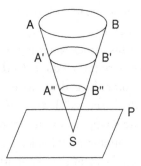

Figure 4

A^1B^1 and A^2B^2, bisecting the second cone. At the point of the cone, S, is the interaction of our present physical perception with the accumulation of all those related memories, which takes place in the plane of our consciousness (or what he calls the representation of the universe). Because memories move down the cone from the past to the present perception and action, we should understand that pure memory for Bergson is both progressive or accumulative. The cone also should symbolise the dynamic nature of memories – by adding new perceptions, we change the nature of those older memories; we unknowingly edit them. According to Deleuze's reading of Bergson, any single memory is always comprised of an entire interlinked sequence of related memories. Conscious thinking, then, occurs when those individual memories are compressed down into a single larger memory that we unconsciously compare and associate with what we physically perceive; pure memory moves down into singular images or instances – what both Deleuze and Bergson refer to as *presentness*.

As he experiences them, Krapp is demonstrating a desire to edit, change, or re-fashion these memories. The purpose of that tape recorder is to edit and revise media. The desire to revise or recompose these memories is clear in *Krapp*. Beckett does not put him on stage simply with a fixed artefact (as he does with the Listener in *Ohio Impromptu*), but with a recorder and microphone. He editorialises in these tapes (rather than simply dictating the present situation), which points to, at least, a level of awareness that these memories are interactive.

In his earlier recording, there are instances where the voice shifts from narrator to editor. As the thirty-nine-year-old Krapp tells about his compulsive drive to eat bananas, the taped voice pauses and suddenly shouts '(*Vehemently.*) Cut 'em out!'[70] as if commanding the future Krapp to stop troubling his stomach. Just a bit later, the taped thirty-nine-year-old voice comments on the taped twenty-nine-year-old's judgement that his youth is over, 'Thank God'.[71] The taped voice pauses, and pointedly comments on the naivety of his younger self. 'False ring there' he explains to what will be his sixty-nine-year-old self.[72] We see this as an ongoing process, not something that he has done once or twice in the past. As our present Krapp begins recording, he almost immediately falls into the same methodology: to editorialise his memories for his future self. Krapp dictates, 'Everything there, everything on this old muckball, all the light and dark and famine and feasting of . . . the ages!', and then in a sudden shout, commands himself to, 'Let that go! Jesus! Take his mind off his homework! Jesus'[73] before he pauses wearily and switches the recorder off momentarily. Then just as his early taped voice tells us he did, Krapp consults his notes scribbled on the back of an envelope. As with the earlier voice, our sixty-nine-year-old Krapp violently advises his future self to suppress any of his 'last fancies' as he shouts, 'Keep 'em under!'[74]

At first glance, that type of editorialising might seem incidental, but early on in the play we see that Krapp (even at thirty-nine) intimately knows that his memories are constantly enveloping and interacting with one another. Like droplets of mercury, his memories are drawn together in a new cohesive amalgam, just as Krapp himself is physically drawn to phantom memories on the tape (we see that Krapp is literally drawn to the recorder as he leans closer and closer, and almost caresses it when Bianca comes up). 'I love to get up and move about in it', the taped voice tells him, 'then back here to . . . (*hesitates*) . . . me. (*pause.*) Krapp'.[75] Just like quicksilver, these individual isolated memories are impossible to pin down. They are, as Bergson theorises, individually ineffable. The younger Krapp tries to express that notion when he says, 'The grain, now what I wonder do I mean by that, I mean . . . (*hesitates*) . . . I suppose I mean those things worth having when all the dust has – when all my dust has settled. I close my eyes and try and imagine them'. The only response he receives to that type of imagining is 'extraordinary silence'.[76] What the thirty-nine-year-old Krapp has stumbled onto here is memory as a durative process. A process that requires the surrounding memory context to have any authentic meaning. One memory is constantly slipping into another, and to pull one out strips it of intrinsic value, and makes it a meaningless symbol.

In *The Creative Mind*, Bergson explains that no one can experience the two identical moments. They might be strikingly similar, as in the two acts of *Waiting for Godot*, but the second moment will always have the memory of the first.[77] The development of Krapp's personality works likewise. There are consistencies in actions, desires, and demeanour, but the drama goes much deeper than depicting a character as a complex or layered self. What it demonstrates is the multiplicity of memory, and how that slips in and out of our consciousness.

We see this first as Krapp demonstrates the way in which these layers of memory accumulate. As he plays the spool from his thirty-ninth birthday, he comes across a word that he, at sixty-nine, doesn't know. '[T]here is of course the house on the canal where mother lay a-dying', the recording says, 'in the late autumn, after her long viduity'. Krapp stops the tape and rewinds it to listen more closely mouthing the word 'viduity' before retrieving an enormous dictionary to look up the word. He reads aloud, 'State – or condition of being – or remaining – a widow – or widower. (*Looks up. Puzzled.*) Being – or remaining? . . . (*Pause. He peers again at dictionary. Reading.*) "Deep weeds of viduity" . . . Also of an animal, especially a bird . . . the vidua or weaver bird . . . Black plumage of male . . . (*He looks up. With relish.*) The vidua bird!' This image of the bird is now part of the memory event and is inextricably linked with the image of his mother in her widow's weeds.[78]

The most important example of this recurrent memory multiplicity is the memory of Bianca. It is here that we can see how Bergson's memory cone actually functions as the memory event occurs. We see sixty-nine-year-old Krapp listening to the recording of his thirty-nine-year-old Krapp listening to himself as a man ten years younger. The tape plays:

> Just been listening to an old year, passages at random. I did not check in the book, but it must be at least ten or twelve years ago. At that time I think I was still living on and off with Bianca in Kedar Street. Well out of that, Jesus yes! Hopeless business. (*Pause.*) Not much about her, apart from a tribute to her eyes. Very warm. I suddenly saw them again. (*Pause.*) Incomparable! (*Pause.*) Ah well . . . (*Pause.*) These old P.M.s are gruesome, but I often find them – (*Krapp switches off, broods, switches on*) – a help before embarking on a new . . . (*hesitates*) . . . retrospect.[79]

The result is the new memory event that Krapp creates for his last tape. The earlier memory has infiltrated his consciousness in a new vital way to actively change his thought process. He sits down to record his thoughts on listening to the younger Krapp, and is suddenly aware of Bianca. Krapp records: 'Just been listening to that stupid bastard I took myself for thirty years ago, hard to believe I was ever as bad as that. Thank God that's all done with anyway. (*Pause.*) The eyes she had!'[80] There are, of course, other, smaller instances: the way he takes notes on envelops, the 'yelp to Providence' and the inside jokes that Krapp joins in on, and so on.[81] Should Krapp record another tape, he will have this new tier of memories to filter the new narration through. Applying Bergson's models it looks something like this:

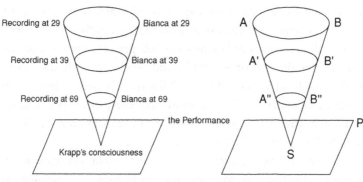

Figure 5

The initial, or early, memory being when he actually lived with and recorded about being with Bianca at age twenty-nine. For Bergson, the earliest recording is the A instance. B then is specific mentioning of Bianca. We don't see this on stage, but understand it through the second layer of memory that brings all of the surrounding perceptions of the relationship with it (i.e., 'Well out of that, Jesus yes!') at age thirty-nine. The second recording Bergson would mark as A^1B^1 because it is always already interacting with the initial instance (AB). A^2B^2 then are the staged experiences that Krapp portrays as he listens to the recording at sixty-nine (which have already been interacting with AB [Krapp at twenty-nine] and A^1B^1 [Krapp at thirty-nine]), and S – the moment of the memory event – is when all of these memories aggregate in the new perception of Bianca at sixty-nine: 'The eyes she had!' This memory event occurs involuntarily for Krapp as the spool collapses, and the aggregate memories coalesce.

As I noted, the spool metaphor is imperfect. Bergson himself was aware that it implied a static or quantitative quality to what should a fluid qualitative multiplicity. This spool metaphor seems to unintentionally imply a storage model of memory. However, Krapp's interaction with the spools as a durative process complicates Bergson's model, and demonstrates how we can use Bergson as a starting point in our understanding of how memory works at a neurological level.

Today cognitive scientists are still divided on the location of the mind and issue of memory. Monist purists, like Mriganka Sur (the Newton Professor of Neuroscience at Massachusetts Institute of

Technology) or Antonio Damásio (head of University of Southern California's Brain and Creativity Institute, and author of *Descartes' Error*), still contend that humans are 100 per cent matter, and the mind is contained entirely within and produced from the brain. Dualists, such as David Chalmers or Vilayanur Ramachandran, really have become something like extraordinarily complex neo-Cartesians. For them qualia[82] (or subjective experiences like memories) are always a non-biological mental phenomena.

Other neurophilosophers, like Dennett, avoid the contention altogether. The mind, or consciousness, for Dennett, in *Consciousness Explained*, is part of the brain, but not necessarily a component part. His interest lies in the structure of consciousness, he refers to human consciousness as 'a huge complex of memes',[83] or a collection of self-replicating cultural ideas competing for existence – especially as they deal with self-conscious physical and emotional exploration and deception.[84] It is noteworthy that the way in which we talk about the interaction of pop-culture phenomena (*viral-videos* or knowing *your meme*) is nearly identical to Dennett's concept of the mind.

On stage, Krapp is demonstrating the inextricable link of the conscious mind (the philosophical mind) and the unconscious (physically regulatory material) brain, which – like Krapp's ledger and spools – are both self-organising systems. Beckett is engaging those same concepts that today's cognitive scientists are still divided on: the location of the mind and issue of memory. The focus here is on the moment of interaction between what Bergson calls matter (what is actual) and memory (what is virtual).

Much of what we feel on a daily basis could be experienced either virtually or actually. Pain, for instance, falls on both sides of this dichotomy. The memory of experiencing pain is something that we can be aware of without actually physically experiencing it, and the brain can even simulate pain in non-existent physical areas (phantom limbs, for instance – or in Krapp's case an entire phantom body). Beckett's work is developing both an examination of qualia and, more importantly, an examination of the moment in which these memories become actualised or spatialised as a physical part of the body (specifically here as Krapp sometimes unhappily *hears* the recitation of his own memories) – they are purely connected to one another.[85]

Daniel Dennett and Marcel Kinsbourne, in 'Time and the Observer: The Where and When of Consciousness in the Brain', explain this spatialisation of memory events in their model of a Multiple Draft memory. For Dennett and Kinsbourne, the action of memory is not a linear system that builds on progressive elements until a whole memory is achieved, rather the memory event is a synchronous accessing of disparate memory elements. These elements are not necessarily connected in a rational way, but are instead triggered by the associations that they have with the event at hand. These elements are then mapped onto specific associative triggers to form a spatialisation of that memory event. They explain this concept thus,

> We perceive – and remember – perceptual events, not a suc-
> cessively analyzed trickle of perceptual elements or attributes
> locked into succession as if pinned into place on a continuous
> film. Different attributes of events are indeed extracted by dif-
> ferent neural facilities at different rates, (e.g. location versus
> shape versus color) and people, if asked to respond to the pres-
> ence of each one in isolation, would do so with different laten-
> cies, depending on which it was, and on other well-explored
> factors. The relative timing of inputs plays a necessary role in
> determining the information or content in experience, but it
> is not obligatorily tied to any stage or point of time during
> central processing. How soon we can respond to one in isola-
> tion, and how soon to the other, does not exactly indicate what
> will be the temporal relationship of the two in percepts that
> incorporate them both.[86]

For Beckett, the actualisation of memory events comes through specific and separate types of spatialisation. The memory event in Beckett is much more specified or localised in the interaction of the body and the mind. This moment of spatialisation transforms Krapp's literally mapped memories (those noted in the ledger and recorded on the tape) in a forced elusive figurativeness. The only entry in the ledger that Krapp is puzzled by is the ironically named 'memorable equinox'. When encountered with locus on which to align these memories – some piece of information that will allow him to end this memory event – Krapp intentionally skips over the sections of the tape:

> This fancy is what I have chiefly to record this evening, against the day when my work will be done and perhaps no place left in my memory, warm or cold, for the miracle that ... (*hesitates*) ... for the fire that set it alight. What I suddenly saw then was this, that the belief I had been going on all my life, namely – (*Krapp switches off impatiently, winds tape forward, switches on again*) – great granite rocks the foam flying up in the light of the lighthouse and the wind-gauge spinning like a propeller, clear to me at last that the dark I have always struggled to keep under is in reality – (*Krapp curses, switches off, winds tape forward, switches on again*) – unshatterable association until my dissolution of storm and night with the light of the understanding and the fire – (*Krapp curses louder, switches off, winds tape forward, switches on again*).[87]

As Dennett and Kinesbourne explain, these memories never truly work in isolation. What a study like theirs illuminates is the interconnectedness of our memories, even those we try to forget. Single, isolated memory, for Beckett, is irrecoverable. It has been too transformed and, like Yeats's 'The Second Coming', cannot hold itself together. The way that Beckett spatialises memory forces a linguistic shift or transformation. Spatialised memory forces language to shift or transform into a type of representative image. This shift is developed abstractly in the creation of aphasic and amnesic characters who render language porous. The moment, or event, of 'actualisation' is where memory slips for these characters. Virtual surroundings become literal in some cases and even more elusively figurative in others.

To be so brief textually, *Krapp's Last Tape* is incredibly complex, but it is not inaccessible. In a November 2008 roundtable discussion on Beckett for the Philoctetes Center, Edward Albee commented that 'everybody goes around saying that Beckett is so obscure. If all of Beckett's plays were presented in living rooms, nobody would find any of them obscure. [. . .] Nobody is clearer. Nobody is more precise with language. Nobody is simpler'.[88] For the depth of the themes and stark presentations of *Krapp*, Beckett's play is a strikingly honest portrayal of what we do when we're alone. It is nearly impossible not to slip into reminiscence while we are alone. Krapp's odd way of eating his banana, or his repetition of words like 'spool', or scanning through his ledger reading aloud his words is something that we all do when we're lost in thought – absent-mindedly wandering around our houses.

Albee's comment is far truer than he realises. With the development of *YouTube*, Krapps of all ages, occupations, and walks of life have been steadily appearing. Kansas State University professor Michael Wesch's 2008 presentation to the Library of Congress, 'An Anthropological Introduction to *YouTube*', looks at the way that Video Blogging (or Vlogging) develops, what he calls, 'new forms of media, new forms of expression, and new forms of identity'.[89] Of course, it is this final idea that I'm so taken with. Thousands of people every day (Wesch's video breaks down the numbers – something like 200,000 three-minute videos) record and produce their own video diary/blog entries. *YouTube* has matured to the point now that we see people producing new vlogs as a response to the 'selves' that they see in their older vlogs, especially, as Wesch points out, their initial or virgin vlogs. Wesch goes on to say that all of the new developments in technology are about linking – not just linking information, but linking people. This is clearly what we see developing on Beckett's stage with Krapp. He is, of course, linking information (or perhaps more properly memories – old versions of memories to new experiences of those memories to create a new memory event), but linking people as well. In this case, it is linking the thirty-nine-year-old Krapp to the sixty-nine-year-old Krapp to create or develop a new identity. To fully understand how Beckett was working with memory, we needed science to catch up to his literature. To imitate Beckett's experiments with memories, we needed technology to catch up to *Krapp's Last Tape*. In both cases, we've been running about fifty years behind. Our new generations of *YouTube*rs, however, have given us a start in the right direction.

CHAPTER 5
INTERVIEWS

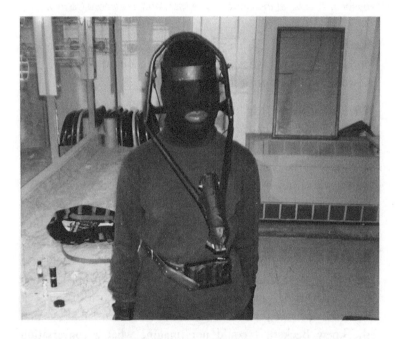

Wendy Salkind as Mouth, in preparation for *Not I*. Director: Xerxes Mehta.
The Maryland Stage Company, Strasbourg and Baltimore, 1996.
Design of Mouth's light: Terry Cobb.

The known difficulties in lighting *Not I* are solved here through the creation of an
instrument that is fixed to the actor's headpiece, thus ensuring an unvarying and
precise focus on the actor's mouth while permitting her freedom of movement.
In performance, the light, shielded by a black cover and set below the spectators'
sight line, is invisible.
Photo: Wendy Salkind.

193

Wendy Salkind on *Not I*

*On 17 September 2011, I interviewed **Wendy Salkind** at her home in Baltimore, Maryland. Salkind, as part of the Maryland Stage Company which took their exciting productions of Beckett's late plays to the Beckett in Strasbourg Festival in 1996 and the Beckett in Berlin Festival and Conference in 2000, played the part of the disembodied Mouth in* Not I *and ghostly first woman in* Play. *In addition to her stage work, Salkind is a Professor in Theatre at the University of Maryland, Baltimore County.*

Katherine Weiss: What was your first encounter with the plays of Samuel Beckett, what were your impressions at that time, and how has your view of Beckett's plays changed?

Wendy Salkind: My first encounter was in a course with Ruby Cohn [author of *Just Play: Beckett's Theatre* (1980) and *A Beckett Canon* (2001)] when I was completing my undergraduate study in theatre at the California Institute of the Arts. I'd already had a course with Ruby in Shakespeare, and in her Modern Dramatists course we read *Endgame*, *Waiting for Godot*, and *Krapp's Last Tape*, but we didn't read *Not I*. What I remember was admiring how methodical Ruby was in her analysis of literature and the ways in which her lectures drew me in to the lack of psychological narrative, the language and the humour of Beckett's plays. Then one day she said, 'Once, when I was having lunch with Sam . . .' She was a private person so I was stunned when I realised that she knew Beckett. I could not imagine what a conversation with him would be like. And that's what really stuck in my mind. [*Laughter.*] So my first impression was that his plays were mysterious and profound. I continue to feel that way, but, being older and having performed some of his plays, I now have a more visceral sense of his writings.

KW: What was the biggest challenge you have faced in preparation when working on Beckett?

WS: Well, with *Not I*, the first big challenge was memorisation of all those incomplete sentences and repetitions. Then I had to find the required speed without losing the memorisation. On top of that was the problem of being able to stay in the play and manage the fear, the terror that the performance created. Similarly in *Play*, the technical demands at times became overwhelming, and the minute my mind shifted out of the play to an awareness of those technical demands, I knew I had the potential to completely lose where I was. Those challenges never disappeared while performing both plays.

KW: Could you talk about the type and amount of research and preparation you did for *Not I* and *Play*?

WS: Certainly. I read the writings of many Beckett scholars, and I read about Beckett's life. I was trying to see if an image would come to me of Mouth from *Not I,* which I felt was really critical. Initially I thought there had to be a real person speaking so that I was not imagining myself as just a disembodied voice. The research during my rehearsals, with the director Xerxes Mehta, involved spending many hours speaking the words of the play one at a time, dot dot dot by dot dot dot, in order to figure out what, exactly, was being described by Mouth, what was the story of this woman, what was her thinking process, and how did Beckett's rhythmic and sonic use of language create a forward movement in the play. We never talked about feelings, only language, structure and some sense of story line. Xerxes is extraordinary in his comprehension of Beckett, so the unravelling of my understanding of both these plays was guided with care and tremendous attention to detail. Then, at a certain point, we agreed I had to forget all the research, and just feel the play in my body.

KW: I've come across actors and directors who insist that stage directions are of little or no importance, while other playwrights, Beckett, of course, and Sam Shepard, for example, insist that actors and directors should serve the text of the playwright's vision. How do you handle working within the strict confines of Beckett's text and the Beckett Estate?

WS: When I first read Beckett's stage directions, I knew that he was trying to avoid a highly emotional, psychological interpretation of these plays. It wasn't until we'd rehearsed both plays a long time that I understood the significance of the speed, and it wasn't until performance that I understood the disembodiment that the plays demand. He provides no stage directions for Mouth in *Not I* and it was through rehearsals that we discovered the necessity of the speed of the speech and the limitations of vocal expression. In *Play* Beckett's stage directions are about the one-second delay to speak once the light is on the face, and he writes that the faces must be impassive and the voices toneless, with rapid tempo throughout. Given the furore of the piece, those constrictions are exceedingly difficult for a performer, but I realised they were essential, absolutely essential. Having performed *Not I* twice, six years apart, I really thought the second time I could get past the terror, it just wouldn't be there, but I was so wrong. I don't know that Beckett understood what he was demanding of the actors with his stage directions. In this country, most actors are trained to interpret language and experience through psychological motivation, through action and reaction that stimulate feeling. With Beckett, it is the structure and the language that drive the action, just as with a musical score. In both these plays you are propelled forward in such a way that you cannot stop. It would ruin the plays to insert a meaningful pause. On another level, if the voice is completely monochromatic, or toneless, then the play becomes purely technical, and the experience of the audience will not be one of being thrown into the nightmare that the characters are experiencing. Without adherence to Beckett's stage directions, there is no fury, no humour, no mystery to these plays.

KW: Your comments remind me of when I directed *Come and Go* with undergraduate students in 2010. The first couple of times we went through the play, the actors wanted to do it with emotion, and they would crack up laughing at each other, because it doesn't work. Yet when they came to the point where they were not speaking with 'colour', as Beckett would say, we discovered that emotion is still present, but the emotion is not expressive. And after every time we rehearsed, they would have this sigh of relief because of the tension that is present when performed this way.

WS: Right, exactly.

KW: When you were interviewed about your performance of *Not I* in the *Baltimore Sun* in 1990, you said that 'Beckett writes about all people who have no voice'. You've hit on something important here. Would you expand on this concept?

WS: It seems to me that part of the struggle for both Mouth and First Woman, the wife, in *Play,* is a desperate need to be heard. And, what occurs in *Not I* is that once the voice erupts, it's an uncontrollable voice, it's a voice that tortures her, it's a voice that demands that she claim her tragic life. While working on the play, the image of the character of Mouth that came to me was a homeless woman in her seventies or a woman who had suffered a stroke. Both were metaphors for the voice that is not heard. His understanding of the ways in which we turn back on our past again and again to relive and to re-examine, never able to articulate in a way that brings us peace, is brilliant and that is what really drives the plays. The experience as an actor was that I couldn't stop my voice, and if I did, I would stop the performance. The danger of that, of being an actor who couldn't control the performance, felt as if my voice was confining and torturing me so that the characters and I experienced the same thing.

KW: In response to Jessica Tandy, who played Mouth in the American première of *Not I*, Beckett wrote to Alan Schneider, who directed this production, to tell his actress that the play should work on the nerves of the audience, not its intellect. How do you feel about Beckett's anti-Brechtian mode? He's often compared to Brecht but at least in his late works he seems very anti-Brecht.

WS: I agree. The audience is never asked to take a step back and consider what is happening and its relevance to the form of theatre or the political, psychological, or social issues at all. Rather, they are immediately attacked by the piece. Beckett engages their senses. The first time we performed *Not I*, there was a woman who crawled out of the audience. I know that a number of people said to me it felt as if they were inside a nightmare. A friend from Ghana told me that he kept seeing images of African masks that frightened him as a child. A number of people said they thought the mouth was moving around the stage, pulsating. One of the things in *Not I*, having never seen it, but the description of what people say, is it takes them a while to realise they will not see a human form behind that disembodied mouth. That kind of peering into the darkness to see what that is and if it will come any closer to them is such an abstraction that they are unaccustomed to, and that alone is unnerving. But I also think, and people have said this too, that when they hear the first scream, there is that feeling that they are rooted in their seats, that they don't know what's going to happen to them.

KW: Have you not seen a video of your performance?

WS: Yes, I have seen the video but the mouth fills the screen so it doesn't give me a sense of what that looked like for the live audience. Looking at the video recently, I realised that the performance is too slow. When we rehearsed the play for the Berlin festival, one day the run through was twelve-and-a-half minutes and both Xerxes and I felt that this was absolutely right. We never knew what the time would be. It varied every time we did it. But after that, any time it was faster than that, it was out of control, and if it was longer, it just started to feel, oddly enough, a little lax. The performance for the video is almost fourteen minutes which I think is because the camera and videographer were right in front of me, so there was yet another tension, and I got through almost the entire play, we were right at the end, when my tongue missed a sound. I instantly picked up the word and went on, but when we finished Xerxes said, 'It's no good, we have to do it again right away'. We did it again right away and I think it started a little too slow.

KW: You are right. It does work very differently on stage.

WS: It's the only play that I've done where I have no idea what that audience experience is like.

KW: When Billie Whitelaw prepared for the role of Mouth she went through a breakdown during one of the rehearsals. It was due, I believe, to sensory deprivation. Indeed, Beckett often put his actors through physical torments. How does *Not I* challenge the actor's endurance of pain? You've already spoken about terror, but could you address other physical reactions to the play and how you handled these?

WS: The sensory deprivation had partially to do with costuming. In order to get the light on my face, I was wearing a kind of metal helmet that was attached to a belt around my waist, and on the belt there was the light that shone on my mouth. I wore the light, so I needed to keep my head still. I felt as if I were in the electric chair. I was on a scaffold that was a number of feet in the air that had no sides to it; it only had a railing. It had to appear as if the mouth was in a void, and I definitely felt like that. It was the only time I've ever performed where I had no sense of the audience and where I was. I was in complete darkness. I can remember feeling as if I was hurling myself toward the audience, so I held onto that railing for dear life. The other problem was that I could see my mouth move, which looked like something that wasn't attached to me, so I felt as if I were outside my body and I had to close my eyes. I performed it with eyes closed and that increased the sense of incredible isolation, which mirrors that of the character and intensified my connection with Mouth. I felt I was absolutely alone and trapped. I had terrible nightmares; they went on for a long time. They started with the typical actor's, 'I'm going to lose my lines on stage', which of course would be disastrous in this play, and they became dreams of flying out into space and dying.

KW: That's interesting because what Beckett does with *Not I* as well as with *Play* is create these plays which are not one-man shows, but in which the figures are ultimately alone. Another figure occupies the stage with you, but you are alone. In any other play if you lost your line, the other actor can pull you out of that awkward spot, or if the line changes it's okay because he still responds. Whereas in *Not I* the two figures on stage do not respond to one another and therefore are not helpful in any way. The auditor's gestures are of *helpless* compassion; he really can't help Mouth.

WS: Because the light is blinding, I couldn't see him or feel him at all. I've never experienced that. Whereas in *Play*, all three of us always sensed the presence of the others. We had an oddly strong feeling that there was dialogue going on. But because of the light coming on and off our faces to trigger our voices, we all felt isolated.

KW: After performing *Not I* and *Play*, do you read or interpret Beckett's works any differently?

WS: I do. Certainly when I returned to reading his prose, I found I read him differently. I have a more visceral experience in reading his texts now. I read them aloud. They need to be read aloud.

KW: One of the techniques you teach is the Alexander technique. How would you describe this technique and how does this technique relate to your work on Beckett?

WS: Alexander technique is a practice to use your thinking in such a way that you can release excess muscular tension and find postural balance and greater physical expression. The problem with both these plays is that the physical limitations placed on the actor generate tremendous emotional tension, which causes physical tension, which compromises breathing. Applying the principles I'd learned from this technique allowed me to experience internal movement and to release some of that performance tension. It is a wonderful technique for actors to learn.

KW: Earlier you spoke about the woman crawling out of the theatre. What kinds of reactions did you receive from Beckett scholars who watched your performance at the Strasbourg Beckett Festival?

WS: What humoured and startled me when we were in Strasbourg, was that there were scholars in the audience who were stunned by the timing, and some of the responses afterwards were, 'Billie [Whitelaw] did it in this amount of time. How was it you were able to do it in twelve and a half minutes and I was able to understand everything you said?' [*Laughter.*] They seemed to experience a kind of delight and awe at this kind of technical proficiency. Now on some level I'm glad that happened, but what was more compelling to me was that finding that twelve and a half minute mark was just magical, mysterious. I have no idea how we got to that. I have no idea why I was able to repeat it and it just started to happen once I was in that piece.

KW: Yet when I watch Billie Whitelaw's version now, I understand everything she says because what those scholars are forgetting, I think, is that they've read the text enough times that they can fill it in; our minds automatically do it. Whereas when I show students a video of the play, they have difficulty understanding it. The more familiar we are with his text, the more we can follow the monologue.

WS: Certainly. But I have to add that meeting and being praised by scholars who I greatly admired, whose writings I'd studied, was quite moving for me. Xerxes has said he thinks that the actor feels this great sense of joy in the performance of this play. I never felt joy, only a great sense of relief. I always felt like I'd run a marathon, or lived through an incredible trauma.

KW: As a final question, I want to give you a chance to express anything we haven't touched on.

WS: What I'd add is that as you approach these plays, you must decipher the story. Certainly in *Play* there is a wonderfully clichéd love triangle, which is easy to figure out. But you have to give careful attention to the kinds of words each of the characters use, and what is repeated and when. There is also some story to the character of Mouth in *Not I*. Beckett gives you clues. There are the literal pieces of history that she grew up in an orphanage and was unloved, and then there is the abstraction of the buzzing and the light that are torturing her. It's not that you can then interpret all of that through that story; it just means it gives you a framework that informs the performance. There has to be a human being behind what's going on.

KW: Exactly. Last fall when I directed Beckett, it was really an eye-opener for me. I had written on and taught these works for some time. As a scholar, I had this really strong feeling that Beckett was about the unknown, and believed that you shouldn't try to decipher the plays too much, but once I was in the theatre, this changed. With *Footfalls* particularly my actress, an undergraduate student, would tell me that parts such as the walking up and down the aisles reminded her of memories of wanting to be married as a child, but here we have a woman, alone, who is re-enacting that dream of marriage. That was her back-story for May. And the performance worked, so I let it be. Ultimately, her back-story was based in the language of the text. By discovering this back-story, she had a sense of who May is.

WS: Right. Sometimes in *Not I*, I'd come upon a repeated image, such as the flowers, she speaks of picking flowers, and I had to figure out why that poetic image is there, and what it suggests to me.

KW: While my actress initially treated me as a well of knowledge, when she asked a question I'd say, 'What do you see in the text?' For me, that process reflects Beckett's refusal to answer questions. He doesn't want to dictate to actors how they should read or interpret the role.

WS: Yes. In *Not I*, the first intelligible word is 'Out', and the first question is what are you in that you're getting out of? Are you already trapped or are you being pushed out, as in a birth? All of those questions came up in rehearsal. The difference in working on any other kind of play is that the actor and director have to find an answer and discover the motivating impulse behind that understanding. In these plays, you recognise the possibilities, you accept the abstraction, and the plays' language and structure guide you.

Bill Largess on *Ohio Impromptu*

*On 17 September 2011, I interviewed **Bill Largess** at the home of Wendy Salkind. While with the Maryland Stage Company, Largess played the part of the Listener in* Ohio Impromptu *and M[an] in* Play, *both of which were featured at the Strasbourg Festival (1996) and the Beckett in Berlin Festival (2000).*

Katherine Weiss: What was your first encounter with the plays of Samuel Beckett? What were your impressions at the time and how has your view of Beckett changed?

Bill Largess: My very first encounter would have been in high school. I took a drama class that was essentially a dramatic literature class. We read pretty widely. The teacher had us read *Waiting for Godot* and told us, 'This is the theatre of the absurd'. We had already read Ionesco, so I was sort of expecting . . . Ionesco and was struck by the fact that it was not at all Ionesco. But my first impression was that I was struck by the humour in *Waiting for Godot*. I didn't expect the vaudeville turns and verbal wit that appears in the play. I was expecting something more apocalyptic and searing. Not that it isn't, but I actually found it very amusing in many ways.

I also was struck by the structure. I happened to connect with this when I was reading plays at that point in my life. I hadn't seen many plays, but I was reading more than I had seen. I was very struck by the structure and the echoing of the ending of the two acts, and the difference between Pozzo and Lucky in the two acts. Beckett accomplished this variation in very simple ways.

Since then, of course, I've seen many of his plays. I guess I can say most of his plays, but certainly not all. I don't know that my initial impression has been proven wrong. There is an enormous amount of wit in these plays. But I am more aware of the pared down quality, the sparseness of the work. The elegance of how much he conveys with so little is something that has really struck me over the years. Having had the chance to do a couple of his plays as an actor, I find that this is a fundamental aspect of his work, which is a wonderful challenge. To call Beckett's writing a simplicity is almost not right. It is easier to write more than it is to write less. The brilliance of how little he writes and still manages to have these powerful plays is something that has really stuck with me.

KW: Could you talk about how you prepared for your role as Listener in *Ohio Impromptu*?

BL: I had seen two productions of the play before I was cast in it, so I sort of had a sense of what works about it. In working with a director like Xerxes [Mehta], the preparation took the form of reading the play over and over but also coming to rehearsal with a very open mind, knowing that this was going to be a real exploration. So I didn't try to make decisions of any kind before coming in. But certainly, given the allusive and enigmatic quality of the story that's being told, and the situation between Reader and Listener, I read it repeatedly. I have to say back then, I didn't particularly research the background of the play, which now I would do. It was not as easy to do without the Internet. Instead, I really focused on what the words were and what happens within the script. Of course in the part of the Listener, what happens is very enigmatic. The preparation took the form of looking into that and trying to come up with possibilities, so when we got into rehearsal we could explore what it might be. Essential, however, was coming in with a very open mind.

KW: In a conversation I've had with Xerxes, he's observed that there's this tension between the actor's inner life and Beckett's horror of the expressive actor, and he believes that this is the key to a successful performance in Beckett's plays. How do you handle this contradiction between the actor's inner life and Beckett's horror of the expressive actor?

BL: An excellent topic for anyone who does Beckett because it is an ongoing question and challenge. I am very much someone who over the years has come to embrace the notion of what the novelist, Isak Dinesen, wrote in *Babette's Feast*, 'The eternal cry of the artist is, let me do my utmost'. Artists want to do as much as they can. What Beckett sets you up to do is a wonderful challenge, or difficulty if you want to think of it as a difficulty. He asks you to do so much, and he insists that on the surface you do so little. In many of the parts I get cast in, I am expressive. But the challenge of being given this circumstance, this set of constraints which Beckett places on all of his characters, certainly the Listener in *Ohio Impromptu,* is wonderful. I feel as though I'm in dialogue with Beckett in which he asks, 'Can you do this? Can you really do this?' I love the opportunity to come back and say, 'I'll try. Let me see if I can do this'. Trying counts. The tension between the actor's impulse and what Beckett lets you do is tough. Once you find your way into it, I think it's immensely rewarding because it's asking you to embrace the tension, embrace the contradiction. I enjoyed that.

KW: Xerxes told me recently that after your performance in Berlin, the scholar Jonathan Kalb wrote to him that yours was the greatest *Ohio Impromptu* he had ever seen because he realised for the first time that the play was about the Listener, not the Reader. In the history of theatre, the character with the most lines is usually the central character. So how, in your opinion, are Beckett and the actor able to destabilise this long tradition in theatre?

BL: In a very simple way, which is that in the course of this very enigmatic encounter between the two characters, if they are two different characters and not the same person, the Listener is in control. Because of the knocks, the Listener controls how the reading proceeds. Even though he does not seem to have control over the story being told, nonetheless, he can stop the Reader and ask for the repeat of what he's heard. The Reader will wait until the Listener decides to continue. The Reader is reading for the Listener's benefit. There's also in Beckett's stage directions the description that the Listener is facing the audience, at an angle, but the Reader is far more turned away from the audience. It's the Listener who is being presented to the audience. Ultimately, the

Reader is not only reading for the Listener's benefit or reading to the Listener, he's also reading about the Listener. It is a story that seems to be about the situation you're seeing on stage. The fact that the Listener is reacting at all indicates to me that essentially the Listener is the central character in the story being told. The Listener has more action. The play is all very simple and pared down, but in terms of the knocking, the stopping the Reader to go back and reread something, the Listener is the one who is more active.

From an actor's standpoint, and this was of course very much something that was discovered in rehearsals with Xerxes, how do you do anything expressive when the Listener is described as having his face covered with his hair hanging down. Beckett has basically taken away facial expressions. He has given the actor essentially these very simple stage directions, the main one is simply, 'Knock'. In rehearsals, Xerxes was very open to and interested in exploring how much, within Beckett's very strict stage directions, variation is available without in any way contradicting the directions. Beckett writes, 'Knock'. Well, what does that mean? How many different kinds of knocks are there? Why does he knock? I can imagine there were productions, like one production by Peter Sellars, where you couldn't even tell that the Listener was doing the knock. It was a very simple uninflected knock each time. The process that we went through led us to a kind of discovery that the knock could be very expressive, that there were very distinctly different reasons for each knock, and that led to a different kind of physicality even without particularly doing anything that contradicted Beckett's description of the scene.

One of the comments I got after a performance (and I wish I knew who this person was) was that he could see the difference in tension in my fist, which I wasn't conscious of. As a more intense or difficult knock was coming up, that audience member could sense my fist tensing more. Xerxes was so insistent that occasionally the knock that allowed the Reader to continue was reluctant. There were a couple knocks which were very difficult. I had heard some part of the reading which was either painful or difficult, where I wasn't ready to go on, and the decision to go on was a very hard one. The danger was I was doing these gentle little knocks which were very powerful if they were audible. Having done a louder knock, a couple of them were really cannon shots, revealed how difficult it was to hear the softer ones. The knock to go on should be a simple little [*Largess knocks gently*] which the audience could hear. But it was so easy to make no noise. Xerxes was very insistent that it had to make some noise.

KW: Was there a mike on the table?

BL: No, there was no mike, no nothing. It was all real sound.

KW: When I directed *Footfalls* in 2010, our sound technician wanted initially to mike the floor. I was immediately against it.

BL: People do that sometimes, but it's not as effective.

KW: You're right. You just don't have the same energy if the footfalls or the knocks are miked.

BL: Xerxes and I agreed that it was in acceptable bounds, because my face was entirely hidden, for moments of expression on my face. We all knew the audience couldn't see my face but the fact that it would affect the energy and the physicality of my body in some way was perfectly acceptable.

I don't know that there was any point where we consciously made the decision and intent that, yes, this is about the Listener. That was a discovery which the audience told us. The difference in the reaction, the fact that it wasn't a simple regular knock, the same thing each time, led them to wonder, why was that knock a more intense reaction. Why was this one a more calm reaction? It's been a long time, but at the time I could've told you distinctly and exactly what each reaction was.

KW: I've come across actors and directors who insist that stage directions and the technical aspects are of little or no importance, while other playwrights, such as Beckett and Sam Shepard, insist that actors and directors should serve the text and the playwright's vision. How do you feel about having to be faithful to the text?

BL: Certainly, it matters on who the playwright is. There are playwrights who don't insist upon that as strongly, or give more vague and general stage directions, and so imply more general freedom. But in the case of someone like Beckett or Shepard where it's distinct and clear, the actions described are part of what the overall vision is. As an actor, you are an interpretive artist. That's going to be the case no matter how you do it, so it becomes a slightly more complex thing. It's like, you have to do this, so in what way does your interpretation come from or inform the play. There's the cliché of the actor saying to the playwright, 'My character wouldn't say that'. That's preposterous. The playwright has written the character's dialogue and you have to figure out why the character says what he does. It's the same thing with the stage directions. When the directions are so integral to the overall piece, particularly if the action doesn't seem to add anything or make sense, it becomes the responsibility of the actor and director to figure out why it's there. It's my job to figure it out, to figure out why and then how do I do it in a way that serves what the character is going through, the action the character is carrying out, and yet, without simply being applied, not just doing it because the playwright said to do it.

KW: Is there anything you would like to add that we haven't touched on?

BL: Only that *Play* and *Ohio Impromptu*, as I have said for years to people who have asked about them or seen references to them, were the hardest plays I ever did and in so many ways the most rewarding and most enjoyable. They are very difficult plays to do well which makes them potentially more exciting and ultimately more rewarding. These productions certainly were. They were very hard, but it was a wonderful experience and I really treasure it.

Wendy Salkind, Peggy Yates and Bill Largess on *Play*

On 17 September 2011, I sat down with **Bill Largess, Wendy Salkind** *and* **Peggy Yates**. *All three actors were cast in Beckett's* Play, *under the direction of Xerxes Mehta. Largess was cast as M, Salkind as M's wife, W1, and Yates as M's mistress, W2. Their production of* Play *toured Strasbourg in 1996 and Berlin in 2000.*

Peggy Yates, Bill Largess, Wendy Salkind (*left to right*) in *Play*.
Director: Xerxes Mehta. Spot operator: Allison Houseworth.
Lighting and Scene design: Terry Cobb. Make-up design: Elena Zlotescu.
The Maryland Stage Company, Baltimore and Berlin, 2000.
Photo: Damon Meledones.

Katherine Weiss: When I directed *Come and Go* and *Footfalls* in 2010, I discovered that working with one actor as opposed to three involved a different kind of collaborative effort. This seems like it would be an interesting process in *Play*. In essence while you're all together on stage, you're not supposed to recognise that there's someone else present. Moreover, there's that fourth player. Beckett designated the light as a player in this strange comedy. Would each of you reflect on how performing as a group that does not acknowledge itself as a group is different or similar to traditional theatre?

Peggy Yates: The fourth person was actually more present than the two other real people, for some reason.

Bill Largess: We address it, for one thing. We talked to the light.

PY: Yes, perhaps that's why. Hearing the other voices obviously fed into my life in the moment. But the light was more present because I was talking directly to it.

BL: The implication being that we're not aware of each other was a challenge because for each of us individually when the light was on we were having this monologue. So there was the question, what is happening when the light was out for each of us. But, of course, the actors are hearing the other actors. It was a balance to find. We worked very hard on finding a level of volume and speed to create the impression that we were all in the same kind of place. From a purely technical standpoint, we were constantly aware of how the others were speaking and how fast it was going. From a character's standpoint, we had to focus on the light. Each struggles with why they're there, why they're talking, and who they're talking to.

Wendy Salkind: I remember the tension I felt once the light was no longer on my face. I had to maintain that inner story so that when the light came back, I could continue my version of the story. But I had to continue to listen to the other two actors, to match certain rhythms, tempo and volume. It seemed that we all sustained a psychological tension that led up to the moment the light returned, feeling like 'I'm going to get my moment here'. [*Laughter.*] In that way there was a connection among us but, of course, we never directly interacted. The only direct interaction was with the light.

KW: Actors respond physically, spiritually, emotionally and intellectually to an imaginary or imaginative situation. The challenge with Beckett is that the situation is often not easy to identify and is often left better unknown. How do you as actors handle the lack of certainty of the situation in Beckett?

PY: That part was hard. At the beginning I wanted to create a story. I wanted to create a fiction that I could follow, the traditional kind of back-story, history: What's my relationship and what do I want? It took a while to let it go and embrace completely the technical aspects of volume and speed because in those technical aspects emotional stuff came up. It was so physically difficult sometimes to maintain the technical that it became part of the emotional situation of the character.

WS: Also, the love triangle was so ordinary and boring, which is kind of the point.

BL: It's almost as if that's what they think is important.

WS: Yes, of course.

BL: The characters are in this strange, hard to describe, situation that they acknowledge. They don't understand why they're there. And they wonder, if I say the right thing will the light stop? I don't know if I thought to make this comparison at the time, but it's a bit like *Ohio Impromptu* where Reader reads the story about the man coming to read the story. Well, we're stuck in these urns, and it's a play about, at least in part, not knowing why we're stuck.

WS: How do I get out, I wondered.

BL: How do I get out? Can I get out? Those are the questions that arose for me. And in a sense, that part is very playable. I remember how angry Wendy's character got at the light. You shout at it. And, Peggy, you try to flirt with it. I try to reason with it. [*Laughter.*] All of which are very playable and, of course, they totally fit the love triangle. It's also amazing how consistent these characters are in terms of what we see them dealing with, which is the memory of the love triangle and then the circumstance they seem to be caught in.

KW: W2 intrudes on this marriage as the light is now intruding on the love triangle.

My next question deals more specifically with the function of the light. The technology of the stage light is an actor and interrogator, and it's been interpreted as such. It's an actor without a face. How do you all understand Beckett's exploration between the human body and stage technology?

WS: I don't know that he knew what technology would be needed to accomplish the image he wanted. He defined a very powerful visual image, and it was essential that the director and designer figure out how to create that image on stage. Any time I've seen Beckett where the visual image is not clean and sparse, the play falls apart instantly. We lose all the conflict because the image controls what happens to the characters. They can use no gestures, no facial expressions, and the minute that light comes on them, they don't know if they are being seen or just blinded. Then when it goes out, it's as if they disappear.

BL: You do disappear.

PY: For the audience, but we're holding onto that thread and when that light comes back on, we're still there. My character still wants to know, still wants out.

KW: Light usually illuminates, brings enlightenment. What happens for the audience is that we don't come any closer to understanding why these figures are there and how they are going to get out. We're not enlightened even when the light is shining on each character.

WS: I remember feeling that the light washed out my face; I remember feeling that it was boring through my brain; that it was just there to torture me. It never occurred to me that it would bring enlightenment to anyone. It was as though the audience was complicit in torturing us because they were out there with that light.

BL: And the notion that we didn't know whether anyone was listening. Are they just like the light? We didn't know.

PY: We don't even know if it is just that. And, then it goes back to repeat in the beginning and the same thing happens again only faster.

BL: And more toneless.

PY: It's interesting to hear that the audience, too, feels the frustration that we were feeling as characters, the frustration that by the end you know no more.

BL: In thinking about some of his other plays in relation to the exploration of the body and theatre technology or stage technology, I think Wendy is right. Beckett had a visual image in mind and he gave a detailed description of how you could do this with urns that sat on top of a platform and everything, but such descriptions are not at all helpful. They reveal how he wants it to look but not how to achieve the look.

PY: He's saying, 'you figure it out'.

BL: *Not I* is another strong example of that. He doesn't give any indication of how you create the image. So it's more about what it's going to look like certainly in terms of the plays where he takes away the body in different ways.

PY: He denies the body.

BL: You can even think of *Endgame* where Hamm can't walk and Clov can't sit down. Taking away the body along with paring away at the words seems to fascinate him. He challenges us to express with less means at our disposal.

WS: Also when you remove the visible body and the gestural body, you remove the observer's ability to find the most ordinary psychological connection to what you're saying. It's as though, for Beckett, the body is only a vehicle for a certain level of experience, but not the expression of that experience.

PY: Yes, the audience is denied the body to help tell the story for them and the actor is denied the body in order to do that same thing. Everything has to come from somewhere else and it's not anywhere that you can easily describe.

WS: Except your experience of the body is much more heightened because you can't use it.

PY: I don't believe there's ever been another play or production that I've ever felt more physically engaged and yet hadn't used my body. Remember, Wendy, in that last performance where you and I dissolved into a bucket of tears. We cried in the urns once the curtain came down because it was such a physical effort and so engaging in so many ways, physically, emotionally, mentally and psychically.

BL: A play to consider in regards to the body is *Catastrophe* where the director manipulates the Protagonist's body. He talks about the light at one point, whether to just focus on his head or his face.

KW: And, there is the canned applause. When the director says, 'There is my catastrophe!', are we, the audience, going to be complicit in this catastrophe or not? And, of course, we applaud, but then we really shouldn't. After all, we've just seen this man tortured on stage. That's a fascinating play. I saw a video of David Warrilow's production. When he raises his head, the audience is confronted with an eye staring back at them. I don't know how the lighting designer achieved the effect; it is remarkable.

WS: I saw that production and he was extraordinary. He looked like a Holocaust victim.

KW: The actor creates an onstage being commonly known as the character, yet in Beckett, as Xerxes Mehta has argued in his scholarly work, there are no characters, or at least none in the traditional sense. These figures are often thought of as ghosts. To what extent did you enter Beckett's after-death world in *Play* and how do you regard the tensions between these inner lives that you create in Beckett's figures, and the fascinating external forms into which you mould yourselves?

PY: I would agree that they are not characters. I wouldn't approach this as I would a traditional play and character.

WS: I agree with Peggy. Although they each have elements of a personality, they are not full characters, and the repetition of the stories, the sense that this conflict will never end, does heighten your awareness that you are only a head, a voice. Peggy and I were talking a moment ago about one rehearsal where we did a psychological improvisation. Xerxes has probably blocked this out. It was an exercise we did which you might do to heighten motivation and interaction between characters. What we can't remember about it is whether it helped us at all. [*Laughter.*] It felt so weird and so wrong.

BL: Yes, I vaguely remember doing it, and think it didn't help really.

PY: It didn't completely inform what we were doing. For me, like Wendy said before, the need to be heard, the need to get out of what box I was in and the inability to be free became the driving force. The technical constraints that were put on us, as far as the speed, the volume and the interaction with the character of light, coloured or became who we were. You're stuck and you want out and you have this driving need that is unquenched – a thirst that you cannot quench. But it is framed in a story of sorts. The story is so simple. It doesn't go away, it's still there, but the real focus and the real drive is getting what you want.

BL: I feel like the after-death quality of the play is a given in the piece. I know we talked about it, asking what is going on with them. Are they in hell? Are they in purgatory? But I don't remember spending a lot of time with that because as W2 says she thought there'd be peace, that it would all be better now. Is that the end of the affair, is that death? What is that? I don't know that they know where they are, exactly. But none of us would have resisted that suggestion, that this is the afterlife.

WS: Right, and it wouldn't help the play to say that's what this is; they've died.

BL: I would even go so far as to use that in trying to talk about *Ohio Impromptu*. Sam McCready, who played Reader, and I used to talk about that; we felt the play had a resolved quality at the end. We didn't articulate that at the time, but we might have gone there with *Play*. That reading is possible but their situation is going to keep going so I don't think it really informed so much.

WS: In that way, the turning back on the story reminded me of those experiences we keep reliving because of some deep guilt, perhaps of something we didn't do or didn't say. Usually, they surface as I'm falling asleep. The memory comes at me and I wonder can I let this go or will it bore into my mind again now? That's what this play felt like.

KW: How do you respond, as actors in *Play*, to being physically restricted?

BL: My memory of the entire experience is of the fact that in order to maintain absolute stillness, because even in those urns we couldn't move, we were given metal bars to hold onto. In my preeminent memory of the whole thing, in rehearsal or performance, all of us basically had to pry our fingers off the bar because we were holding on so tight; we essentially couldn't let go.

PY: Literally, we couldn't move. I had to stay there a few minutes and say to myself, 'Come on. You can let go now'.

BL: And it hurt.

PY: Do you remember doing a run without the bar in the urns? I felt like I was going to fall into or push over the urn because it's not natural to be completely still. Maybe ideally, if you worked on this for years you would get to a place where you were so free, so still and so calm that you wouldn't need the support. Maybe? Let me take that back.

KW: You definitely couldn't do it with the speed of speech you all reached.

PY: Exactly.

WS: Part of the feeling of moving forward or falling is because the effort to be heard makes you jut your head forward, wanting to grab that light.

PY: When I remember they put the bars in, I thought, oh, thank God something to hold onto, but then it became a clutching of sorts. When I think of this play, I think the first thing my hands do is this. [*She balls her hands into fists.*]

KW: Would you talk about the make-up. Your faces looked as though they were part of the urns. How was that accomplished?

WS: It was Elmer's glue and oatmeal.

PY: And then around the mouth was latex.

BL: Because the oatmeal would've swelled and fallen off if we'd used any water-based make-up. We used grease paint on top of the latex, then we added the Elmer's glue and finally the oatmeal. The colour was cadaver grey.

PY: How appropriate!

WS: We literally had to cover our entire faces with Elmer's glue.

BL: And pat on the oatmeal.

WS: Or there was Peggy's technique where she'd roll her face in a plate of oatmeal flakes. [*Laughter by all.*]

PY: We had to blow dry our faces so that the Elmer's glue didn't completely dry. If it was too wet it would set.

WS: But if it was too dry it would crack and fall off.

BL: The reason for the latex around our mouths was because the oatmeal in that area had to be a little more fixed. As inexpressive as we were, our lips had to move. Otherwise the little flakes of oatmeal would start to crack off. In a couple of run-throughs they popped off. [*Laughter.*]

WS: This was a horrible feeling because you felt so exposed.

BL: We had those stocking caps on as well to hide our hair. At the end of the night, we took those stocking caps off, and then, it was just like *Mission Impossible*, you could peel off the glue. A couple of times, if you were really careful you could get the whole mask off. I only accomplished it once or twice.

PY: I always felt like this was probably really good for my skin.

WS: That's what Elena Zlotescu, the make-up designer, said. I was trying to remember if we tried anything else.

BL: We tried all latex once and we despised that. It was horrible because it stinks so badly. The oatmeal stuck on great, but it took forever and it was expensive too. We learned that we had to do the grease paint around our eyes first because once you got the oatmeal around your eyes, you couldn't quite get enough grease paint in. So when we peeled it off, we still had grey around our eyes and a little around our mouths.

WS: I was thinking that we'd have trouble taking this production to another country now because we wouldn't be able to bring the oatmeal with us on the plane, as we did flying to Berlin.

BL: We would, and, remember, those big bottles of Elmer's glue.

WS: And the oatmeal couldn't be instant. We discovered it had to be regular oatmeal.

PY: Not five minutes, not one minute.

BL: Regular rolled oats. Once in a while, this even happened in a couple of performances, you'd feel the oatmeal mask crack and you'd think I hope it's not falling off.

PY: Right, it's not like you can use your mouth less. So if you felt it going, it was like, oh well, here we go. [*Laughter.*]

BL: It took forever because of the time it took to dry between each step. Am I remembering it right; it was ninety minutes to get it all done? At least an hour. Then I had to get it off while Sam [McCready] would do *That Time* because I'd have to do *Ohio Impromptu*. Fortunately, the make-up for *Ohio Impromptu* was just white make-up.

KW: Often, when analysing Beckett, one forgets his humour. Would you all talk about the humour of the play from the actor's perspective?

WS: Yes, we really discovered that in rehearsal once we could play it at full speed. And there were times we just lost it because of the humour.

BL: The absurdity of the love triangle, and of the man's lies. He's just lying back and forth to both of the women. You know, it's funny. And then there's Erskine . . . showing people in and showing people out.

PY: And my depiction of W1, who Wendy played, not being all that positive [*Laughter*]. Puffy face, and so forth.

BL: And vice versa.

WS: The language of the women's accusations is so excessive, and then there is M's hiccup, that barely interrupts the pace.

KW: And also, M's ridiculous rationale for what's happened to the two women. Perhaps, he says, they're sitting together, drinking tea. [*Laughter.*] As though they have become friends.

BL: Yes, that green tea they both so liked.

WS: It was shocking the first time we performed and the audience laughed, because, in conventional plays, you've been trained to allow time for laughter before you go back to the dialogue or action. That would be impossible in this play. So if they laugh, and they miss what's been said, they'll get another chance to hear it again in the repeat.

BL: The instinct to stop for the laughter is strong but you just have to plough ahead. I'll throw in one more thing. It's as much textual as anything else. Some of the humour comes (and this is the thing I love) from the audience's reaction to the repeat. It's a little while before the audience knows they're hearing the same thing, and it's the moments of laughter that lets them know the same little joke is being retold. Once in a while there would be a little murmur in the audience: 'They've gone back to the beginning. Oh no!'

WS: It could be their realisation that they're just as trapped as are we.

BL: I think that once at the University of Maryland, Baltimore County theatre when we performed it, when we started a false third repeat, there was an 'Oh no!' in the audience.

WS: We did have an experience in rehearsals, at least Peggy and I did – I don't know if it happened to you, Bill – where we each just blanked for a moment. It was horrifying; it was just a dead stop. And Xerxes didn't do anything. He didn't say, okay, let's take it back. It was just like we all stopped, waiting, what do we do? Would this come back? Of course, the light stayed on your face because it was your turn to talk. So, the light is there and you can't talk. It was like the rehearsal process completely mirrored what was happening in this play.

PY: I think that was when I stopped thinking of it as a comedy because there was so much fear. There was always that threat of not staying in character, of starting to get so fast you felt out of control. That fear was always hovering on the edge.

BL: There really was the tendency to speed up which was not good. We fought that a lot and at first we would constantly go too fast. I don't know that one would do it differently now, our lighting person, Alli Houseworth, rehearsed with us from the very beginning.

WS: She memorised the entire play.

BL: She had three buttons whereas now I think it would just be three cues: go go go. I don't think she ever made a mistake.

PY: Never. I don't think she ever did in rehearsal or performance, not ever a hitch.

WS: I think that blanking out moment had to do with getting caught up in what was happening with the two of you and losing my stream of thought when the light was off of me.

BL: I think it was in the performance that ended with you two in tears, that the light came up on me and there was an infinitesimal moment of me not speaking just because my mind had wandered a tiny bit. I had listened to something someone else had said. For the rest of it my heart was beating. And I think it was partly because it was a performance in which we had sped up. We were going very fast. It was very exciting; it was very thrilling in a way. But, again, as I said, I heard something that one of you said and all of a sudden I was like 'ahhh'.

WS: When we sped up, it was white-knuckle time for Xerxes. I could hear him thinking, 'I don't think they can keep control of it at that speed'.

BL: It was like a rollercoaster when it got fast!

WS: And you knew too. As soon as it started you knew you couldn't slow down from there.

BL: Because it was supposed to be quicker the second time through.

PY: And if you slowed down or sped up, the danger is for Alli who has to keep going in kind of a flow. If it's going a tiny bit faster for a few seconds that amounts to a lot faster.

WS: She was phenomenal, the way she did that.

KW: Would you all like to add anything else to the discussion? Otherwise, I'll turn this interrogator, the voice recorder, off. [*Laughter.*]

WS: I would say there was an element of fun in *Play* that didn't exist in *Not I*. It was kind of comradely that I knew the minute I stepped up in that urn, that we were all about to enter this tremendously difficult experience together. It felt a little like a marathon.

PY: I think of the play as going down in this sled that you can't stop; the slalom doesn't stop until the end when it's over. Performing *Play* is like stepping into a sled.

BL: I also remember the experience of getting into place before the show, and as I stepped into the urn, [*he takes a deep breath*] my heart began to race a little. It was almost better once we started. It was waiting backstage for the curtain to open that was the worst.

Sam McCready on *That Time* and *Ohio Impromptu*

On 16 September 2011, I visited the Irish actor, **Sam McCready***, at his home in Baltimore. After scones and coffee, prepared by his wife, actress Joan McCready, we went to Sam's study which contained books by and on W.B. Yeats and Samuel Beckett, among other Irish writers. McCready was part of the Maryland Stage Company which took their exciting productions of Beckett's late plays to the Beckett in Strasbourg Festival in 1996 and the Beckett in Berlin Festival and Conference in 2000. McCready played Reader in* Ohio Impromptu *and Listener in* That Time. *He also acted in other Beckett plays, including* Krapp's Last Tape *at Trinity College, Hartford, directed by Arthur Feinsod.*

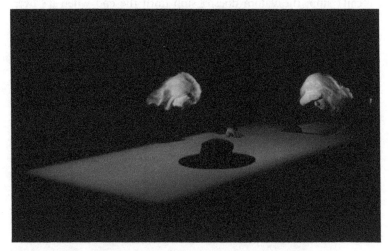

Sam McCready as Reader and Bill Largess as Listener in *Ohio Impromptu*.
Director: Xerxes Mehta. Lighting and Scene design: Terry Cobb.
Costume design: Elena Zlotescu. The Maryland Stage Company, Baltimore and Berlin, 2000; Strasbourg, 1996 (with Michael Stebbins as Listener); Baltimore, 1990 (with Walter Bilderback as Listener).
Photo: Robert Dold.

Katherine Weiss: What was your first encounter with the plays of Samuel Beckett?

Sam McCready: The first time I encountered Beckett was in the late 1950s when I saw a production in Belfast of *Waiting for*

Godot. It was the first Irish production. I had heard a great deal about the play and I was delighted when I had the opportunity to see it.

KW: What were your impressions at that time?

SMC: I was thoroughly confused; it was all very new and quite different from anything I had seen before. You must remember that I was still at college and my experience of plays was Shakespeare and the classic plays by Sheridan, Oscar Wilde, Bernard Shaw and Sean O'Casey. In *Godot*, there didn't appear to be any real plot and the set was an empty space with a withered tree at the back. Yet the characters, principally Vladimir and Estragon, were familiar to me possibly because they came from an Irish theatre tradition, as in the plays of J.M. Synge. I enjoyed their dialogue although I didn't always understand what they were talking about. Who was Godot? Why did they want to find Godot? The questions appeared important but the play didn't provide any obvious answers.

I enjoyed Pozzo, the braggart, and Lucky, the elderly man in rags, with a rope around his neck, and a long, long speech, longer than any I had ever heard in the modern theatre. I understood the master/slave relationship but what were they doing on an Irish country road? The play provided no answers and it was, for me, a rude awakening; I was witnessing a piece of modernist theatre, a theatre of symbol and image that was defying the rules of conventional theatre as I knew them. I had many questions in my head as I left the theatre.

KW: How have your views of Beckett's plays changed since then?

SMC: I think I'm still confused! Seriously, since that time, some fifty years ago, I have come to realise a little more about what Beckett is about. His theatre engages me emotionally, intellectually and spiritually through the use of language and symbol, sound and silence, movement and stillness, light and space – all the devices of the modern theatre. As I reflect on that first experience of *Waiting for Godot*, I see the figure of Pozzo as a symbol of modern materialism, while Lucky, with that rope around his neck, is a dependent slave, attached to his master, unable to break free. I have learned to 'read' the symbols, in the same way as I 'read' modern painting; there is no one explanation, no one interpretation and the experience of the plays, especially in performance, is richer for that reason.

KW: When you first saw *Waiting for Godot*, had you already decided to become an actor or did watching it change that?

SMC: No, I was already very committed to the theatre as a profession before I saw *Godot* but seeing the play encouraged me to look beyond some of the conventional theatre I was doing and to strive to do more demanding plays. Interestingly in that production, the actors, many of whom I knew, were coming very fresh to Beckett; they didn't have theories and scholarly ideas to get in the way of their intuitive response to the characters. They approached the play like any other play and somehow it worked for the audience. Indeed, Patrick Magee, an Irish actor, who made such a speciality of Beckett (he performed in *Krapp's Last Tape* and *That Time*, both of which were written for him), told me he found nothing fancy or intellectual about Beckett's characters. 'I'm an actor', he said, 'I'm offered the part, I learn it; I listen to the director, and I do what I can. I find the character but what happens to the character in the play is not my concern – that's for the playwright or the audience to think about'. And he went on, 'Do you know who you are as a person, do you know what you're doing every minute of the day? Of course not. Neither does the character'. I was lucky enough to act with Magee in a number of radio productions and his approach was always the same. He never argued or fought with the director, he never became obsessed with a character, he learned the lines, he followed the director's blocking, but intuitively he inhabited the character and ensured he always said the lines clearly. For me, as an actor, Beckett is just another playwright, like Shakespeare. Shakespeare makes demands on the actor; Ibsen, Oscar Wilde, Arthur Miller, all of these playwrights make demands. Beckett makes demands; I must respond to those demands while at the same time remembering he is just another playwright.

KW: Would you discuss your preparation and research for the reader in *Ohio Impromptu*, as well as for Krapp in *Krapp's Last Tape* and Listener in *That Time*.

SMC: I ask myself, 'Who is this person? Where are they? What do they want? What do they need?' And that's how I approach Beckett's characters. But, in terms of the study of Beckett's plays, he throws up certain problems. In *Ohio Impromptu*, for example, he keeps interrupting the narrative with knocks and some of the lines are repeated. When I tried to read it straight through, I found it impossible to get a clear narrative, so I had to ignore the knocks and the repetitions in order to find the simple story. The same thing with *That Time*, which I think is a beautiful work. In the play, there are three voices and each of them is speaking part of the narrative, a series of interlinking monologues. When I tried to read the play straight through, it was totally confusing; I couldn't make sense of it until I isolated the narrative of each of the three Voices, A, B and C, and studied them separately. When I was rehearsing the play, I looked only at Voice A and read that monologue through; then Voice B; and finally Voice C. Then I had to record each of the voices, suggesting a different age or mood for each monologue; only in performance, when I listened to the three voices on tape, was I able to get an overall sense of the narrative. With *Krapp's Last Tape*, because Krapp has recorded a narration at various stages of his life, I am asked as an actor to age through each of these narratives, while in performance, I have to be aware of Krapp in the present, listening to old recordings, making a new recording. These demands, I believe, are specific to Beckett.

For me, Beckett's language is extraordinarily simple. What he does with that language, of course, is mesmeric, with its rhythms, its allusions, its ambiguities, its fascinating use of repetition. There is a phrase from *Ohio Impromptu*, 'White nights now again his portion'. When I first read the play, I didn't know what 'white nights' meant, perhaps other people did, but I didn't. With research I discovered it was a direct translation from the French *nuits blanches*, which I understand means sleepless nights, nightmares. White and nights, two simple words, but rich with meaning when used by Beckett. As an actor, if there is any word I don't understand in a play, I have to find out what the word means. Now it so happens I'm Irish; the language that Beckett uses in the three plays I am speaking about is largely familiar to me; the idiom is familiar. The language is part of me, I use it every day. But I would think for an actor who is not Irish, there are a number of expressions and idioms which might be unfamiliar and need research.

KW: Xerxes Mehta has observed that there is a tension between the actor's inner life and Beckett's horror of the expressive actor. He believes that this may be the key to the successful performance of Beckett's plays. How do you handle the tension between the actor's need to create an inner life and Beckett's horror of the expressive actor?

SMC: That's a difficult and complex question to answer. What Xerxes describes represents what is surely the greatest challenge for the actor in Beckett. When I work on Beckett, I start as I would for any role; I work on the material imaginatively, emotionally and physically – not necessarily in that order. I use my imagination a great deal. I can't read words without my imagination seeing a picture. As an actor, I move around, my body is an expressive instrument, and I explore my emotional range. Those are all the skills of what we might call the expressive actor and I use them all in my work on Beckett in rehearsal. But what I have to do with Beckett in performance, to follow Xerxes's thesis, as I understand it, is to deny all those things; to deny my imagination, to deny the colour that comes from emotion and feelings and, of course, I have to deny myself the conventional physical vocabulary which an actor is trained to use.

When I am acting the Beckett character, while I am speaking the words, I must say to my body, my imagination, my feeling, 'No,

I mustn't use you; I mustn't go there'. It is a kind of holding back, it is a denial of all I represent as an actor. My voice is naturally rich and resonant, but I must try to deny that voice in performance. I try to find a dryer, colder, less expressive voice and that is totally against everything I do. It is a struggle and out of that struggle a tension is created between the inner life of the character and my desire to be expressive. Being of mature years myself, much of what Beckett writes is within my experience, the pull of memory, the isolation, the loneliness and so on. When I speak about sitting on a stone, going into the wetness, the dampness, the rain, going into a library, an art gallery, returning home, as the character does in *That Time*, I cannot help but create in my inner mind the associations I have with these experiences and yet I must hold them back, to distil them as it were, to allow the Beckett character to speak through me and yet not be coloured by me. As a Beckett actor, I am the medium through which the character speaks.

I also have to mention that my experience of the theatre is deeply rooted in the plays of William Butler Yeats; he is my major study. In his *Happy Days,* Beckett, as you know, quotes from Yeats's play *At the Hawk's Well.* The phrase that he quotes – 'I call to the eye of the mind' – is for me a mantra which I use when performing Beckett. I am the medium, calling to the imagination of the audience, images, feelings, thoughts and sensations. I am not acting these things out, externalising them; I am calling them up, inducing, through the words, a state of reverie or dream. Through my experience of Yeats, aspects of the Beckettian theatre which may be less familiar to others are, in fact, very familiar to me; the importance of stillness, the use of a mask-like, expressionless face, the negation of personality. Whether or not Beckett was influenced by Yeats is not a central issue. Beckett comes out of a theatre tradition in which Yeats is a major player, and to me, as an actor, many aspects of the Beckettian theatre are familiar to me through Yeats.

KW: That's really interesting. Xerxes and I were trying to think of who Beckett reads in terms of playwrights. Very few scholars actually write about which plays Beckett had seen or which plays

Beckett had in his library. They talk about the poetry and novels he read but they don't talk about the plays very much. And there is a lot of resonance between him and Yeats.

SMC: The most obvious one is in Yeats's *Purgatory*, isn't it; two tramps, a man and his son, a withered tree . . .

KW: A stone.

SMC: A stone.

KW: The only difference is that in *Purgatory* there is a house and sometimes it's performed without a house.

SMC: In the first production, there was the exterior of a house on stage but since then the house has been left to the imagination; all that is on stage are the withered tree and the stone. With Yeats there is that wonderful economy we also find in Beckett; the one-act play, the central action represented by one or two characters, the symbolic action.

KW: Did you experience any physical challenges in Beckett's plays, and if so, how did you handle them?

SMC: In *That Time* I was standing on a high platform in darkness, my head lit by a single spotlight. I had to keep absolutely still, my eyes closed for most of the play, and occasionally open them, while taking deep breaths. This may seem very simple, but to have your eyes closed when you're in total darkness for a long time, lit by a single spotlight and listening to a recorded voice (your own) coming from speakers, can become an unsettling, disorientating experience; you feel as if you're levitating. In *Ohio Impromptu*, sitting with one hand on my forehead, while I read and turned the pages from a large book, responding to the knocks from the Listener, all in near total stillness, and then, at a particular moment, taking the hand down, looking at the Listener and holding that look, unblinking, unmoving, while the stage lights dimmed very slowly, that was quite demanding – but I loved the experience of it. How did I handle these challenges? By listening intently to the recordings in *That Time* and focusing on my task to respond to the Listener in *Ohio Impromptu*. Focus on the character and that distracts you from thinking about yourself.

One thing I haven't touched on and one that frustrates me very much with Beckett is that he uses much recorded speech which the actor has to record in rehearsals and listen to on stage. That appears very easy. As an actor in a conventional play, you usually learn the lines during the rehearsals and by the opening you've grown into them. Now the problem with Beckett is that you have to record the speeches early in the rehearsal process so that you can actually rehearse the play. The lines have been set in stone, as it were, by the time you perform for an audience, and you have to listen to your own voice over and over, knowing there are other choices you would have made if you had been able to record the lines at the Dress Rehearsal or been able to say them 'live' in performance. You are always reminded that while you are taking part in a live performance, living in the moment, you are also dealing with something very mechanical, something fixed over which you have no control. As an actor I find that frustrating and if that's part of the tension of your earlier question, it's certainly there.

KW: It is common knowledge that an actor responds physically, spiritually, emotionally and intellectually to an imaginative or an imaginary situation as you, yourself, pointed out. The challenge with Beckett is that the situation is often not easy to identify, and is often better left unknown. How do you as an actor handle the lack of interpretive certainty in Beckett?

SMC: There are sequences that I don't understand as an actor. But as an actor I have to create an understanding for myself, otherwise I will just be saying words. I make the meaning for myself and I play that meaning. Beckett denied any kind of interpretation, and Xerxes Mehta, our director, while creating a situation in which we discuss the play, in no way imposes an interpretation on his actors. He creates an environment in which the actor is allowed to find his own meaning and to play that meaning. I must make decisions about the character I am playing, I must have something concrete, something very human, something simple to hang on to before I can play the character. And I must trust the language. If I say it simply and directly, avoiding any nuance of interpretation, I believe the audience will make sense of it.

KW: It struck me that your magnificent *Ohio Impromptu*, which I saw in Berlin, was like a Rembrandt painting.

SMC: Oh yes, absolutely.

KW: And in fact the situation of this play can be a painterly one. It's not about an action unravelling; it's about reading, about narrative, about listening, but not a physically outward action in the traditional sense. And again it seems like this image, or after-image, is almost ghostly. How do you as an actor master such an image without ending up being static?

SMC: In *Ohio Impromptu*, *That Time* and *Krapp's Last Tape*, memory is a central theme. I really connect with this. In the end that's all we have in life, memories, and when we die, the memory will be no more. Not a cheerful thought. Although I am static in *That Time*, the inner life of the character is in the image, and repress it how I will, it will still speak to the audience. In *Ohio Impromptu* I feel my personal story is being narrated, that I am reading from the book of my life, and the devastation of the final line, 'Nothing is left to tell' and the closing of the book, signify that my life is over. I believe I am reading to my other self, my alter ego, until there is nothing more to say and that is the end. Again, I believe the inner life of the character will speak out of the stillness.

KW: Beckett shied away from interpreting his plays for actors and directors. How important is the process of interpretation to the actor, and was Beckett's refusal to answer the questions a flaw or a virtue?

SMC: A virtue. To me the writer is the writer and the actor the actor. The writer writes and the actor interprets; it's a happy collaboration. Beckett has no responsibility to say what his play is about; what he wants to say is in the play. A play, as in a work of contemporary art, is open to many interpretations, and is the greater for it.

KW: Occasionally I meet people who argue that there is no freedom in Beckett, and thus no joy in acting or directing in Beckett. His plays are technical, as we've discussed. They're controlled to a further extent than most playwrights, some would say. However, I have found that there is great emotion in Beckett. Emotion in Beckett is expressed in the technique. We have touched on some of this already. The holding back of the conventional forms of expressing emotions results in a greater emotion in the audience. I would like you to talk a little more about how you handled the technique of this control.

SMC: As I've said, the Beckett texts encourage the actor to draw on a rich emotional life and the denial of those inner feelings in performance creates an exciting tension. Stillness, for example, is not a static condition; it is rich and full. Stillness enables the actor to have tremendous concentration and to place a focus on the words and the ideas that may be diffused by the actor moving around. Stillness is a virtue, if the actor knows how to handle it. The control which Beckett imposes on you is in fact a liberation. Beckett defines the limits; accept those limits and you become alive in a fresh, unencumbered way. I appreciate Beckett's specificity yet his stage directions are still open to interpretation. In *Footfalls*, for example, he specifies the number of paces, but we have to decide for ourselves 'what length are the paces'. How heavy should the knocks be in *Ohio Impromptu*? How strong is the miked breathing in *That Time*? Those are the director's choices.

KW: Directors who say they wouldn't direct Beckett's plays because in Beckett there is no artistic freedom forget that Beckett changed his own stage directions according to the spaces in which he was directing. Crucial to your choices is knowing what's on the page so that if a change is suggested it is one that is informed.

SMC: You're absolutely right. If you make any changes, they have to be true to the intention of Beckett, and therefore you must know your text intimately. I'm sure you have followed the Gate productions which were filmed for the *Beckett on Film* project in 2000; those I've seen, I have thought unsatisfactory. In *Ohio Impromptu*, the same actor plays both roles, Reader and Listener. The play is filmed in close up, and the actor is dressed informally. The production may satisfy some viewers but it's not Beckett.

KW: In Berlin in 2000, one of the hot topics was about this particular production of *Ohio Impromptu*. Some people loved it because it was the same actor which supported their reading that the two figures in the play are the same person, and some people wondered, 'Do we know that?' I thought about that a lot. Even if what we are seeing on stage is one person rather than two, when we project an image of ourselves outward we never see ourselves the way we really are. You only have to look in a mirror, or listen to yourself on tape, to realise this. That's part of the reason why Beckett didn't put a mirror in front of the Reader.

SMC: I don't think you can film Beckett satisfactorily. Beckett wrote for the theatre (apart from the pieces he wrote for television) and his work can only be fully understood in the theatre.

KW: Part of the beauty about the late works, like in *Ohio Impromptu*, is that distance; you don't see the faces clearly. When I'm an audience member, I'm drawn in by the fact that I can project my own face onto those characters because I recognise the emotion. But they are emotions that we don't readily want to feel so we do hold them back. That's the tension, too, for me as a viewer.

To conclude, is there anything you would like to add that we haven't discussed?

SMC: I want to just make one further comment in relation to Beckett and Yeats. I want to mention the theory of dreaming back, a Buddhist belief in which, after death, a person returns to a place of trauma and relives the experience over and over. I have found this belief useful in performing Beckett. You have said that when seeing our production of *Ohio Impromptu* in Berlin, you found the characters ghostly. Interestingly, when I'm doing *Ohio Impromptu*, I connect with that sense of dreaming back, believing that I am not a living human being but a soul, a ghost reliving an action which is occurring again and again and again in the hope that one day I will be released. Dreaming back is central to Yeats's later plays and I think it's present in Beckett's later plays also. I don't have to prove it but for me, as an actor, it is something I can hold on to.

CONCLUSION

The quantity and quality of Samuel Beckett's literary output is astonishing. Along with writing prose and poetry, Beckett produced a vast collection of dramatic literature, writing not only stage plays (of which he is most known for) but also plays for radio and television. Beckett even ventured into cinema with one short film. *Film*, while not discussed at length in this book, reveals Beckett's interest in exploring technology thematically and formally.

Beckett's dramatic works do not exist in a vacuum. They are in conversation with theory and philosophy. We find, for example, the philosopher Walter Benjamin and Henri Bergson in dialogue with Beckett. Benjamin and Beckett question the role of technology in relation to the storyteller, particularly the post-war storyteller. And, Bergson's investigation of memory may have inspired Beckett's exploration of memory and the tape recorder as discussed by Dustin Anderson in Chapter 4. Additionally, post-World War Two thinkers, such as Gilles Deleuze and Félix Guattari, Cathy Caruth and Dominick LaCapra, among others, enrich a reading of Beckett's use of technology as seen in his later works. These theorists learn from Beckett what it means to exist in a highly technological modern world, full of uncertainty and trauma. Beckett has been a frequent study of philosophers such as Alain Badiou who, as Graley Herren points out in Chapter 4, has misread Beckett's concept of love in the teleplays. What we discover when reading or seeing Beckett's plays is that the plays lend themselves to complex theoretical and philosophical inquiry.

What makes Beckett remarkable as a playwright is not only his understanding of theoretical and philosophical concepts or his fine exploration of language. Beckett was deeply invested in putting his plays into performance. He had an acute awareness of how his work should look and went to great lengths to ensure that his plays were done well. Beckett often directed his own stage and television plays and corresponded with actors and directors, offering what assistance he could. Nicholas Johnson and Xerxes Mehta address the challenges in directing Beckett in Chapter 4 and actors Sam McCready, Bill Largess, Wendy Salkind and Peggy Yates speak about their experiences as actors in Beckett's late plays in Chapter 5. Along with revealing how they created their roles, these theatre professionals discuss the make-up and costuming as well as the humour and terror of *Play*, *Not I*, *That Time* and *Ohio Impromptu*.

Both theory and performance studies are essential to this study of Beckett. They help to inform Beckett's use of technology to challenge the conventions of the stage, radio and television. He pushes the limits of each dramatic form, minimalising the action and picture before the audience. In doing this, Beckett challenges many of the conventions the audience takes for granted. We are shown how political tyranny and personal ghosts haunt his protagonists. We witness his storytellers struggling to create tales that they hope will relieve and liberate them from their current agony. And we discover that writing, for Beckett, is a technological production that illuminates the audiences' process of reading images and making connections where there may possibly be none.

The underlining paradox in Beckett's exploration of technology is that even when his machines fail, as seen in all his dramatic texts to a greater or lesser extent, these machines are still rooted in ideas surrounding authority and authorship. Although much of the writing in the twentieth century has tried to destabilise notions of clock and chronicle time as authorial, this destabilisation found in *Waiting for Godot* and *Endgame* can only be a philosophical one, Beckett reveals. Beckett's agenda is not one of deconstructing concepts of time. Rather, he exposes the process of inscription into timepieces (*Waiting for Godot*, *Endgame* and *Happy Days*), tape recorders (*Krapp's Last Tape*) and photographic images (the teleplays) and challenges this inscribed authority through the inevitable 'winding down' of watches and clocks in works.

The winding and breaking down of technology is heightened in Beckett's radio plays. There is humour in the sounds of the faltering machines in *All That Fall* and *The Old Tune*. Beckett saturates his radio plays with sound, crucial to the radio play. But by doing so in uncommon ways, Beckett makes his listeners aware of the mechanisms that go into constructing his plays about the process of constructing stories. All the voices in the radio plays are under the obligation to tell a tale of some sort. While the stories begin, putter out, falter, the audience is challenged to follow and piece the narratives together.

The act of inscription becomes the focal point of Beckett's teleplays. By the time Beckett is writing for television, he becomes intrigued by the interrogation of the spectator as a voyeur in the act of surveillance and inscription. Surveillance, in these works, is related closely to the act of reading images. Deleuze and Guattari's system of faciality and their metaphor of the white wall/black hole become extremely helpful to understanding how we read faces and sur*faces* and how Beckett stages this process of reading. In projecting death-masks and impenetrable ghostly images on screen, Beckett exposes all acts of reading as struggling to reconstruct authority, and by exposing the mechanisms involved in inscribing meaning onto the white surface of the face and the sealing of the black holes of the eyes, Beckett suggests that all humanity is locked into systems of authority. Making sense is what we are programmed to do, and yet, when confronted with Beckett's puzzles our ability to reason is shown as a faltering mechanism.

The frequency with which technological images and language appear and break down in Beckett's dramatic writing constitute more than just a minor theme in his work. The consistency of these technologies reveals Beckett's overarching concern over textual authority. It is through his employment of technology that he can interrogate the machines upholding authorial structures, exposing their mechanisms and as such awakening the absent-minded spectators and readers. But regardless of the heightened awareness of the mechanisms upholding authorial systems and thus the ability to break down these structures, Beckett unnervingly reveals in his late works, such as *Catastrophe* and *What Where*, that the spectators remain enclosed in the process of inscribing meaning onto surfaces.

NOTES

Introduction

1. See James McNaughton, 'Beckett, German Fascism, and History: The Futility of Protest', *Samuel Beckett Today/Aujourd'hui*, Vol. 15 (2005), pp. 101–16 and Mark Nixon, 'Between Gospel and Prohibition: Beckett in Nazi Germany 1936–1937' in Seán Kennedy and Katherine Weiss (eds), *Samuel Beckett: History, Memory, Archive*, New York: Palgrave/Macmillan, 2009, pp. 31–46.
2. Terry Eagleton, 'Political Beckett?', *New Left Review*, Vol. 40 (2006), p. 48.
3. The Croix de Guerre recognises individuals who fought against the Axis Forces during World War Two.
4. The Médaille de la Reconnaissance, a medal to honour civilians who came to the aid of those injured, disabled, or in danger, was founded in 1917.
5. See, for example, Seán Kennedy and Katherine Weiss (eds), *Samuel Beckett: History, Memory, Archive*. New York: Palgrave/Macmillan, 2009.
6. Ruby Cohn (ed), *Samuel Beckett: Disjecta*. New York: Grove Press, 1984, pp. 171–2.
7. James Knowlson, *Damned to Fame: The Life of Samuel Beckett*. New York: Touchstone, 1996, p. 71.
8. For studies that discuss the intersections between Yeats's theatre and Beckett, see Emily Atkins, '"Study that Tree": The Iconic Stage in *Purgatory* and *Waiting for Godot*', *South Carolina Review*, Vol. 40, No. 2 (2008), pp. 66–77; and Terence Brown, 'W.B. Yeats and Samuel Beckett', *Yeats: An Annual of Critical and Textual Studies*, Vol. 10 (1992), pp. 190–2.
9. John Haynes and James Knowlson, *Images of Beckett*. Cambridge: Cambridge University Press, 2003, pp. 53–5.
10. For more on Yeats's influence on Beckett, see John P. Harrington, 'The Irish Beckett' in John P. Harrington (ed), *Modern and Contemporary Irish Drama*, 2nd ed. New York and London: Norton, 2009, pp. 525–30; and Anthony Roche, *Contemporary Irish Drama: From Beckett to McGuinness*. New York: St. Martin's Press, 1995, pp. 15–35.
11. Knowlson, *Damned to Fame*, p. 71.
12. Cohn (ed), *Disjecta*, p. 82.
13. Cohn (ed), *Disjecta*, p. 82.
14. École Normale Supérieure, located in Paris, France, is a prestigious public university designed to provide higher education and research for students seeking careers in education.
15. James Acheson, *Samuel Beckett's Artistic Theory and Practice: Criticism, Drama and Early Fiction*. Basingstoke: Macmillan, 1997, p. 6.
16. Knowlson, *Damned to Fame*, p. 125.
17. Knowlson, *Damned to Fame*, p. 328.
18. In the first of Beckett's 'Three Dialogues' with Georges Duthuit, Beckett voiced the artist's struggle to create as 'The Expression that there is nothing to express,

nothing with which to express, nothing from which to express, no power to express, no desire to express, together with the obligation to express' (Qtd in Cohn (ed), *Disjecta*, p. 139).

19. Knowlson, *Damned to Fame*, p. 249.
20. Knowlson, *Damned to Fame*, p. 250.
21. Knowlson, *Damned to Fame*, p. 328; David Pattie, *The Complete Critical Guide to Samuel Beckett*. London and New York: Routledge, 2000, p. 73.
22. Knowlson, *Damned to Fame*, p. 328.
23. Pattie, *Complete Critical Guide to Samuel Beckett*, p. 73.
24. Samuel Beckett, *Eleutheria*. New York: Foxrock Inc., 1995, p. 1.
25. Knowlson, *Damned to Fame*, p. 329.
26. Knowlson recalls that Roger Blin wanted to stage *Eleutheria* but felt that the play had 'too many characters for his limited resources'. *Damned to Fame*, p. 348.
27. In the American première of *Waiting for Godot* in 1956, directed by Alan Schneider, more than a third of the audience left during the intermission, prompting Beckett to write to Schneider that 'Success and failure on the public level never mattered much to me, in fact I feel much more at home with the latter, having breathed deep of its vivifying air all my writing life up to the last couple of years'. See Maurice Harmon (ed), *No Author Better Served: The Correspondence of Samuel Beckett and Alan Schneider*. Cambridge, MA: Harvard University Press, 1998, p. 8.
28. Ronan McDonald, *The Cambridge Introduction to Samuel Beckett*. Cambridge: Cambridge University Press, 2006, p. 53.
29. Qtd in Knowlson, *Damned to Fame*, p. 385.
30. Qtd in Knowlson, *Damned to Fame*, p. 385.
31. S.E. Gontarski, *The Intent of Undoing in Samuel Beckett's Texts*. Bloomington: Indiana University Press, 1985.
32. See Knowlson, *Damned to Fame*, pp. 477–9, 534–5, 552–4; Jonathan Bignell, *Beckett on Screen: The Television Plays*. Manchester: Manchester University Press, 2010.
33. Reinhart Müller-Freienfels, 'Samuel Beckett: "We do it to have fun together": Erinnerungen an Beckett in Stuttgart', unpublished typescript, Historisches Archiv, SWR [formerly SDR], 1988.
34. Martin Esslin, *The Theatre of the Absurd*, 3rd edition. London: Penguin, 1991, p. 25.
35. Esslin, *Theatre of the Absurd*, p. 26.
36. Esslin, *Theatre of the Absurd*, pp. 90–1.
37. Pattie, *Complete Critical Guide to Samuel Beckett*, pp. 114–15.
38. McDonald, *Cambridge Introduction to Samuel Beckett*, p. 25.
39. Samuel Beckett, 'The Capital of the Ruins' in S.E. Gontarski (ed), *The Complete Short Prose 1929–1989*, New York: Grove Press, 1995, p. 278.
40. Beckett, 'The Capital of the Ruins', p. 278.
41. Walter Benjamin, 'The Work of Art in the Age of Mechanical Reproduction' in Hannah Arendt (ed), *Illuminations*, trans. Harry Zohn, New York: Schocken, 1969, p. 241.
42. Cohn (ed), *Disjecta*, p. 19.
43. Knowlson, *Damned to Fame*, p. 505.

Chapter 1

1. Knowlson, *Damned to Fame*, p. 328.
2. Samuel Beckett, *Waiting for Godot*. New York: Grove Press, 1954, p. 25. In Beckett's revision of the play published in Dougald McMillan and James Knowlson's *The Theatrical Notebooks of Samuel Beckett: Waiting for Godot*. London: Faber and Faber, 1993, he omitted this reference and the numerous threatening cracks of the whip.
3. Beckett, *Waiting for Godot*, p. 16.
4. Beckett, *Waiting for Godot*, p. 22.
5. Jonathan Kalb, 'The Mediated Quixote: The Radio and Television Plays, and *Film*' in John Pilling (ed), *The Cambridge Companion to Beckett*, Cambridge: Cambridge University Press, 1994, p. 136.
6. Beckett, *Waiting for Godot*, p. 20.
7. Beckett, *Waiting for Godot*, p. 25.
8. Beckett, *Waiting for Godot*, p. 25.
9. Beckett, *Waiting for Godot*, p. 25.
10. Harmon (ed), *No Author Better Served*, p. 2.
11. Beckett, *Waiting for Godot*, p. 25.
12. Beckett, *Waiting for Godot*, p. 24.
13. McMillan and Knowlson, *Theatrical Notebooks*, p. 34. The stage direction '*He taps with finger on watch*' was added to the revised text as recorded in McMillan and Knowlson's study of the *Waiting for Godot* Production Notebooks.
14. Beckett, *Waiting for Godot*, p. 31.
15. McMillan and Knowlson, *Theatrical Notebooks*, p. xvi.
16. Beckett, *Waiting for Godot*, p. 19.
17. Richard Schechner, 'Godotology: There's Lots of Time in *Godot*', *Modern Drama*, Vol. 9, No. 3 (1966), p. 269.
18. Beckett, *Waiting for Godot*, p. 24.
19. Beckett, *Waiting for Godot*, p. 24.
20. Beckett, *Waiting for Godot*, p. 48.
21. Beckett, *Waiting for Godot*, p. 31.
22. Jean Baudrillard, *The System of Objects,* trans. James Benedict. London: Verso, 1996, p. 24.
23. Beckett, *Waiting for Godot*, p. 58.
24. Beckett, *Waiting for Godot*, p. 8.
25. Beckett, *Waiting for Godot*, p. 9.
26. Beckett, *Waiting for Godot*, p. 9.
27. Samuel Beckett, *En attendant Godot*. Paris: Les Éditions de Minuit, 1952, p. 12; Samuel Beckett, *Stücke, Kleine Prosa, Auswahl in einem Band*, trans. Erika and Elmar Tophoven. Frankfurt am Main: Suhrkamp Verlag, 1969, p. 136.
28. Ruby Cohn, *Just Play: Beckett's Theater*. Princeton, NJ: Princeton University Press, 1980, p. 40.
29. Beckett, *Waiting for Godot*, p. 57.
30. Beckett, *Waiting for Godot*, p. 58.
31. Beckett, *Waiting for Godot*, p. 10.
32. Dougald McMillan and Martha Fehsenfeld, *Beckett in the Theatre*. London: Calder, 1988, p. 60. McMillan and Fehsenfeld reproduce this exchange between Didi and Gogo from the unpublished manuscript.

33. Beckett, *Waiting for Godot*, p. 10.
34. Beckett, *Waiting for Godot*, p. 33.
35. Beckett, *Waiting for Godot*, p. 58.
36. Beckett, *Waiting for Godot*, p. 58.
37. Sidney Homan, *Beckett's Theaters: Interpretations for Performance*. Lewisburg, PA: Bucknell University Press, 1984, p. 32.
38. Homan, *Beckett's Theaters*, p. 41. Homan points out that the audience shares the activity of waiting with the actors on stage. This technique resulted in varied responses. During the American première of *Waiting for Godot* at the Coconut Grove, the audience walked out, while the San Quentin inmates took the play to heart.
39. Vivian Mercier, 'The Uneventful Event' (1956) in Lance St. John Butler (ed), *Critical Essays on Samuel Beckett: Critical Thought Series 4*, Aldershot: Scolar Press, 1993, p. 29. Mercier's italics.
40. See Ruby Cohn, *Back to Beckett*. Princeton, NJ: Princeton University Press, 1973, p. 152; and Michael Worton, '*Waiting for Godot* and *Endgame*: Theatre as Text' in John Pilling (ed), *The Cambridge Companion to Beckett*, Cambridge: Cambridge University Press, 1994, p. 71. Cohn reveals that Beckett's own comments about *Endgame*, in part to explain the play's title, reflect the play's staging of authority:

> Hamm is a king in this chess game lost from the start. From the start he knows he is making loud senseless moves. That he will make no progress at all with the gaff. Now at the last, he makes a few senseless moves as only a bad player would. A good one would have given up long ago. He is only trying to delay the inevitable end. Each of his gestures is one of the last useless moves which put off the end. He is a bad player.

Worton explains that two kings are left on the board 'only when two bad players are playing. [. . .] [T]hey can never end the game but merely engage in an infinite series of movements around the chess-board'.
41. Samuel Beckett, *Endgame* and *Act Without Words 1*. New York: Grove, 2009, pp. 8, 90.
42. Beckett, *Endgame*, p. 57.
43. For an informative discussion of Hamm as a ham actor who attempts to play the role of Hamlet, see Cohn, *Back to Beckett*, p. 145.
44. Beckett, *Endgame*, p. 60.
45. Beckett, *Endgame*, pp. 59–60.
46. Beckett, *Endgame*, p. 10.
47. Beckett, *Endgame*, p. 11.
48. Beckett, *Endgame*, p. 66.
49. David H. Hesla, *The Shape of Chaos: An Interpretation of the Art of Samuel Beckett*. Minneapolis: University of Minnesota Press, 1971, p. 7.
50. Cohn (ed), *Disjecta*, p. 145.
51. Beckett, *Endgame*, p. 66.
52. Beckett, *Endgame*, p. 7.
53. Worton, '*Waiting for Godot* and *Endgame*', p. 79. Worton points out that this choice suggests that 'the mechanical has replaced the artistic'.
54. Beckett, *Endgame*, p. 80.
55. Beckett, *Endgame*, p. 56.
56. In the *Beckett on Film* production of *Endgame* (2000) when Clov places the clock on the ashbin, the clock's ticking makes an extraordinary hollow sound which

echoes eerily, reminding the audience of the passing of clock time in addition to the inevitable decay and death of the apocalyptic staged world.

57. Beckett, *Endgame*, pp. 20, 40.
58. Worton, '*Waiting for Godot* and *Endgame*', p. 69.
59. Worton, '*Waiting for Godot* and *Endgame*', p. 79.
60. Beckett, *Endgame*, p. 37.
61. Beckett, *Endgame*, p. 8.
62. Beckett, *Endgame*, p. 93.
63. Cohn, *Just Play*, p. 45.
64. Similarly, each act of *Happy Days*, Beckett's first play to feature a woman in the central role, opens with the piercing ring of a bell. Sounding like an amplified alarm clock, this bell awakens Winnie and forces her to begin her daily routines.
65. Beckett, *Endgame*, p. 93.
66. Beckett, *Endgame*, p. 77.
67. For example, see Paul Lawley, 'Stages of Identity: From *Krapp's Last Tape* to *Play*' in John Pilling (ed), *The Cambridge Companion to Beckett*, Cambridge: Cambridge University Press, 1994, p. 91; Steven Connor, *Samuel Beckett: Repetition, Theory and Text*. Oxford: Basil Blackwell, 1988, p. 129.
68. Samuel Beckett, *Krapp's Last Tape and Other Dramatic Pieces*. New York: Grove, 2009, p. 4.
69. Beckett, *Krapp's Last Tape and Other Dramatic Pieces*, p. 3.
70. Beckett, *Krapp's Last Tape and Other Dramatic Pieces*, p. 7.
71. Beckett, *Krapp's Last Tape and Other Dramatic Pieces*, p. 7.
72. Cohn, *Just Play*, p. 51.
73. N. Katherine Hayles, 'Voices Out of Bodies: Audiotape and the Production of Subjectivity' in Adalaide Morris (ed), *Sound States: Innovative Poetics and Acoustical Technologies*, Chapel Hill: University of North Carolina Press, 1997, p. 81.
74. Beckett, *Krapp's Last Tape and Other Dramatic Pieces*, p. 10.
75. Beckett, *Krapp's Last Tape and Other Dramatic Pieces*, p. 5.
76. Beckett, *Krapp's Last Tape and Other Dramatic Pieces*, p. 4.
77. Beckett, *Krapp's Last Tape and Other Dramatic Pieces*, p. 4.
78. Beckett, *Krapp's Last Tape and Other Dramatic Pieces*, p. 5.
79. Lawley, 'Stages of Identity', p. 91.
80. For a discussion on Krapp as author and editor, see Lawley, 'Stage of Identity', pp. 90–1. For a discussion on the medium of audiotape and editing, see Hayles, 'Voices Out of Bodies', p. 77.
81. Beckett, *Krapp's Last Tape and Other Dramatic Pieces*, p. 10.
82. Beckett, *Krapp's Last Tape and Other Dramatic Pieces*, p. 10.
83. Beckett, *Krapp's Last Tape and Other Dramatic Pieces*, p. 10.
84. See James Knowlson and John Pilling, *Frescoes of the Skull: The Later Prose and Drama of Samuel Beckett*. London: John Calder, 1979, pp. 84–92.
85. Beckett, *Krapp's Last Tape and Other Dramatic Pieces*, p. 5.
86. Beckett, *Krapp's Last Tape and Other Dramatic Pieces*, p. 3.
87. Beckett, *Krapp's Last Tape and Other Dramatic Pieces*, p. 6.
88. Samuel Beckett, *Proust*. New York: Grove Press, 1957, p. 2.
89. Beckett, *Krapp's Last Tape and Other Dramatic Pieces*, p. 5.
90. Beckett, *Krapp's Last Tape and Other Dramatic Pieces*, p. 7.
91. Beckett, *Krapp's Last Tape and Other Dramatic Pieces*, p. 5.

92. Katharine Worth, *Samuel Beckett's Theatre: Life Journeys.* Oxford: Oxford University Press, 1999, pp. 99–100.
93. Beckett, *Krapp's Last Tape and Other Dramatic Pieces*, p. 8.
94. James Knowlson, *Theatrical Workbook I: Samuel Beckett's Krapp's Last Tape.* London: Brutus Books Ltd., 1980, p. 105.
95. Knowlson, *Theatrical Workbook I*, pp. 97–8.
96. Cohn, *Just Play*, p. 246; Knowlson and Pilling, *Frescoes of the Skull*, p. 84.
97. Knowlson, *Theatrical Workbook I*, p. 62.
98. Beckett does not reproduce the modernists' 'paranoid version' of technology, but rather creates a work that is structured on these fears and concerns. For more, see Michael Davidson, 'Technologies of Presence: Orality and the Tapevoice of Contemporary Poetics' in Adalaide Morris (ed), *Sound States: Innovative Poetics and Acoustical Technologies*, Chapel Hill: University of North Carolina Press, 1997, p. 99.
99. Knowlson, *Theatrical Workbook I*, p. 64.
100. Beckett, *Krapp's Last Tape and Other Dramatic Pieces*, p. 4.
101. Hayles, 'Voices Out of Bodies', p. 82.
102. Beckett, *Krapp's Last Tape and Other Dramatic Pieces*, p. 5.
103. Beckett, *Krapp's Last Tape and Other Dramatic Pieces*, p. 10.
104. Knowlson, *Theatrical Workbook I*, p. 42.
105. Tim Armstrong, *Modernism, Technology and the Body: A Cultural Study.* Cambridge: Cambridge University Press, 1998, p. 65.
106. Anson Rabinbach, *The Human Motor: Energy, Fatigue, and the Origins of Modernity.* Berkeley: University of California Press, 1992, p. 117.
107. Armstrong, *Modernism, Technology and the Body*, p. 65.
108. Beckett, *Krapp's Last Tape and Other Dramatic Pieces*, p. 11.
109. For a further discussion of Fanny and the parallels to Krapp's name and constipation, see S.E. Gontarski, 'Crapp's First Tapes: Beckett's Manuscript Revisions of *Krapp's Last Tape*', *Journal of Modern Literature*, Vol. 6, No. 1 (1977), p. 67.
110. For a discussion on constipation as time hoarded, see Phil Baker, *Beckett and the Mythology of Psychoanalysis.* Basingstoke: Macmillan, 1997, pp. 50–63.
111. Knowlson and Pilling, *Frescoes of the Skull*, p. 82.
112. Beckett, *Krapp's Last Tape and Other Dramatic Pieces*, p. 10.
113. Beckett, *Krapp's Last Tape and Other Dramatic Pieces*, p. 12.
114. Beckett International Foundation, University of Reading, MS UoR 2101.
115. Knowlson, *Damned to Fame*, p. 580.
116. Gaby Wood, *Living Dolls: A Magical History of the Quest for Mechanical Life.* London: Faber and Faber, 2002, pp. 24–5.
117. Wood, *Living Dolls*, p. xvi.
118. Cathy Caruth, *Unclaimed Experience: Trauma, Narrative and History.* Baltimore, MD and London: Johns Hopkins University Press, 1996, pp. 2–3.
119. Adam Phillips, 'Close-Ups', *History Workshop Journal*, Vol. 57 (2004), p. 142.
120. Phillips, 'Close-Ups', p. 146.
121. Antonia Rodríguez-Gago, 'The Embodiment of Memory (and Forgetting) in Beckett's Late Women's Plays', *Assaph: Studies in the Theatre*, Vol. 17–18 (2003), p. 116.
122. Phillips, 'Close-Ups', pp. 147–8.
123. See the Introduction for more on Beckett's involvement with and impressions of Saint-Lô.

124. Phyllis Gaffney, *Healing Amid the Ruins: The Irish Hospital at Saint-Lô*. Dublin: A&A Farmar, 1999, p. 76.
125. Qtd in Knowlson, *Damned to Fame*, p. 313.
126. Beckett, 'The Capital of the Ruins', p. 277.
127. Samuel Beckett, *Happy Days*. New York, Grove Press, 1989, p. 7.
128. Beckett, *Happy Days*, p. 9.
129. Beckett, *Happy Days*, p. 64.
130. S.E. Gontarski, *Beckett's Happy Days: A Manuscript Study*. Columbus: Ohio State University Libraries, 1977, pp. 37–8.
131. Beckett, *Happy Days*, p. 8.
132. Beckett, *Happy Days*, p. 12.
133. Beckett, *Happy Days*, p. 10.
134. See Gontarski, *The Intent of Undoing*, pp. 74–5, 83; Derek Goldman, 'What was that Unforgettable Line?: Remembrances from the Rubbleheap', *The South Atlantic Quarterly*, Vol. 103, No. 1 (2004), pp. 45–55; Cohn, *Back to Beckett*, pp. 180–3.
135. Beckett, *Proust*, p. 8.
136. Beckett, *Happy Days*, pp. 39–40.
137. Fiona Shaw, Interview, New York Public Radio, 2008, accessed 12 April 2010, www.youtube.com/watch?v=Px0QLQwL8Oc, 12 April 2010.
138. Beckett, *Happy Days*, p. 13.
139. Beckett, *Happy Days*, p. 33.
140. Beckett, *Happy Days*, p. 33.
141. Beckett, *Happy Days*, p. 33.
142. Gontarski, *Intent of Undoing*, p. 80.
143. Beckett, *Happy Days*, p. 15.
144. Beckett, *Happy Days*, pp. 16, 17.
145. Beckett, *Happy Days*, p. 19.
146. Gontarski tells us that in an earlier draft of *Happy Days* the 'sexual overtones . . . were more explicit' (*Intent of Undoing*, p. 81).
147. Beckett, *Happy Days*, p. 54.
148. Lawley, 'Stages of Identity', p. 98. Despite their avoidance to define Winnie's Mildred story, Knowlson and Pilling argue that it gives 'expression to the fear, violence, and suffering that, in Beckett's view, seems to be an unavoidable accompaniment to procreation, birth and being' (*Frescoes of the Skull*, p. 97).
149. Beckett, *Happy Days*, p. 55.
150. Beckett, *Happy Days*, p. 55.
151. Beckett, *Happy Days*, p. 58.
152. Beckett, *Happy Days*, p. 41.
153. Beckett, *Happy Days*, pp. 42–3.
154. Beckett, *Happy Days*, p. 58.
155. Beckett, *Happy Days*, p. 44.
156. Beckett, *Happy Days*, p. 59.
157. Samuel Beckett, *Ends and Odds: Nine Dramatic Pieces*. New York: Grove Press, 1981, pp. 44, 48.
158. Samuel Beckett, *Cascando and Other Short Dramatic Pieces*. New York: Grove Press, 1969, p. 54.
159. Beckett, *Cascando and Other Short Dramatic Pieces*, p. 59.
160. Beckett, *Cascando and Other Short Dramatic Pieces*, p. 62.

161. Harmon (ed), *No Author Better Served*, p. 145. In a letter to Alan Schneider dated 26 November 1963, Beckett wrote: 'The man on the light should be regarded as a fourth player and must know the text inside and out'.
162. Beckett, *Cascando and Other Short Dramatic Pieces*, p. 62.
163. Rudolf Arnheim, *Film*, trans. L.M. Sieveking and Ian F.D. Morrow. London: Faber and Faber, 1933, pp. 17–38.
164. Andreas Huyssen, *After the Great Divide: Modernism, Mass Culture and Postmodernism*. Basingstoke: Macmillan, 1988, p. 75.
165. Beckett, *Cascando and Other Short Dramatic Pieces*, p. 49.
166. Beckett, *Cascando and Other Short Dramatic Pieces*, p. 51, 52.
167. Beckett, *Cascando and Other Short Dramatic Pieces*, p. 54.
168. Benjamin, 'The Work of Art', pp. 228–9.
169. Beckett, *Cascando and Other Short Dramatic Pieces*, p. 53.
170. Beckett, *Cascando and Other Short Dramatic Pieces*, p. 55.
171. Beckett, *Cascando and Other Short Dramatic Pieces*, pp. 60–1.
172. Beckett, *Proust*, p. 9.
173. Beckett, *Cascando and Other Short Dramatic Pieces*, p. 58.
174. George Devine's manuscript notes relating to the London première of *Play* at the Old Vic, 1963, Beckett International Foundation, University of Reading, MS UoR 1581/15.
175. Beckett, *Cascando and Other Short Dramatic Pieces*, p. 55.
176. Beckett returns to using props in his short play of 1982, *Catastrophe*.
177. Jacques Derrida, *Archive Fever: A Freudian Impression*, trans. Eric Prenowitz. Chicago, IL: University of Chicago Press, 1996, p. 19.
178. Samuel Beckett, *Come and Go: A Dramaticule*. London: Calder and Boyars, 1973, pp. 9, 11, 13.
179. Knowlson and Pilling, *Frescoes of the Skull*, p. 121.
180. Beckett, *Come and Go*, p. 9.
181. Beckett, *Come and Go*, p. 11.
182. Knowlson suggests that this and other episodes of breaking off love are traces of Beckett's relationship with his cousin, Peggy Sinclair, and another young love of his, Ethna MacCarthy. For more, see *Damned to Fame*, pp. 397–9.
183. Beckett, *Krapp's Last Tape and Other Dramatic Pieces*, p. 5.
184. Beckett, *Come and Go*, p. 13.
185. Beckett, *Come and Go*, p. 14.
186. Keir Elam asserts that a possible reading of 'rings' is 'a sign, perhaps, that they are all married or engaged', but admits that the image is 'also a possible pun, as if to say that they have formed analogous and still-remembered rings in the past'. See Keir Elam, 'Dead Heads: Damnation-Narration in the "Dramaticules"' in John Pilling (ed), *The Cambridge Companion to Samuel Beckett*, Cambridge: Cambridge University Press, 1994, p. 148.
187. Elam, 'Dead Heads', p. 148.
188. Knowlson and Pilling, *Frescoes of the Skull*, p. 122.
189. Xerxes Mehta, '"Down, all going down . . .": The Spiral Structure of Beckett's Theater' in S.E. Gontarski (ed), *A Companion to Samuel Beckett*, Oxford: Wiley-Blackwell, 2010, p. 386.
190. Dominick LaCapra, *Writing History, Writing Trauma*. New York and Baltimore: Johns Hopkins University Press, 2001, p. 21.
191. Derrida, *Archive Fever*, p. 11.

192. Beckett, *Ends and Odds*, pp. 44, 48.
193. Knowlson and Pilling, *Frescoes of the Skull*, p. 221.
194. Beckett, *Ends and Odds*, p. 46.
195. Connor, *Samuel Beckett*, p. 202.
196. Connor, *Samuel Beckett*, p. 202.
197. Beckett, *Ends and Odds*, p. 45.
198. Beckett, *Ends and Odds*, p. 42.
199. Walter D. Asmus, 'Practical Aspects of Theatre, Radio and Television: Rehearsal notes for the German première of Beckett's *That Time* and *Footfalls* at the Schiller-Theater Werkstatt, Berlin', trans. Helen Watanabe, accessed 6 September 2011, www.english.fsu.edu/jobs/num02/Num2WalterAsmus.htm. 6 September 2011.
200. Knowlson, *Damned to Fame*, p. 544.
201. Beckett, *Ends and Odds*, pp. 14–15.
202. Beckett, *Ends and Odds*, pp. 44, 48.
203. Knowlson tells us that 'Beckett insisted to Dr Müller-Freienfels that "the sex of the hands [in *Nacht und Träume*] must remain uncertain. One of our numerous teasers"'. *Damned to Fame*, p. 600.
204. Elaine Scarry, *The Body in Pain: The Making and Unmaking of the World*. New York and Oxford, Oxford University Press, 1985, p. 4.
205. Beckett, *Ends and Odds*, p. 47.
206. Beckett, *Ends and Odds*, p. 47.
207. Beckett, *Ends and Odds*, pp. 46–7.
208. Elam, 'Dead Heads', p. 157.
209. Jonathan Boulter, 'Archives of the End: Embodied Histories in Samuel Beckett's Plays' in Seán Kennedy and Katherine Weiss (eds), *Samuel Beckett: History, Memory, Archive*, New York: Palgrave/Macmillan, 2009, pp. 131–4. Others, too, have imagined May as dead, a ghost haunting the old home or church. See, for example, Connor, *Samuel Beckett*, pp. 170–1.
210. Beckett, *Ends and Odds*, p. 47.
211. Seán Kennedy, 'Does Beckett Studies Require a Subject?' in Seán Kennedy and Katherine Weiss (eds), *Samuel Beckett: History, Memory, Archive*, New York: Palgrave/Macmillan, 2009, p. 15.
212. Beckett, *Ends and Odds*, p. 14.
213. Beckett, *Ends and Odds*, p. 47.
214. Beckett, *Ends and Odds*, p. 48.
215. Beckett, *Ends and Odds*, p. 46.
216. Beckett, *Ends and Odds*, p. 47.
217. Beckett, *Ends and Odds*, p. 47.
218. Beckett, *Ends and Odds*, p. 47.
219. Knowlson and Pilling, *Frescoes of the Skull*, p. 221.
220. Gontarski, *Intent of Undoing*, p. 74.

Chapter 2

1. Harmon (ed), *No Author Better Served*, p. 24.
2. Knowlson, *Theatre Workbook I*, p. 46.
3. Beckett, *Krapp's Last Tape and Other Dramatic Pieces*, p. 17.

4. Beckett, *Krapp's Last Tape and Other Dramatic Pieces*, p. 20.
5. Linda Ben-Zvi, 'Samuel Beckett's Media Plays', *Modern Drama*, Vol. 28, No. 1 (1985), pp. 24–5.
6. Beckett, *Krapp's Last Tape and Other Dramatic Pieces*, pp. 17–18.
7. Beckett, *Krapp's Last Tape and Other Dramatic Pieces*, p. 18.
8. Beckett, *Krapp's Last Tape and Other Dramatic Pieces*, p. 18.
9. Beckett, *Krapp's Last Tape and Other Dramatic Pieces*, p. 18.
10. Louise O. Cleveland, 'Trials in the Soundscape: The Radio Plays of Samuel Beckett', *Modern Drama*, Vol. 11, No. 3 (1968), p. 272.
11. Beckett, *Krapp's Last Tape and Other Dramatic Pieces*, pp. 15, 16.
12. Beckett, *Krapp's Last Tape and Other Dramatic Pieces*, p. 19.
13. Beckett, *Krapp's Last Tape and Other Dramatic Pieces*, p. 19.
14. Beckett, *Krapp's Last Tape and Other Dramatic Pieces*, p. 19.
15. Beckett, *Krapp's Last Tape and Other Dramatic Pieces*, pp. 19–20.
16. Beckett, *Krapp's Last Tape and Other Dramatic Pieces*, p. 23.
17. Beckett, *Krapp's Last Tape and Other Dramatic Pieces*, p. 25.
18. Beckett, *Krapp's Last Tape and Other Dramatic Pieces*, p. 25.
19. Beckett, *Krapp's Last Tape and Other Dramatic Pieces*, p. 25.
20. W.H. Lyons, 'Backtracking Beckett' in C.A. Burns (ed), *Literature and Society: Studies in Nineteenth and Twentieth Century French Literature, Presented to R.J. North*, Birmingham: John Goodman & Sons, 1980, pp. 1–7.
21. Cleveland, 'Trials in the Soundscape', p. 273.
22. Beckett, *Krapp's Last Tape and Other Dramatic Pieces*, p. 27.
23. Walter Benjamin, 'On Some Motifs in Baudelaire' in Hannah Arendt (ed), trans. Harry Zohn, *Illuminations*, New York: Schocken, 1969, p. 191.
24. Beckett, *Krapp's Last Tape and Other Dramatic Pieces*, p. 49. Dan's description is echoed in *The Unnamable* translated into English by Beckett in 1959. The narrator of *The Unnamable* reveals that he resides in 'a hard shut dry cold black place, where nothing stirs, nothing speaks, and that I listen, and that I seek, like a caged beast born of caged beasts born of caged beasts born of caged beasts born in a cage and dead in a cage, born and then dead, born in a cage and then dead in a cage, in a word like a beast, in one of their words, like such a beast'. Samuel Beckett, *Trilogy: Molloy, Malone Dies, The Unnamable*. London: Calder, 1994, p. 390.
25. Beckett, *Krapp's Last Tape and Other Dramatic Pieces*, p. 20.
26. Beckett, *Krapp's Last Tape and Other Dramatic Pieces*, p. 21.
27. Ben-Zvi, 'Samuel Beckett's Media Plays', p. 28. Linda Ben-Zvi argues that the audience hears 'a world that exists within the skull of Maddy Rooney'.
28. Beckett, *Krapp's Last Tape and Other Dramatic Pieces*, p. 50.
29. Beckett, *Krapp's Last Tape and Other Dramatic Pieces*, p. 26.
30. Beckett, *Krapp's Last Tape and Other Dramatic Pieces*, p. 34.
31. Thomas F. Van Laan, '*All That Fall* as "a Play for Radio"', *Modern Drama*, Vol. 28, No. 1 (1985), p. 41.
32. Beckett, *Krapp's Last Tape and Other Dramatic Pieces*, p. 34.
33. Beckett, *Krapp's Last Tape and Other Dramatic Pieces*, p. 34.
34. Beckett, *Krapp's Last Tape and Other Dramatic Pieces*, pp. 44, 45, 46.
35. Beckett, *Krapp's Last Tape and Other Dramatic Pieces*, p. 46.
36. Cohn (ed), *Disjecta*, p. 145.
37. Beckett, *Krapp's Last Tape and Other Dramatic Pieces*, p. 43.
38. Beckett, *Krapp's Last Tape and Other Dramatic Pieces*, p. 48.

39. Beckett, *Krapp's Last Tape and Other Dramatic Pieces*, p. 55.
40. For example, see Ben-Zvi, 'Samuel Beckett's Media Plays', pp. 29–30; Kalb, 'Mediated Quixote', p. 127; Van Laan, *'All That Fall'*, p. 39.
41. See John Fletcher et al., *A Student's Guide to the Plays of Samuel Beckett*. London: Faber and Faber, 1978, p. 82; Knowlson, *Damned to Fame*, p. 387. Knowlson suggests that although Dan may not have intended to murder the child, he is responsible for its death.
42. Everett Frost argues, 'The last thing we hear is *not* the scene lingering for a fade after Maddy and Dan have left it (a common strategy in radio) but, rather, the storm – the natural world as it atomizes Maddy's mind as a result of this tragic recognition (an oblivion that is, perhaps, as welcome as it is terrible)'. Everett Frost, 'A "Fresh Go" for the Skull: Directing *All That Fall*, Samuel Beckett's Play for Radio' in Lois Oppenheim (ed), *Directing Beckett*, Ann Arbor: University of Michigan Press, 1997, p. 207.
43. Beckett, *Krapp's Last Tape and Other Dramatic Pieces*, p. 37.
44. Beckett, *Krapp's Last Tape and Other Dramatic Pieces*, p. 59.
45. Beckett, *Krapp's Last Tape and Other Dramatic Pieces*, p. 59.
46. Kalb, 'Mediated Quixote', p. 129.
47. Wanda Avila, 'The Poem within the Play in Beckett's *Embers*', *Language and Style: An International Journal*, Vol. 17, No. 3 (1984), p. 194.
48. Beckett, *Krapp's Last Tape and Other Dramatic Pieces*, p. 66.
49. Paul Lawley, '*Embers*: An Interpretation', *Journal of Beckett Studies*, Vol. 6 (1980), p. 12.
50. Beckett, *Krapp's Last Tape and Other Dramatic Pieces*, p. 60.
51. Beckett, *Krapp's Last Tape and Other Dramatic Pieces*, p. 60.
52. Beckett, *Krapp's Last Tape and Other Dramatic Pieces*, p. 71.
53. Fletcher et al., *A Student's Guide*, p. 166.
54. Cohn (ed), *Disjecta*, p. 172.
55. For further studies that explore ghosts in *Embers*, see Kalb, 'Mediated Quixote', p. 130 and Lawley, '*Embers*: An Interpretation', p. 10.
56. Beckett, *Krapp's Last Tape and Other Dramatic Pieces*, p. 75.
57. Beckett, *Krapp's Last Tape and Other Dramatic Pieces*, p. 75.
58. Dominique Laporte, *History of Shit*, trans. Nadia Benabid and Rodolphe el-Khoury. Cambridge, MA: MIT Press, 2000, p. 10.
59. Clas Zilliacus, 'Samuel Beckett's *Embers*: "A Matter of Fundamental Sounds"', *Modern Drama*, Vol. 13, No. 2 (1970), p. 221.
60. Samuel Beckett, *The Old Tune*. London: Calder, 1999, p. 5.
61. Beckett, *The Old Tune*, p. 12.
62. Beckett, *The Old Tune*, pp. 6, 10, 20.
63. Walter Benjamin, 'The Storyteller' in Hannah Arendt (ed), trans. Harry Zohn, *Illuminations*, New York: Schocken, 1969, p. 91.
64. Beckett, *The Old Tune*, p. 6.
65. Beckett, *The Old Tune*, pp. 6–7.
66. Beckett, *The Old Tune*, p. 5.
67. Beckett, *The Old Tune*, p. 5.
68. Beckett, *The Old Tune*, p. 9; Vivian Mercier, *Beckett/Beckett*. London: Souvenir Press, 1977, pp. 42–3. Mercier points out that Gorman and Cream 'use a number of Dublin expressions that can be found in the works of O'Casey and Joyce – and perhaps a few that can't'.

69. Beckett, *The Old Tune*, p. 7.
70. Beckett, *The Old Tune*, pp. 11, 13, 14, 18.
71. Clas Zilliacus, 'Scoring Twice: Pinget's *La manivelle* and Beckett's *The Old Tune*', *Moderna Sprak*, Vol. 68 (1974), pp. 3–4.
72. Benjamin, 'On Some Motifs in Baudelaire', p. 191.
73. Beckett, *The Old Tune*, p. 10.
74. Benjamin, 'The Storyteller', p. 87.
75. Beckett, *The Old Tune*, pp. 19–20.
76. Benjamin, 'The Storyteller', p. 84.
77. Benjamin, 'The Storyteller', p. 84.
78. Benjamin, 'The Storyteller', p. 88.
79. Acheson, *Samuel Beckett's Artistic Theory*, p. 6.
80. Beckett, *The Old Tune*, p. 6.
81. Beckett, *The Old Tune*, p. 6.
82. Beckett, *The Old Tune*, p. 7.
83. Beckett, *The Old Tune*, p. 15.
84. Beckett, *The Old Tune*, p. 16.
85. Beckett, *The Old Tune*, p. 16.
86. Beckett, *The Old Tune*, pp. 11–12.
87. Beckett, *The Old Tune*, p. 6.
88. Beckett, *The Old Tune*, pp. 19–20.
89. Beckett, *The Old Tune*, p. 20.
90. For a discussion of Beckett's use of music, see the critical work of Catherine Laws and Michael Maier.
91. Cohn (ed), *Disjecta*, p. 139.
92. Beckett, *Ends and Odds*, p. 116.
93. Frost, 'A "Fresh Go"', p. 361, n. 6. Everett Frost states: 'Correspondence at the BBC and a discussion with the author confirmed that *Rough for Radio I* is an early attempt at the play that became *Cascando*. In 1985 Beckett described it to me as "unfinished and now unfinishable" and requested that we not include it in *The Beckett Festival of Radio Plays*'.
94. Fletcher et al., *A Student Guide*, p. 161.
95. I would like to thank Dr Edith Seier for her linguistic insight.
96. Beckett, *Ends and Odds*, p. 120.
97. Beckett, *Ends and Odds*, p. 120.
98. Beckett, *Ends and Odds*, p. 121.
99. Beckett, *Ends and Odds*, p. 122.
100. Beckett, *Ends and Odds*, p. 121.
101. Beckett, *Ends and Odds*, p. 122.
102. Beckett, *Cascando and Other Short Dramatic Pieces*, p. 9.
103. Beckett, *Cascando and Other Short Dramatic Pieces*, p. 16.
104. Beckett, *Cascando and Other Short Dramatic Pieces*, p. 25.
105. Beckett, *Ends and Odds*, p. 129.
106. Beckett, *Ends and Odds*, p. 129.
107. Martin Esslin, 'Beckett's *Rough for Radio*', *Journal of Modern Literature*, Vol. 6 (1977), p. 99.
108. Beckett, *Cascando and Other Short Dramatic Pieces*, p. 15.
109. See Armstrong, *Modernism, Technology and the Body*, pp. 31–2, 36–41.
110. Beckett, *Ends and Odds*, p. 135.

111. Beckett, *Ends and Odds*, p. 138.
112. Beckett, *Ends and Odds*, p. 138.
113. Beckett, *Cascando and Other Short Dramatic Pieces*, p. 23.
114. Beckett, *Cascando and Other Short Dramatic Pieces*, p. 32.
115. Beckett, *Cascando and Other Short Dramatic Pieces*, p. 32.
116. Beckett, *Cascando and Other Short Dramatic Pieces*, p. 9.
117. Beckett, *Cascando and Other Short Dramatic Pieces*, p. 11.
118. Beckett, *Cascando and Other Short Dramatic Pieces*, p. 13.
119. Beckett, *Cascando and Other Short Dramatic Pieces*, pp. 18–19.
120. Beckett, *Cascando and Other Short Dramatic Pieces*, pp. 31–2. In 'dread nay', written thirteen years after *Words and Music*, the line 'no sense gone' echoes 'No sense no need'. Samuel Beckett, *Collected Poems in English and French*. London: John Calder, 1977, p. 34.
121. Curiously, Henry explains that the sound we hear is 'So unlike the sea' (Beckett, *Krapp's Last Tape and Other Dramatic Pieces*, p. 59); however, in the original production of 1959 the sound we hear is so like the sea.
122. Beckett, *Cascando and Other Short Dramatic Pieces*, p. 32.
123. Acheson, *Samuel Beckett's Artistic Theory*, p. 6.

Chapter 3

1. In his subsequent work with the SDR, Beckett accepted their modest honorariums. Refusing the monetary reward in 1965 was related to his uncertainty as to whether he could do the job adequately.
2. Beckett directed *He Joe* twice, once in 1965 and a second time in 1979.
3. Müller-Freienfels, 'Samuel Beckett', p. 1. All translations from this text are mine.
4. Müller-Freienfels, 'Samuel Beckett', pp. 1–2.
5. Müller-Freienfels, 'Samuel Beckett', p. 3.
6. For example, see S.E. Gontarski, 'The Anatomy of Beckett's *Eh Joe*', *Modern Drama*, Vol. 26, No. 4 (1983), p. 433; Rosette Lamont, 'Beckett's *Eh Joe*: Lending an Ear to the Anima' in Linda Ben-Zvi (ed), *Women in Beckett: Performance and Critical Perspectives*, Urbana: University of Illinois Press, 1990, p. 229.
7. Beckett, *Cascando and Other Short Dramatic Pieces*, p. 35.
8. Beckett, *Cascando and Other Short Dramatic Pieces*, p. 36.
9. Beckett, *Cascando and Other Short Dramatic Pieces*, p. 41.
10. Beckett, *Cascando and Other Short Dramatic Pieces*, p. 35.
11. Graley Herren, *Samuel Beckett's Plays on Film and Television*. New York, Palgrave/Macmillan, 2007, p. 52.
12. Beckett, *Cascando and Other Short Dramatic Pieces*, p. 35.
13. Beckett, *Cascando and Other Short Dramatic Pieces*, p. 36.
14. Susan Sontag, *On Photography*. Harmondsworth: Penguin, 1977, p. 5.
15. Beckett, *Cascando and Other Short Dramatic Pieces*, p. 36.
16. Toby Zinman, '*Eh Joe* and the Peephole Aesthetic', *Samuel Beckett Today/Aujourd'hui*, Vol. 4 (1995), p. 53.
17. Clas Zilliacus, *Beckett and Broadcasting: A Study of the Works of Samuel Beckett for and in Radio and Television*. Åbo: Åbo Akademi, 1976, p. 191.
18. Zilliacus, *Beckett and Broadcasting*, p. 190.

19. Beckett, *Cascando and Other Short Dramatic Pieces*, p. 37.
20. Herren, *Beckett's Plays on Film and Television*, p. 52.
21. Beckett, *Cascando and Other Short Dramatic Pieces*, p. 36.
22. Beckett, *Cascando and Other Short Dramatic Pieces*, p. 39.
23. Beckett, *Waiting for Godot*, p. 58.
24. Beckett, *Cascando and Other Short Dramatic Pieces*, p. 41.
25. Beckett, *Cascando and Other Short Dramatic Pieces*, p. 41. The title of the teleplay in French is *Dis Joe* which translates into 'say Joe'. In a sense, the voice attempts to reactivate Joe into an author so that he can be done with his past memories.
26. Beckett, *Cascando and Other Short Dramatic Pieces*, p. 40.
27. Beckett, *Cascando and Other Short Dramatic Pieces*, p. 40.
28. Beckett, *Cascando and Other Short Dramatic Pieces*, p. 38.
29. Gilles Deleuze and Félix Guattari, *A Thousand Plateaus: Capitalism and Schizophrenia*, trans. Brian Massumi. London: Athlone Press, 1999, pp. 167–80, 186–90.
30. Beckett, *Cascando and Other Short Dramatic Pieces*, p. 36.
31. Graley Herren, 'Unfamiliar Chambers: Power and Pattern in Samuel Beckett's *Ghost Trio*', *Journal of Beckett Studies*, Vol. 8, No. 1 (1998), p. 74.
32. Martin Esslin, 'Visions of Absence: Beckett's *Footfalls*, *Ghost Trio* and . . . *but the clouds* . . . ' in Ian Donaldson (ed), *Transformations in Modern European Drama*, Atlantic Highlands: Humanities, 1983, pp. 126–7.
33. Beckett, *Ends and Odds*, p. 57.
34. Beckett, *Ends and Odds*, p. 55.
35. Beckett, *Ends and Odds*, p. 55.
36. James Knowlson, '*Ghost Trio/Geister Trio*' in Enoch Brater (ed), *Beckett at 80/ Beckett in Context*, Oxford and New York: Oxford University Press, 1986, p. 198.
37. Beckett, *Ends and Odds*, p. 59.
38. Knowlson, '*Ghost Trio/Geister Trio*', p. 200.
39. Cited from Sontag, *On Photography*, p. 158.
40. Beckett, *Ends and Odds*, p. 55.
41. Beckett, *Ends and Odds*, p. 55.
42. Knowlson, '*Ghost Trio/Geister Trio*', p. 203.
43. Beckett, *Ends and Odds*, p. 55.
44. Beckett, *Ends and Odds*, p. 53.
45. Beckett, *Ends and Odds*, p. 60.
46. Beckett, *Ends and Odds*, p. 57.
47. While the teleplay was originally written in English, Beckett directed a German translation of the work for the SDR three months prior to the BBC production. In the German production, there is no shot of the cassette player.
48. Herren, 'Unfamiliar Chambers', p. 86.
49. Beckett, *Ends and Odds*, p. 58.
50. Herren, *Beckett's Plays on Film and Television*, p. 81.
51. Beckett, *Ends and Odds*, p. 64.
52. Herren, 'Unfamiliar Chambers', p. 91.
53. Beckett, *Ends and Odds*, p. 59.
54. Beckett, *Ends and Odds*, p. 58.
55. Knowlson, '*Ghost Trio/Geister Trio*', p. 199.
56. Beckett, *Ends and Odds*, p. 75.
57. Hans H. Hiebel, 'Beckett's Television Plays and Kafka's Late Stories', *Samuel Beckett Today/Aujourd'hui*, Vol. 6 (1997), p. 336. Hiebel argues that the camera

becomes Beckett's writing instrument in the production of *Quad* through the alterations that arose in the filming of the teleplay.

58. Beckett, *Ends and Odds*, p. 70.
59. Beckett, *Ends and Odds*, p. 72.
60. Beckett, *Ends and Odds*, pp. 72, 75.
61. Beckett, *Ends and Odds*, p. 71.
62. Beckett, *Ends and Odds*, pp. 71, 72.
63. Richard Bruce Kirkley, 'A Catch in the Breath: Language and Consciousness in Samuel Beckett's . . . *but the clouds* . . . ', *Modern Drama*, Vol. 35, No. 4 (1992), pp. 609–10.
64. Beckett, *Ends and Odds*, p. 72.
65. Beckett, *Waiting for Godot*, p. 58.
66. Beckett, *Ends and Odds*, pp. 72, 74.
67. Beckett, *Ends and Odds*, p. 71. This phrase is yet another example of M's use of arcane phrases; the phrase means 'to come home at nightfall'.
68. Beckett, *Ends and Odds*, pp. 72–3, 75.
69. Daniel Katz, 'Mirror Resembling Screens: Yeats, Beckett and . . . *but the clouds* . . . ', *Samuel Beckett Today/Aujourd'hui*, Vol. 4 (1995), p. 86.
70. Beckett, *Ends and Odds*, p. 74.
71. Beckett, *Ends and Odds*, p. 75.
72. For a detailed discussion of Beckett's deconstruction of Yeats's 'The Tower', see Herren, *Beckett's Plays on Film and Television*, pp. 93–122.
73. See Knowlson, *Damned to Fame*, pp. 608–9.
74. Beckett, *Ends and Odds*, p. 74.
75. Beckett, *Ends and Odds*, p. 75.
76. Stan Douglas, 'Shades of Masochism: Samuel Beckett's Teleplays', *Photofile* Vol. 30 (1990), p. 23.
77. Armstrong, *Modernism, Technology and the Body*, p. 232.
78. Beckett, *Ends and Odds*, p. 71.
79. Beckett, *Ends and Odds*, p. 71.
80. Herren, *Beckett's Plays for Film and Television*, p. 100.
81. Beckett, *Ends and Odds*, p. 71.
82. Beckett, *Ends and Odds*, p. 72.
83. Beckett, *Ends and Odds*, p. 74.
84. Beckett, *Ends and Odds*, p. 74.
85. Beckett, *Ends and Odds*, p. 74.
86. Enoch Brater, *Beyond Minimalism: Beckett's Late Style in the Theater*. New York: Oxford University Press, 1987, p. 102.
87. Beckett, *Ends and Odds*, p. 69.
88. Beckett, *Ends and Odds*, p. 73.
89. Roland Barthes, *Camera Lucida: Reflections on Photography*, trans. Richard Howard. London: Jonathan Cape, 1982, p. 97.
90. Brater, *Beyond Minimalism*, p. 100.
91. Elizabeth Klaver, 'Samuel Beckett's *Ohio Impromptu, Quad*, and *What Where*: How It Is in the Matrix of Text and Television', *Contemporary Literature*, Vol. 32, No. 3 (1991), p. 375. Klaver suggests that the printed text of *Quad* is 'a blueprint in which the architecture of the piece is described in diagrams and in mathematical codes which direct the series of permutations'.
92. Samuel Beckett, *Collected Shorter Plays*. New York: Grove Press, 1984, p. 305.

93. Samuel Beckett, *Three Plays: Ohio Impromptu, Catastrophe, What Where*. New York: Grove Press, 1984, p. 59.

94. Beckett, *Collected Shorter Plays*, p. 305.

95. See, for example, Catherina Wulf, 'At the Crossroads of Desire and Creativity: A Critical Approach to Samuel Beckett's Television Plays "Ghost Trio," ". . . but the clouds . . ." and "Nacht und Träume"', *Samuel Beckett Today/Aujourd'hui*, Vol. 3 (1994), pp. 56–65.

96. Beckett, *Collected Shorter Plays*, p. 305.

97. Beckett, *Collected Shorter Plays*, p. 305.

98. Beckett, *Collected Shorter Plays*, p. 305.

99. Samuel Beckett, *Nohow On: Company, Ill Seen Ill Said, Worstward Ho*. New York: Grove Press, 1996, p. 90.

100. Beckett, *Collected Shorter Plays*, p. 305.

101. Knowlson, *Damned to Fame*, pp. 599–600.

102. Knowlson, *Damned to Fame*, p. 600.

103. Herren, *Beckett's Plays on Film and Television*, p. 187.

104. Beckett, *Collected Shorter Plays*, p. 305.

105. Enoch Brater, 'Toward a Poetics of Television Technology: Beckett's *Nacht und Träume* and *Quad*', *Modern Drama*, Vol. 28, No. 1 (1985), p. 49.

106. Beckett, *Three Plays*, p. 59.

107. Müller-Freienfels, 'Samuel Beckett', p. 17.

108. Müller-Freienfels, 'Samuel Beckett', p. 17.

109. Knowlson interprets *Quad 1* and *2* as 'Dantesque about its imagery, with the figures resembling Gustave Doré's engravings of Dante and Virgil in Hell'. *Damned to Fame*, p. 592. He continues, quoting a letter Beckett wrote to the Polish translator of his novella *Company*, that 'Dante and Virgil in Hell always go to the left (the damned direction), and in Purgatory always to the right'. Along these lines, Gensch's own comments on *Quad 1* and *2* are fitting. He explained these two works as possibly images of
> eternity . . . They all move in their circle counter clockwise. It is said that Beckett had said, 'like in Dante's inferno'. In Dante all the souls also travel counter clockwise. It was also on account of practical reasons; they must decide on a direction or else they would run into each other. However, one can describe the teleplay as representing Hell, the eternal, eternity, or the purposeless walking done in hell. (Interview with Gogo Gensch, 2007)

110. Since there is no dialogue in *Quad 1* or *2*, and since the focus is on movement, Beckett employed professional ballet dancers to take on the roles of the four figures.

111. It was specifically *Quad 1* that gave Beckett the most problems. The invention of *Quad 2* was only later conceived of after Müller-Freienfels who, along with his friend Roman Brotman, had seen *Quad 1* on the black and white television monitor, informed Beckett that the play looked equally impressive in monochrome (Interview with Gogo Gensch, 2007).

112. In Gensch's memory 'the main problems were that of the fixed camera position which was fixed relatively quickly, and the coordination between the percussions and the dancers which was much more difficult to solve' (Interview with Gensch, 2007).

113. Hans H. Hiebel, '*Quadrat 1 + 2* as a Television Play', *Samuel Beckett Today/ Aujourd'hui: Beckett in the 1990s*, Vol. 2 (1993), p. 338.

114. Klaver, 'Samuel Beckett's *Ohio*', p. 378.

115. Beckett much admired the work of Charlie Chaplin and even desired to cast Chaplin in his film, titled *Film* (1964). Chaplin refused the offer. His second choice, Jack MacGowan's schedule was too full, and so the role went to Buster Keaton. Knowlson, *Damned to Fame*, p. 464.

116. Knowlson, *Damned to Fame*, p. 592.

117. Cohn (ed), *Disjecta*, p. 145.

118. Knowlson attests to the ghostly nature of *Quad 1* and *2*. Eckart Voigts-Virchow has examined television, more generally, as 'dead, a non-presence – but one that does its best to seem alive'. For him, Beckett's teleplays destabilise the pretence of liveliness. Eckart Voigts-Virchow, 'Face Values: Beckett, Inc., The Camera Plays, and Cultural Liminality', *Journal of Beckett Studies*, Vol. 10, No. 1–2 (2000–2001), p. 124.

119. Beckett's apartment in Paris overlooked the exercise yard of Santé Prison. According to Knowlson, the 'thought of men living in cages so close at hand filled him with real distress'. *Damned to Fame*, p. 426. Gensch also referred to Santé Prison in my interview with him. He explains that one can relate *Quad 1* and *2* to the fact that Beckett lived 'across from a prison and always heard how the prisoners walked in circles the entire day'.

120. Knowlson, *Damned to Fame*, p. 593.

121. Herren, *Samuel Beckett's Play*, p. 138.

122. Beckett, *Collected Shorter Plays*, p. 211.

123. Most notable of the Beckett archival projects is the Beckett International Foundation housed at The University of Reading. This collection, of which Beckett generously donated many of his manuscripts and typescripts, was founded in 1971. Although Beckett never visited the Foundation, his friendship with James Knowlson and his own former academic training surely provided him with an awareness of the ramifications of archives.

124. Cited in Martha Fehsenfeld, '"Everything Out but the Faces": Beckett's Reshaping of *What Where* for Television', *Modern Drama*, Vol. 29, No. 2 (1986), p. 229.

125. Fehsenfeld, 'Everything Out', p. 230.

126. Fehsenfeld, 'Everything Out', p. 231.

127. Fehsenfeld, 'Everything Out', p. 232.

128. Fehsenfeld, 'Everything Out', p. 239.

129. Fehsenfeld, 'Everything Out', p. 230.

130. Graley Herren, *Ghosts in the Machine: A Study of Samuel Beckett's Plays for Television*. unpublished manuscript, 2002, p. 107.

131. Beckett, *Three Plays*, pp. 42, 44.

132. Beckett, *Three Plays*, p. 42.

133. Beckett, *Three Plays*, p. 45.

134. Beckett, *Three Plays*, p. 47.

135. Beckett, *Three Plays*, p. 52.

136. Samuel Beckett, '*What Where*: The Revised Text', ed. S.E. Gontarski, *Journal of Beckett Studies*, Vol. 2, No. 1 (1992), pp. 2–10. The words 'what' and 'where' appear on nearly every one of the teleplay's eight pages, and therefore, no page numbers are given.

137. Fehsenfeld, 'Everything Out', p. 230. Fehsenfeld points out that the megaphone on stage was 'painted lampblack'.
138. Herren, *Ghosts in the Machine*, p. 110.
139. See: Fehsenfeld, 'Everything Out', p. 235; Klaver, 'Samuel Beckett's *Ohio*', p. 380; Herren, *Ghosts in the Machine*, p. 107.
140. Beckett, *Three Plays*, p. 59.
141. In the 2000 *Beckett on Film* production, the decision was made to film the stage version of the text in a library of the future. This choice produces a sci-fi reading of the play. The room, for example, embarrassingly resembles something out of *Star Trek*. The only redeeming quality of the film is the close-up of the black megaphone, which gives the impression that the surface of this object is a black whirlpool ready to suck in all matter.
142. Klaver, 'Samuel Beckett's *Ohio*', p. 378.
143. Fehsenfeld, 'Everything Out', p. 237.
144. Herren, *Ghosts in the Machine*, pp. 121–2.
145. Fehsenfeld, 'Everything Out', p. 234.
146. V (the megaphone), too, is replaced by a face, but his face, unlike the B-ms, is larger and distorted. Jim Lewis explains that V's grotesque death-mask was achieved 'by using a mirror-reflected image plus [an] old pane of glass'. Fehsenfeld, 'Everything Out', p. 236.
147. Fehsenfeld, 'Everything Out,' p. 236. Fehsenfeld's italics.
148. Cohn (ed), *Disjecta*, pp. 171–2.
149. Beckett, *Three Plays*, p. 59.
150. Harmon (ed), *No Author Better Served*, p. 24. In a letter to Alan Schneider dated 29 December 1957, Beckett wrote: 'If people want to have headaches among the overtones, let them. And provide their own aspirin'.
151. Beckett considered having V open and close his eyes as Listener does in *That Time*, but in the end decided that V's eyes should remain closed throughout. As I have argued elsewhere, while the closing of Listener's eyes in *That Time* suggest that he struggles to shut out the past to keep the memories from absorbing into his present, the opening of his eyes is inevitable. They are 'automatic expressions [that] produce faciality as an abstract machine. . . . [I]t is an inscription of horror; it is the face' underneath the death-mask. Katherine Weiss, 'Bits and Pieces: The Fragmented Body in Samuel Beckett's *Not I* and *That Time*', *Journal of Beckett Studies*, Vol. 10, No. 1–2 (2000–2001), p. 193. In *What Where*, Beckett similarly uses the face. By closing his eyes, V, on the one hand, tries to shut out the possibility of absorbing into the system he inscribes and, on the other hand, he inscribes himself into the system he tries to flee. He becomes a prisoner behind the mask.

Chapter 4

1. See S.E. Gontarski, 'Greying the Canon: Beckett and Performance' in S.E. Gontarski and Anthony Uhlmann (eds), *Beckett After Beckett*, Gainesville: University Press of Florida, 2006, p. 141.
2. I am referring here to a dominant structure of economic life in the late twentieth and early twenty-first centuries, particularly in the culturally hegemonic societies

Notes

of the United States and Europe; it is not intended to exclude the experiences of those who come from cultures that self-identify as non-capitalist. The circulation of this term can be traced to Frederic Jameson, *Postmodernism, or The Cultural Logic of Late Capitalism*. London and New York: Verso, 1991.

3. For a useful précis of this history, see Dennis Kennedy, 'Directing/Director' in Dennis Kennedy (ed), *The Oxford Encyclopedia of Theatre and Performance*, Oxford: Oxford University Press, 2004, pp. 376–7.
4. Samuel Beckett, *Endgame*. London: Faber and Faber, 1964, p. 7.
5. For extended quotations from the programme notes and a thorough analysis of this controversy, see Jonathan Kalb, *Beckett in Performance*. Cambridge: Cambridge University Press, 1987, p. 79.
6. Beckett began directing in the mid-1960s, first with *L'Hypothèse* by Robert Pinget in Paris in 1965, and then from 1967 at the Schiller Theatre in Berlin. For a complete list of his productions, see C.J. Ackerley and S.E. Gontarski (eds), *The Faber Companion to Samuel Beckett*, London: Faber and Faber, 2006, pp. 141–4.
7. Ackerley and Gontarski (eds), *The Faber Companion*, p. 310.
8. Edward Beckett, 'Letter to the editor', *The Guardian*, 24 March 1994, p. 25.
9. See Matthew Feldman, 'Beckett and Popper, or, "What Stink of Artifice": Some Notes on Methodology, Falsifiability, and Criticism in Beckett Studies', *Samuel Beckett Today/Aujourd'hui*, Vol. 16 (2006), pp. 373–91.
10. Beckett, *Krapp's Last Tape and Other Dramatic Pieces*, p. 3.
11. For a more thorough exploration of these issues, see Nicholas Johnson, 'Analogue Krapp in a Digital Culture', *Journal of Beckett Studies*, Vol. 20, No. 2 (2011), pp. 213–20.
12. Beckett, *Waiting for Godot*, p. 58.
13. Xerxes Mehta, 'Ghosts' in Lois Oppenheim (ed), *Directing Beckett*, Ann Arbor: University of Michigan Press, 1994, p. 170. Mehta's essay is also reprinted in this book.
14. Kalb, *Beckett in Performance*, p. 71.
15. Herbert Blau, 'Interview with Herbert Blau' in Lois Oppenheim (ed), *Directing Beckett*, Ann Arbor: University of Michigan Press, 1994, p. 56.
16. Cohn (ed), *Disjecta*, p. 139.
17. Beckett, *Waiting for Godot*, p. 42.
18. Alain Badiou, *Being and Event*, trans. Oliver Feltham. London: Continuum, 2005, p. 391.
19. Samuel Beckett, *Proust* (1931) in Paul Auster (ed), *The Selected Works of Samuel Beckett, Volume IV: Poems, Short Fiction, Criticism*, New York: Grove Press, 2010, p. 534.
20. Beckett, *Proust*, p. 540.
21. Samuel Beckett, *First Love* (1946) in Paul Auster (ed), *The Selected Works of Samuel Beckett, Volume IV: Poems, Short Fiction, Criticism*, New York: Grove Press, 2010, p. 234.
22. Beckett, *Ends and Odds*, p. 15.
23. Alain Badiou, *On Beckett*, Alberto Toscano and Nina Power (eds), trans. Bruno Bosteels. Manchester: Clinamen Press, 2003, p. 15.
24. Badiou, *On Beckett*, p. 4.
25. Badiou, *On Beckett*, p. 5.
26. Badiou, *On Beckett*, p. 17.
27. Badiou, *On Beckett*, p. 28.

257

28. Badiou, *On Beckett*, pp. 27–8.
29. Badiou, *On Beckett*, p. 28.
30. Badiou, *On Beckett*, p. 28.
31. Leonard Cohen, 'Anthem' (1992) in *Stranger Music: Selected Poems and Songs*. New York: Vintage, 1994, p. 373.
32. Beckett, *Cascando and Other Short Dramatic Pieces*, p. 37.
33. Beckett, *Cascando and Other Short Dramatic Pieces*, p. 37.
34. Beckett, *Ends and Odds*, p. 44.
35. Beckett, *Cascando and Other Short Dramatic Pieces*, p. 37.
36. Beckett, *Cascando and Other Short Dramatic Pieces*, p. 39.
37. Badiou, *On Beckett*, p. 15.
38. Badiou, *On Beckett*, p. 28.
39. Badiou, *On Beckett*, p. 27.
40. Beckett, *Ends and Odds*, p. 55.
41. Beckett, *Ends and Odds*, p. 75.
42. Beckett, *Ends and Odds*, p. 72.
43. Beckett, *Ends and Odds*, p. 74.
44. Badiou, *On Beckett*, p. 28.
45. Beckett, *Collected Shorter Plays*, p. 305.
46. Badiou, *On Beckett*, p. 27.
47. Beckett, *Collected Shorter Plays*, pp. 91–3.
48. Badiou, *On Beckett*, p. 17.
49. Knowlson, *Damned to Fame*, p. 593.
50. Samuel Beckett, *Worstward Ho* (1983) in Paul Auster (ed), *The Selected Works of Samuel Beckett, Volume IV: Poems, Short Fiction, Criticism*, New York: Grove Press, 2010, p. 471.
51. Badiou, *On Beckett*, p. 28.
52. Beckett, *Cascando and Other Short Dramatic Pieces*, p. 38.
53. Badiou, *On Beckett*, pp. 4–5.
54. Andrew Gibson, *Beckett and Badiou: The Pathos of Intermittency*. Oxford: Oxford University Press, 2006, p. 209.
55. Shane Weller, *Beckett, Literature, and the Ethics of Alterity*. Basingstoke: Palgrave Macmillan, 2006, p. 2.
56. Simon Critchley, *Very Little . . . Almost Nothing: Death, Philosophy, Literature*. Second edition. London: Routledge, 2004, pp. xxiii–xxiv.
57. Simon Critchley, 'On the Ethics of Alain Badiou' in Gabriel Riera (ed), *Alain Badiou: Philosophy and Its Conditions*, Albany, NY: SUNY Press, 2005, p. 233.
58. Critchley, 'On the Ethics', p. 232.
59. Beckett, *Proust*, p. 534.
60. Badiou, *On Beckett*, p. 28.
61. Badiou, *On Beckett*, p. 5.
62. Beckett, *Proust*, p. 538.
63. 'The 50 Most Stylish Men of the Past 50 Years', *Gentleman's Quarterly*, Comer, Elkins, French, et al. (eds) (October 2007).
64. Henri Bergson, *Time and Free Will: An Essay on the Immediate Data of Consciousness*, trans. F.L. Pogson. London: George Allen and Unwin, 1910, pp. 76–7.
65. Bergson, *Time and Free Will*, pp. 18–19.
66. Henri Bergson, *The Creative Mind: An Introduction to Metaphysics*. New York: Kensington/Citadel Press, 1928, p. 165.

67. Bergson, *Creative Mind*, p. 165.
68. Patrick McNamara, *Mind and Variability: Mental Darwinism, Memory, and the Self*. Westport: Praeger, 1999, p. 37.
69. Henri Bergson, *Matter and Memory*, trans. Paul and Palmer. Cambridge: Zone Books, 2002, p. 152.
70. Beckett, *Krapp's Last Tape and Other Dramatic Pieces*, p. 5.
71. Beckett, *Krapp's Last Tape and Other Dramatic Pieces*, p. 10.
72. Beckett, *Krapp's Last Tape and Other Dramatic Pieces*, p. 6.
73. Beckett, *Krapp's Last Tape and Other Dramatic Pieces*, p. 10.
74. Beckett, *Krapp's Last Tape and Other Dramatic Pieces*, p. 10.
75. Beckett, *Krapp's Last Tape and Other Dramatic Pieces*, p. 6.
76. Beckett, *Krapp's Last Tape and Other Dramatic Pieces*, p. 6.
77. Bergson, *Creative Mind*, p. 164.
78. Beckett, *Krapp's Last Tape and Other Dramatic Pieces*, p. 7.
79. Beckett, *Krapp's Last Tape and Other Dramatic Pieces*, p. 6.
80. Beckett, *Krapp's Last Tape and Other Dramatic Pieces*, p. 10.
81. Beckett, *Krapp's Last Tape and Other Dramatic Pieces*, p. 6.
82. Qualia is a hotly debated concept, and few scientists or philosophers agree on what it is. For Daniel Dennett, in Marcel & Bisiach's *Consciousness in Modern Science*, qualia are ineffable, intrinsic, private, and are directly or immediately knowable in consciousness. For V.S. Ramachandran and E.M. Hubbard, in 'Synaesthesia: A Window Into Perception, Thought and Language', *Journal of Consciousness Studies*, Vol. 8, No. 12 (2001), qualia are irrevocable and indubitable; unconsciously, but intentionally created; open-ended upon creation; and contained within short-term memory. Ramachandran and Hirstein's 'Three Laws of Qualia: What Neurology Tells Us about the Biological Functions of Consciousness, Qualia and the Self' in *Journal of Consciousness Studies*, Vol. 4, No. 5–6 (1997) explains the concept of qualia most directly: 'Qualia are the "raw feels" of conscious experience: the painfulness of pain, the redness of red. Qualia give human conscious experience the particular character that it has. For instance, imagine a red square; that conscious experience has (at least) two qualia: a colour quale, responsible for your sensation of redness, and a shape quale, responsible for the square appearance of the imagined object' (p. 430).
83. Daniel Dennett, *Consciousness Explained*. Boston: Little, Brown, Co., 1992, p. 210.
84. Dennett, *Consciousness Explained*, p. 428.
85. While these experiences seem the same, the second instance leaves out the phenomena or internal subjective experience. The awareness might be removable from the material brain, but the experience is not possible without the component material parts. In this way, we see the interaction of the mind/consciousness and the brain/body. The memory of experiencing pain is something that we can be aware of without actually physically experiencing it, and the brain can even simulate pain in non-existent physical areas (phantom limbs, for instance – or in Krapp's case a phantom body). Beckett's work, I contend, is developing both an examination of qualia and, more importantly, an examination of the moment in which memory becomes actualised as a physical part of the body (specifically here as Krapp sometimes unhappily *hears* the recitation of his own memories). Up to this point, Deleuze's concept of the machinic and rhizomatic multiplicity – based on Bergson's spectrum of duration – has been the most useful model to understand how this everyday process is actualised. Cognitive science has presented us with

another alternative in conceptualising this process though.

86. Daniel Dennett and M. Kinsbourne, 'Time and the Observer: The Where and When of Consciousness in the Brain', *Behavioral and Brain Science*, Vol. 15, No. 2 (1995), p. 245.

87. Beckett, *Krapp's Last Tape and Other Dramatic Pieces*, pp. 8–9.

88. 'I'll Go On: An Afternoon of Samuel Beckett', participants Albee, Bishop, Epstein, Oppenheim, Turturro, Philoctetes Center, 22 Nov 2008.

89. Michael Wesch, 'An Anthropological Introduction to *YouTube*', Library of Congress, 23 June 2008.

CHRONOLOGY OF SELECTED EVENTS, PERFORMANCES AND PUBLICATIONS

1906   Born in Foxrock, County Dublin on Good Friday, 13 April. Samuel Barclay Beckett was the second and last child of May and Bill Beckett. His older brother, Frank, was born in 1902. Beckett's relationship with his mother was often strained; she was a devout Protestant who disapproved of Beckett's love for his first cousin, Peggy Sinclair, and for Suzanne Deschevaux-Dumesnil, the French pianist who later became Beckett's wife. For his father, Beckett had many fond memories, often alluding to him in his prose texts.

1920 to 1923   Sent to join his brother, Frank, at the Portora Royal School. The decision to send the Beckett boys to this prestigious boarding school in Enniskillen was largely a reaction to the political turmoil in Dublin which resulted from the 1916 Easter Rebellion.

1923 to 1926   Studied Modern Languages (French and Italian) at Trinity College Dublin. Two of his instructors, Thomas Rudmose-Brown and Bianca Esposito, influenced him greatly. Rudmose-Brown's interest in French poetry cultivated Beckett's love of poetry. Esposito introduced Beckett to Dante's *Divine Comedy*, a crucial literary influence on which Beckett drew on for the rest of his writing career.

1926   Awarded the Trinity College Foundation Scholarship in June for his exceptional academic performance. Beckett embarked on his first trip to France, in which he cycled around the country.

1927   Sent by his father on a vacation to Italy so that Beckett would improve his Italian. While in Italy, Beckett visited many art galleries in Florence and went hiking in Northern Italy. Upon returning to

Dublin, Beckett studied for his final exams and passed with high marks. Graduated from Trinity College with a BA, first in the First Class in December. He is awarded Trinity College's Gold Medal for academic achievement.

1928   Appointed to teach high-school English and French at the elite Campbell College in Belfast. After only two terms (January to September), he returned to Dublin. Thereafter Beckett travelled to Austria to visit his cousin, Peggy, who was studying music and dance at Schule Hellerau-Laxenburg, before going to Paris.

On Rudmose-Brown's recommendation, Beckett was appointed the Trinity Exchange Lecturer in English at Paris's École Normal Supérieure, a university that prepared its students for careers in teaching, that October. While Beckett disliked the life of the academic, he was pleased to have the chance to live in Paris for the year. It was during this first stay in Paris that Beckett met Thomas MacGreevy, the Irish poet, and James Joyce, the Irish novelist. Beckett became close friends with MacGreevy with whom he corresponded until MacGreevy's death.

1929   Published first critical essay, 'Dante ... Bruno . Vico .. Joyce' and his first work of fiction, 'Assumption', in the literary magazine, *transition*.

1930   Wrote 'Whoroscope' in the summer. The poem was awarded ten pounds and published by Hours Press.

Returned to Dublin in September to take a position as Lecturer in French at Trinity College.

1931   Became involved in the theatre event which Trinity's Modern Languages Society, made up of staff and students, performed each February at the Peacock Theatre in Dublin. Although Beckett played Don Diegue in the burlesque rewrite of *Le Cid* (renamed *Le Kid*), he only contributed minimally to the event, rarely attending rehearsals. This marked Beckett's first and only attempt at acting and was his first venture in theatre.

In March, Beckett had a row with his mother over some of his writing, which she found horrifying and disgusting.

Miserable as a lecturer and with being in Dublin, Beckett fled to Germany for his Christmas holidays. In December, he resigned from his post at Trinity College.

1931 to 1933   Travelled to Germany to visit his uncle, William 'Boss' Sinclair, and his cousin, Peggy Sinclair. Beckett was very much in love with Peggy. His close relationship with the Sinclairs, who were Jewish, explained, in part, Beckett's later work with the French Resistance. It was during this time, moreover, that Beckett wrote his first novel, *Dream of Fair to Middling Women*; the novel was not published until 1992, three years after Beckett's death.

1932   Began translating literary works into French. He and his friend, Alfred Peron, were the first to translate parts of James Joyce's *Finnegans Wake* into French. Their translation, however, was not published.

1933   Death of Peggy Sinclair of pulmonary tuberculosis in May.
   Death of Beckett's father, Bill Beckett, of a heart attack on 26 June.

1934   To help Beckett cope with the death of his father and cousin as well as panic attacks and mysterious illnesses that Beckett suffered from, the twenty-seven-year-old Beckett left for London in January to undergo two years of psychotherapy at the Tavistock Clinic. His doctor, Wilfred Bion, followed the theories of Sigmund Freud and C.G. Jung. In Dublin such treatment was still illegal.
   Published his collection of short stories, *More Pricks Than Kicks* by Chatto and Windus in May.

1935   Invited as Bion's guest to C.G. Jung's lecture for the Institute of Psychological Medicine of the Tavistock Clinic. The epiphany Jung had during this lecture – that one of his patients suffered from never having been born – haunted Beckett for years to come.

1936 to 1937   Travelled throughout Germany. Much of his trip was spent visiting art galleries, collecting art catalogues, and keeping notes of his impressions of the works he saw in his diaries. During his travels, he became increasingly aware of the threat of Germany's relatively new government, the Third Reich. Impressions of the radio broadcasts he heard of Hitler and Goebbels were also recorded in his diaries.

1937   Attempted to write *Human Wishes*, a play about the relationship between Dr Johnson and Mrs Hester Thrale. Only a fragment of the play was completed.

Returned to Dublin after his tour of Germany only to leave shortly thereafter. Leaving Dublin, Beckett returned to Paris to settle down.

1938   On 7 January, Beckett was stabbed by a pimp. The knife missed his lung and heart by a fraction of a hair. While in the hospital he was visited by many, including an acquaintance, Suzanne Deschevaux-Dumesnil, who later became Beckett's wife.

1939   England declared war on Germany on 3 September.

1940   In June, Beckett headed for the south of France with Suzanne as they feared for their safety at the fall of France. In October, he and Suzanne returned to their apartment.

1941   Death of James Joyce in January.

Joined the French Resistance. Beckett's decision to join the Resistance Cell, Gloria SMH, came shortly after his friend Paul Leon was arrested.

In February, Beckett began writing *Watt*.

1942 to 1945   Gloria SMH was betrayed. On 16 August, Beckett and Suzanne narrowly escaped the Gestapo, fleeing on foot to the village of Roussillon in the south of France. It was there that Beckett met Henri Hayden, the Polish-born painter with whom he remained friends for many years.

1945   Awarded the Croix de Guerre for his Resistance work.

Completed *Watt* in March.

Returned to Paris with Suzanne. Worried about the health of his mother, Beckett visited Dublin via London. While in the bombed out city of London, Beckett was detained by immigration authorities who were suspicious of his Irish passport and French address. Such post-World War Two suspicions also made returning to Paris, where

Suzanne was awaiting him, difficult. Beckett overcame this challenge when he joined the Irish Red Cross in August; that same month he was sent to Saint-Lô, Normandy, to help reconstruct the hospital there.

1946 Arrived back in Paris. Beckett completed his first novel in French, *Mercier et Camier* (*Mercier and Camier*).

1947 Completed his first play in French, *Eleutheria*.

1948 Began writing *En attendant Godot* (*Waiting for Godot*).

1950 Death of Beckett's mother on 25 August.

1953 *En attendant Godot* premièred on 19 January at the Théâtre de Babylone in Paris under the direction of Roger Blin. Reactions to the play were mixed.

Had a small house built in Ussy-sur-Marne, France.

1954 Death of Beckett's brother, Frank, in September.

1955 *Waiting for Godot* premièred in London on 3 August under the direction of Peter Hall.

Completed *Fin de partie* (*Endgame*).

1956 *Waiting for Godot* premiered in America at the Coconut Grove Playhouse in Miami, Florida, on 3 January under the direction of Alan Schneider. Despite the poor audience response to the play, the fiasco led to a close correspondence between Schneider and Beckett. Schneider went on to direct several of the American premieres of Beckett's plays.

Wrote *All That Fall*, a play for radio for the BBC Third Programme from July through September. Later this year, Beckett wrote *Acte sans paroles I* in French, with music by his cousin John Beckett, and *Acte sans paroles II*.

1957 *All That Fall* was first broadcasted by the BBC Third Programme on 3 January.

1958 *Fin de partie* and *Act Without Words I* début at the Royal Court Theatre in London.

Completed *Krapp's Last Tape* which débuted the same year at the Royal Court Theatre.

Withdrew from Dublin's International Theatre Festival and forbade all subsequent productions of his plays in Ireland for many years thereafter. Beckett's decision was based on his disgust with the Festival's removal of James Joyce and Sean O'Casey from the programme after being urged to do so by the Archbishop of Dublin.

The English translation of *Endgame* was staged in London after long battles with the Lord Chamberlain's office over what the office considered blasphemous dialogue.

Met Barbara Bray who worked at the BBC. Beckett and Bray began a love affair that would last the rest of his life.

1959   Sent *Embers* to Donald McWhinnie at the BBC. The radio play was broadcast on the Third Programme. *Embers* won the RAI Prize in the Prix Italia Contest of this year.

Bestowed with an honorary doctorate degree from Trinity College in June. While in Dublin to receive the doctorate, Beckett met up with many of his Irish friends.

1960   *Act Without Words II* was performed at the Institute of Contemporary Arts, London.

French première of *La dernière bande* (*Krapp's Last Tape*).

Met the famous philosopher of the Frankfurt School, Theodor Adorno, at the Suhrkamp Publishing House in Frankfurt. Suhrkamp was hosting an event to honour Beckett.

In winter, Beckett bought a car and moved with Suzanne to a larger apartment where he would live out the rest of his life.

1961   Married Suzanne in March to ensure that she would receive the rights and monetary support if he were to die before her. While living as a married man, he also helped his mistress, Barbara Bray, move to Paris.

Shared the Prix International des Éditeurs with Jorge Luis Borges.

Happy Days premiered at the Cherry Lane Theatre on 17 September in New York.

Rough for Radio I was written in French.
Words and Music was completed.

1962 Translated *Happy Days* (*Oh les beaux jours*) into French.

1962 to 1963 *Words and Music* was broadcast on the BBC Third Programme.
Cascando was written in French.
Completed *Play* which was first performed at the Ulmer Theatre in Germany.

1964 The English translation of *Cascando* was broadcast on the BBC Third Programme.
French première of *Play (Comédie)*.
London première of *Play* at the Old Vic. Beckett attended rehearsals for this production at which time he met Billie Whitelaw; he admired her performance in rehearsals greatly.
Travelled to New York City, his first and only trip to America, to assist in the filming of *Film*, directed by Alan Schneider and starring Buster Keaton. Beckett wrote the short film script for Barney Rosset of Grove Press.

1965 Sent John Calder a new short play, *Come and Go*, for the opening of Calder's theatre in Soho, London.
Wrote his first teleplay, *Eh Joe*, which was broadcast on BBC television.

1966 Directed *He, Joe* (*Eh Joe*) for the Süddeutscher Rundfunk (SDR) in Stuttgart, Germany, at the invitation of Reinhart Müller-Freienfels, the broadcasting system's artistic director. This endeavour resulted in a long commitment of working together with the SDR.

1967 Directed *Endspiel* (*Endgame*) at the Schiller-Theater Werkstatt in Berlin, Germany. This production marked Beckett's first solo directorial début. Its success led to more directorial work of his plays at the Berlin theatre.
In spring, diagnosed with glaucoma. Death of Thomas MacGreevy.

1969 Wrote *Breath* for Kenneth Tynan's *Oh! Calcutta!*

Directed *Das letzte Band* (*Krapp's Last Tape*) at the Schiller-Theater Werkstatt in Berlin with Martin Held as Krapp.

Received the Nobel Prize for Literature on 23 October. Beckett sent his French publisher, Jérôme Lindon, to accept the award for him.

1971 Flew to Berlin to direct *Glückliche Tage* (*Happy Days*) at the Schiller-Theater Werkstatt.

1972 Wrote *Not I* in the spring after recovering from two successful cataract surgeries. Later this year, *Not I* premièred at the Lincoln Center in New York City under the direction of Alan Schneider and starring Jessica Tandy.

1973 *Not I* staged in January at the Royal Court in London, with Billie Whitelaw in the lead role and Beckett as director.

1975 Directed *Warten auf Godot* (*Waiting for Godot*) at the Schiller-Theater Werkstatt with Walter Asmus assisting in March. The two became friends and worked together on other projects.

1975 Met Rick Cluchey, a felon who began acting in prison with the San Quentin Drama Workshop. Cluchey was in Paris, starring in a production of *Endgame* at the American Center.

Wrote *Footfalls* for Billie Whitelaw.

After *Warten auf Godot* opened in Berlin, Beckett left for Paris to direct Madeleine Renaud, the first French Winnie of *Happy Days*, in *Pas Moi* (*Not I*).

Billie Whitelaw's television version of *Not I* is completed.

1976 Wrote and completed *Ghost Trio*.

Donald McWhinnie directed *That Time* for London's Royal Court Theatre. The play was staged alongside the début of *Footfalls*, which Beckett directed and Whitelaw starred in.

Rough for Theatre I and *Rough for Theatre II* were published. Although the date the plays were written is unknown, it is thought that both were most likely completed in the late 1950s.

Rough for Radio II was broadcasted on the BBC Third Programme; the play was believed to be written in the early 1960s.

1977   Completed . . . *but the clouds* . . . .

Beckett was deeply concerned about the unrest in South Africa and as such allowed *Waiting for Godot* to be performed in Cape Town as a political allegory. His political engagement was also apparent in his friendship with Anton Libera. Beckett extended a formal invitation in the hopes that the Polish translator would be permitted to travel to Berlin to see *That Time* and *Footfalls* in order to assist him with translating these plays into Polish. However, Libera's passport was withheld by Polish officials.

Directed Cluchey in *Krapp's Last Tape* in Berlin.

1978   Directed *Spiel* (*Play*) in Berlin's Schiller-Theater Werkstatt.

1979   Wrote *A Piece of Monologue* for David Warrilow of the Mabou Mines theatre company. The monologue was performed at the LaMama Theatre Club, one of New York City's famous Off-Broadway theatres. Two years prior Warrilow staged Beckett's short story 'The Lost Ones' with great success.

Directed Whitelaw in *Happy Days* for the Royal Court.

1981   Wrote *Rockaby* for Whitelaw and Daniel Labeille. In conjunction with the State Universities of New York (SUNY), Labeille wanted a play by Beckett for a theatre festival he was putting on in New York for Beckett's seventy-fifth birthday.

Directed Cluchey in *Endgame*.

Wrote *Ohio Impromptu* for S.E. Gontarski who organised the International Symposium at Ohio State University to honour Beckett on his seventy-fifth birthday.

Wrote and directed *Quadrat 1* and *Quadrat 2* (*Quad 1* and *Quad 2*) for the SDR.

1982   Wrote *Catastrophe*, a short play which Beckett dedicated to Václav Havel, a Czech writer who was under house arrest at the time. Havel later became the first elected president of Czechoslovakia. The play was performed at a benefit put on by the International Association for the Defence of Artists.

Sent *Nacht und Träume* to the SDR.

1983 Completed *What Where*. *What Where* and *Catastrophe* were staged in America with glowing reviews.

1984 Death of Roger Blin, the first director to stage *En attendant Godot*. *What Where* was adapted for television and filmed at the SDR for Germany under the title *Was Wo*.

1986 Beckett was diagnosed with emphysema and moved into a nursing home in Paris.

1987 Won the Common Wealth Award in Dramatic Arts. He gave the entire award of $11,000 to Cluchey, who since had been pardoned by the governor of California.

1989 Death of Suzanne on 17 July; death of Beckett on 22 December.

FURTHER READING

Biography and history

Bair, Deirdre, *Samuel Beckett: A Biography*. London: Harcourt Brace, 1978.
Cronin, Anthony, *Samuel Beckett: The Last Modernist*. London: Harpers Collins, 1997.
Eagleton, Terry, 'Political Beckett?', *New Left Review*, Vol. 40 (2006), pp. 67–74.
Gaffney, Phyllis, *Healing Amid the Ruins: The Irish Hospital at Saint-Lô*. Dublin: A&A Farmar, 1999.
Gontarski, S.E., *The Intent of Undoing in Samuel Beckett's Dramatic Texts*. Bloomington: Indiana University Press, 1985.
Kennedy, Seán and Katherine Weiss (eds), *Samuel Beckett: History, Memory, Archive*. New York: Palgrave/Macmillan, 2009.
Knowlson, James, *Damned to Fame: The Life of Samuel Beckett*. New York: Touchstone, 1996.

Stage plays: *Waiting for Godot, Endgame*

Asmus, Walter D., 'Beckett Directs Godot' in S.E. Gontarski (ed), *On Beckett: Essays and Criticism*, New York: Grove Press, 1986, pp. 280–90.
Atkins, Emily, '"Study That Tree": The Iconic Stage in *Purgatory* and *Waiting for Godot*', *South Carolina Review*, Vol. 40, No. 2 (2008), pp. 66–77.
Bradby, David, *Waiting for Godot*. Cambridge: Cambridge University Press, 2001.
Fernández Quesada, Nuria, 'Under the Aegis of the Lord Chamberlain and the Franco Regime: The Bowdlerisation of *Waiting for* Godot and *Endgame*' in Catherine O'Leary and Alberto Lázaro (eds), *Censorship Across Borders: The Reception of English Literature in Twentieth-Century Europe*, Newcastle upon Tyne: Cambridge Scholars, 2011, pp. 193–209.
Füger, Wilhelm, 'The First Berlin *Godot*: Beckett's Debut on the German Stage', *Samuel Beckett Today/Aujourd'hui*, Vol. 11 (2001), pp. 57–63.
Jones, Louisa, 'Narrative Salvation in *Waiting for Godot*', *Modern Drama*, Vol. 17, No. 2 (1974), pp. 179–88.
Koshal, Erin, '"Some Exceptions" and the "Normal Thing": Reconsidering *Waiting for Godot*'s Theatrical Form through Its Prison Performances', *Modern Drama*, Vol. 53, No. 2 (2010), pp. 187–210.
Köster, Maria Rita Teixeira Silva, 'Conor McPherson's View of *Endgame* by Samuel Beckett', *Ilha do Desterro: A Journal of Language and Literature*, Vol. 58 (2010), pp. 381–96.

McDonald, Ronan, '*Waiting for Godot*: A Modern Tragedy?' in Giuseppe Serpillo and Donatella Badin (eds), *The Classical World and the Mediterranean*, Cagliari: Tema, 1996, pp. 270–6.

McMillan, Dougald and James Knowlson, *The Theatrical Notebooks of Samuel Beckett: Waiting for Godot*. London: Faber and Faber, 1993.

Prince, Eric, 'Forty Years On: Peter Hall's Godot', *Journal of Beckett Studies*, Vol. 8, No. 2 (1999), pp. 45–60.

Schechner, Richard, 'Godotology: There's Lots of Time in *Godot*', *Modern Drama*, Vol. 9, No. 3 (1966), pp. 268–76.

Torrance, Robert M., 'Modes of Being and Time in the World of Godot', *Modern Language Quarterly*, Vol. 28 (1967), pp. 77–95.

Stage plays: *Krapp's Last Tape, Happy Days, Play*

Admussen, Richard L., 'The Manuscripts of Beckett's *Play*', *Modern Drama*, Vol. 16, No. 1 (1973), pp. 23–7.

Campbell, Julie, 'The Semantic Krapp in *Krapp's Last Tape*', *Samuel Beckett Today/ Aujourd'hui*, Vol. 6 (1997), pp. 63–71.

Catanzaro, Mary F., 'Disconnected Voices, Displaced Bodies: The Dismembered Couple in Beckett's *Krapp's Last Tape, Happy Days*, and *Play*' in Michael J. Meyer (ed), *Literature and the Grotesque*, Amsterdam: Rodopi, 1995, pp. 31–51.

Eastman, Richard M., 'Samuel Beckett and *Happy Days*', *Modern Drama*, Vol. 6, No. 4 (1964), pp. 417–24.

Goldman, Derek, 'What Was That Unforgettable Line?: Remembrances from the Rubbleheap', *The South Atlantic Quarterly*, Vol. 103, No. 1 (2004), pp. 45–55.

Gontarski, S.E., 'Crapp's First Tapes: Beckett's Manuscript Revisions of *Krapp's Last Tape*', *Journal of Modern Literature*, Vol. 6, No.1 (1977), pp. 61–8.

Gontarski, S.E., *Beckett's Happy Days: A Manuscript Study*. Columbus: Ohio State University Libraries, 1977.

Gontarski, S.E., 'Literary Allusions in "Happy Days"' in S.E. Gontarski (ed), *On Beckett: Essays and Criticism*, New York: Grove Press, 1986, pp. 308–24.

Knowlson, James, *Theatre Workbook I Samuel Beckett: Krapp's Last Tape*. London: Brutus Books Ltd., 1980.

Knowlson, James (ed), *Happy Days: The Production Notebook of Samuel Beckett*. New York: Grove Press, 1986.

Malkin, Jeanette R., 'Matters of Memory in *Krapp's Last Tape* and *Not I*', *Journal of Dramatic Theory and Criticism*, Vol. 11, No. 2 (1997), pp. 25–39.

Pountney, Rosemary, 'Samuel Beckett's Interest in Form: Structural Patterning in *Play*', *Modern Drama*, Vol. 19, No. 3 (1976), pp. 237–44.

Worth, Katharine, 'Past into Future: *Krapp's Last Tape* to *Breath*' in James Acheson and Kateryna Arthur (eds), *Beckett's Later Fiction and Drama: Texts for Company*, London: Macmillan, 1987, pp. 18–34.

Late stage plays

Asmus, Walter D., 'Practical Aspects of Theatre, Radio and Television: Rehearsal notes for the German première of Beckett's *That Time* and *Footfalls* at the Schiller-Theater Werkstatt, Berlin', trans. Helen Watanabe, accessed 14 July 2012, www.english.fsu. edu/jobs/num02/Num2WalterAsmus.htm.

Brater, Enoch, 'The I in Beckett's *Not I*', *Twentieth Century Literature*, Vol. 20, No. 3 (1974), pp. 189–200.

Diamond, Elin, '"what?. . . who?. . . no!. . . she!": The Fictionalizers in Beckett's Plays' in Ruby Cohn (ed), *Samuel Beckett: A Collection of Criticism*, New York: McGraw-Hill, 1975, pp. 111–19.

Gontarski, S.E., '"Making Yourself All Up Again": The Composition of Samuel Beckett's *That Time*', *Modern Drama*, Vol. 23, No. 2 (1980), pp. 112–20.

Knowlson, James and John Pilling, *Frescoes of the Skull: The Later Prose and Drama of Samuel Beckett*. London: John Calder, 1979.

McMullan, Anna, *Theatre on Trial: Samuel Beckett's Later Drama*. London: Routledge, 1993.

Mehta, Xerxes, 'Shapes of Suffering: Image/Narrative/Impromptu in Beckett's *Ohio Impromptu*', *Journal of Beckett Studies*, Vol. 6, No. 1 (1996), pp. 97–118.

Rodríguez-Gago, Antonia, 'The Embodiment of Memory (and Forgetting) in Beckett's Late Women's Plays', *Assaph: Studies in the Theatre*, Vol. 17–18 (2003), pp. 113–26.

States, Bert O., '*Catastrophe*: Beckett's Laboratory/Theatre', *Modern Drama*, Vol. 30, No. 1 (1987), pp. 14–22.

Weiss, Katherine, 'Bits and Pieces: The Fragmented Body in Samuel Beckett's *Not I* and *That Time*', *Journal of Beckett Studies*, Vol. 10, No. 1–2 (2000–2001), pp. 187–95.

Radio plays

Avila, Wanda, 'The Poem within the Play in Beckett's *Embers*', *Language and Style: An International Journal*, Vol. 17, No. 3 (1984), pp. 193–205.

Campbell, Julie, 'Staging *Embers*: An Act of Killing?' *Samuel Beckett Today/Aujourd'hui*, Vol. 7 (1998), pp. 91–104.

Cleveland, Louise O., 'Trials in the Soundscape: The Radio Plays of Samuel Beckett', *Modern Drama*, Vol. 11, No. 3 (1968), pp. 267–82.

Cousineau, Thomas, 'The Significance of Repetition in Beckett's *Embers*', *Southern Humanities Review*, Vol. 19, No. 4 (1985), pp. 313–21.

Esslin, Martin, 'Beckett's *Rough for Radio*', *Journal of Modern Literature*, Vol. 6 (1977), pp. 95–103.

Fletcher, John and Peter Lewis, 'Beckett and the Medium: *Rough for Radio?*' in Peter Lewis (ed), *Papers of the Radio Literature Conference 1977*, Durham: Department of English, 1978, pp. 157–73.

Frost, Everett, 'Fundamental Sounds: Recording Samuel Beckett's Radio Plays', *Theatre Journal*, Vol. 43, No. 3 (1991), pp. 361–76.

Frost, Everett, 'A "Fresh Go" for the Skull: Directing *All That Fall*, Samuel Beckett's Play for Radio' in Lois Oppenheim (ed), *Directing Beckett*, Ann Arbor: University of Michigan Press, 1997, pp. 186–219.

Frost, Everett, 'Mediating On: Beckett, *Embers*, and Radio Theory' in Lois Oppenheim (ed), *Samuel Beckett and the Arts: Music, Visual Arts, and Non-Print Media*, New York: Garland, 1999, pp. 311–31.

Lawley, Paul, '*Embers*: An Interpretation', *Journal of Beckett Studies*, Vol. 6 (1980), pp. 9–36.

Lyons, W.H., 'Backtracking Beckett' in C.A. Burns (ed), *Literature and Society: Studies in Nineteenth and Twentieth Century French Literature, Presented to R.J. North*, Birmingham: John Goodman & Sons, 1980, pp. 1–7.

Perloff, Marjorie, 'The Silence That is Not Silence: Acoustic Art in Samuel Beckett's *Embers*' in Lois Oppenheim (ed), *Samuel Beckett and the Arts: Music, Visual Arts, and Non-print Media*, New York: Garland, 1999, pp. 248–68.

Pountney, Rosemary, '*Embers*: An Interpretation', *Samuel Beckett Today/Aujourd'hui*, Vol. 2 (1993), pp. 269–73.

Van Laan, Thomas F., '*All That Fall* as "a Play for Radio"', *Modern Drama*, Vol. 28, No. 1 (1985), pp. 38–47.

Worth, Katharine, 'Beckett and the Radio Medium' in John Drakakis (ed), *British Radio Drama*, Cambridge: Cambridge University Press, 1981, pp. 191–217.

Worth, Katharine, 'Women in Beckett's Radio and Television Plays' in Linda Ben-Zvi (ed), *Women in Beckett: Performance and Critical Perspectives*, Urbana: University of Illinois Press, 1990, pp. 236–42.

Zilliacus, Clas, 'Samuel Beckett's *Embers*: "A Matter of Fundamental Sounds"', *Modern Drama*, Vol. 13, No. 2 (1970), pp. 216–25.

Zilliacus, Clas, '*All That Fall* and Radio Language' in Lois Oppenheim (ed), *Samuel Beckett and the Arts: Music, Visual Arts, and Non-print Media*, New York: Garland, 1999, pp. 295–310.

Teleplays

Ben-Zvi, Linda, 'Samuel Beckett's Media Plays', *Modern Drama*, Vol. 28, No. 1 (1985), pp. 22–37.

Ben-Zvi, Linda, '*Not I*: Through a Tube Starkly' (1992) in Jennifer Birkett and Kate Ince (eds), *Samuel Beckett: Longman Critical Readers*, London: Longman, 2000, pp. 259–65.

Bignell, Jonathan, 'Beckett in Television Studies', *Journal of Beckett Studies*, Vol. 10, No. 1–2 (2000–2001), pp. 105–18.

Esslin, Martin, 'Visions of Absence: Beckett's *Footfalls*, *Ghost Trio* and . . . *but the clouds* . . .' in Ian Donaldson (ed), *Transformations in Modern European Drama*, Atlantic Highlands: Humanities, 1983, pp. 119–29.

Fehsenfeld, Martha, '"Everything Out but the Faces": Beckett's Reshaping of *What Where* for Television', *Modern Drama*, Vol. 29, No. 2 (1986), pp. 229–40.

Gontarski, S.E., 'The Anatomy of Beckett's *Eh Joe*', *Modern Drama*, Vol. 26, No. 4 (1983), pp. 425–34.

Herren, Graley, 'Madness in the Method: Re-Visions of *Eh Joe* in Recent Productions', *Samuel Becket Today/Aujourd'hui*, Vol. 7 (1998), pp. 105–19.

Herren, Graley, 'Ruptures and Rituals: Beckett's Re-vision of Yeats in . . . *but the clouds . . .* ', *Nua: Studies in Contemporary Irish Writing*, Vol. 1, No. 2 (1998), pp. 29–46.

Herren, Graley, 'Unfamiliar Chambers: Power and Pattern in Samuel Beckett's *Ghost Trio*', *Journal of Beckett Studies*, Vol. 8, No. 1 (1998), pp. 73–100.

Herren, Graley, 'Ghost Duet, or Krapp's First Videotape', *Samuel Beckett Today/ Aujourd'hui*, Vol. 11 (2001), pp. 159–66.

Herren, Graley, '*Nacht und Träume*: Beckett's Agony in the Garden', *Journal of Beckett Studies*, Vol. 11, No. 1 (2001), pp. 54–70.

Herren, Graley, *Samuel Beckett's Plays on Film and Television*. New York: Palgrave/ Macmillan, 2007.

Hiebel, Hans H., '*Quadrat 1 + 2* as a Television Play', *Samuel Beckett Today/Aujourd'hui*, Vol. 2 (1993), pp. 335–43.

Klaver, Elizabeth, 'Samuel Beckett's *Ohio Impromptu*, *Quad*, and *What Where*: How It Is in the Matrix of Text and Television', *Contemporary Literature*, Vol. 32, No. 3 (1991), pp. 366–82.

Knowlson, James, '*Ghost Trio/Geister Trio*' in Enoch Brater (ed), *Beckett at 80/Beckett in Context*, Oxford and New York: Oxford University Press, 1986, pp. 193–207.

McMullan, Anna, 'Versions of Embodiment/Visions of the Body in Beckett's . . . *but the clouds . . .* ', *Samuel Beckett Today/Aujourd'hui*, Vol. 6 (1997), pp. 353–64.

Malkin, Jeanette R., 'Matters of Memory in *Krapp's Last Tape* and *Not I*', *Journal of Dramatic Theory and Criticism*, Vol. 11, No. 2 (1997), pp. 25–39.

Weiss, Katherine, 'Animating Ghosts in Samuel Beckett's *Ghost Trio* and . . . *but the clouds . . .* ', *Journal of Beckett Studies*, Vol. 18, No. 1–2 (2009), pp. 105–22.

Zinman, Toby, '*Eh Joe* and the Peephole Aesthetic', *Samuel Beckett Today/Aujourd'hui*, Vol. 4 (1995), pp. 53–64.

On performance

Chabert, Pierre, 'The Body in Beckett's Theatre', *Journal of Beckett Studies*, Vol. 8 (1982), pp. 23–8.

Chabert, Pierre, 'Samuel Beckett as Director', trans. M.A. Bonney and James Knowlson, in James Knowlson (ed), *Samuel Beckett: Krapp's Last Tape: A Theatre Workbook*, London: Brutus Books Ltd., 1980, pp. 85–107.

Cousineau, Thomas, 'An Interview with Pierre Chabert', *Journal of Beckett Studies*, Vol. 4, No. 1 (1994), pp. 119–31.

Gontarski, S.E., 'The Body in the Body of Beckett's Theater', *Samuel Beckett Today/ Aujourd'hui*, Vol. 11 (2001), pp. 169–77.

Gussow, Mel, *Conversations With and About Beckett*. New York: Grove Press, 1996.

Harmon, Maurice (ed), *No Author Better Served: The Correspondence of Samuel Beckett and Alan Schneider*. Cambridge: Harvard University Press, 1998.

Haynes, John and James Knowlson, *Images of Beckett*. Cambridge: Cambridge University Press, 2003.

Homan, Sidney, *Beckett's Theaters: Interpretations for Performance*. Lewisburg, PA: Bucknell University Press, 1984.

Kalb, Jonathan, *Beckett in Performance*. Cambridge: Cambridge University Press, 1991.

McMillan, Dougald and Martha Fehsenfeld, *Beckett in the Theatre*. London: Calder, 1988.

McMullan, Anna, 'Virtual Subjects: Performance, Technology, and the Body in Beckett's Late Theatre', *Journal of Beckett Studies*, Vol. 10, No. 1–2 (2000–2001), pp. 165–72.

Mehta, Xerxes, '"Down, all going down . . .": The Spiral Structure of Beckett's Theater' in S.E. Gontarski (ed), *A Companion to Samuel Beckett*, Oxford: Wiley-Blackwell, 2010, pp. 372–88.

Postlewait, Thomas, 'Self-Performing Voices: Mind, Memory, and Time in Beckett's Drama', *Twentieth Century Literature: A Scholarly and Critical Journal*, Vol. 24 (1978), pp. 473–91.

Pountney, Rosemary, *Theatre of Shadows: Samuel Beckett's Drama 1956–1976*. Towota: Barnes and Noble, 1988.

Siess, Jürgen, 'Staging of Institutional Tensions in Beckett's Plays', *Samuel Beckett Today/Aujourd'hui*, Vol. 6 (1997), pp. 45–53.

Tönnies, Merle, 'The Spectator as Participant: The Role of Integrating Audience Laughter in Samuel Beckett's Drama', *Forum Modernes Theater*, Vol. 11, No. 2 (1996), pp. 185–96.

Worth, Katharine, *Samuel Beckett's Theatre: Life Journeys*. Oxford: Oxford University Press, 1999.

On theory and aesthetics

Acheson, James, *Samuel Beckett's Artistic Theory and Practice: Criticism, Drama and Early Fiction*. Basingstoke: Macmillan, 1997.

Boulter, Jonathan, *Beckett: A Guide for the Perplexed*. London: Continuum, 2008.

Brater, Enoch, *Beyond Minimalism: Beckett's Late Style in the Theater*. New York: Oxford University Press, 1987.

Bryden, Mary, *Women in Samuel Beckett's Prose and Drama*. Basingstoke: Macmillan, 1993.

Cohn, Ruby, *Back to Beckett*. Princeton: Princeton University Press, 1973.

Cohn, Ruby, *Just Play: Beckett's Theater*. Princeton, NJ: Princeton University Press, 1980.

Cohn, Ruby, 'Beckett's Theatre Resonance' in Morris Beja, S.E. Gontarski and Pierre Astier (eds), *Samuel Beckett: Humanistic Perspectives*, Columbus: Ohio State University Press, 1983, pp. 3–15.

Connor, Steven, *Samuel Beckett: Repetition, Theory and Text*. Aurora: The Davies Group, 2007.

Esslin, Martin, *The Theatre of the Absurd*, 3rd edition. London: Penguin, 1991.

Levy, Shimon, *Samuel Beckett's Self-Referential Drama: The Three I's*. New York: St. Martin's, 1990.

Maude, Ulrika, *Beckett, Technology and the Body*. Cambridge: Cambridge University Press, 2009.

Simon, Bennett 'The Fragmented Self, the Reproduction of the Self, and Reproduction in Beckett and in the Theater of the Absurd' in Joseph H. Smith (ed), *The World of Samuel Beckett*, Baltimore, MD: Johns Hopkins University Press, 1990, pp. 157–80.

Sobosan, Jeffrey G., 'Time and Absurdity in Samuel Beckett', *Thought: A Review of Culture and Idea*, Vol. 49 (1974), pp. 187–95.

Essay collections

Gontarski, S.E. (ed), *A Companion to Samuel Beckett*. Chichester: Wiley-Blackwell, 2010.

Pilling, John (ed), *The Cambridge Companion to Beckett*. Cambridge: Cambridge University Press, 1994.

St. John Butler, Lance (ed), *Critical Essays on Samuel Beckett: Critical Thought Series 4*. Aldershot: Scolar Press, 1993.

Student guides

Fletcher, John et al., *A Student's Guide to the Plays of Samuel Beckett*. London: Faber and Faber, 1978.

Harrington, John P. (ed), *Modern and Contemporary Irish Drama*, 2nd edition. New York and London: Norton, 2009.

McDonald, Ronan, *The Cambridge Introduction to Samuel Beckett*. Cambridge: Cambridge University Press, 2007.

Pattie, David, *The Complete Critical Guide to Samuel Beckett*. London and New York: Routledge, 2000.

INDEX

O'Casey, Sean 4–5, 15, 225,
249 n.68, 266
Juno and the Paycock 4–5
Windfalls 4
Old Vic 246 n.174, 267
Oppenheim, Lois 135
Orwell, George 160

Pattie, David 6–7, 9
Pelorson, Georges 5
Peron, Alfred 263
Phillips, Adam 40–1
Pilling, John 245 n.148
Pinget, Robert 66, 79, 80,
257 n.6
La manivelle 66, 79, 80
L'Hypothèse 257 n.6
Pinter, Harold 8
Post, C.W. 37
postmodernism 100, 155,
166–7, 169, 175–6, 179,
256–7 n.2
post-war 1, 3, 7, 14, 80, 154,
162, 236, 264
Proust, Marcel 165, 176–7,
179–80
Provincetown Playhouse 36
purgatory 47, 106, 216,
254 n.109

Rabinbach, Anson 37
Ramachandran, Vilayanur 188,
259 n.82
Reavey, Jean 128
Renaud, Madeleine 268
Richardson, Dorothy 114–15
Rodríguez-Gago, Antonia 40

Rosset, Barney 128, 267
Royal Court Theatre 39–40,
265, 266, 268, 269
Rudmose-Brown, Thomas 261,
262

Said, Edward 166
Saint-Lô, Normandy 11–12,
41–2, 85, 244 n.123, 265
San Quentin Drama Workshop
162, 242 n.38, 268
Scarry, Elaine 60
Schechner, Richard 19
Schiller-Theater Werkstatt 29,
36, 59, 247 n.199, 257 n.6,
267, 268, 269
Schneider, Alan 18, 36, 66,
128, 162, 197, 240 n.27,
246 n.161, 256 n.150, 265,
267, 268
Schubert, Franz 3, 118, 171
self-reflexive 12, 15, 50, 66–7,
75, 96, 98
Sellars, Peter 207
Shakespeare, William 3, 194,
225, 226
Hamlet 242 n.43
Shaw, Fiona 43
Shaw, George Bernard 225
Shenker, Israel 5, 85, 95
Shepard, Sam 195, 208–9
Sheridan, Richard B. 225
Simmel, Georg 72
Sinclair, Peggy 246 n.182, 261,
263
Sinclair, William 'Boss' 263
Sisyphus 25

CREDITS